Business Planning

for Managers and Entrepreneurs

About the Author

Pierre A. Lurin is a Partner at INVESTAURA Management Consultants, a consultancy specialising in Mergers and Acquisitions, Corporate Development and Enterprise Performance Management. He started his career in the UK with Analysys Mason, a consultancy specialising in telecommunications strategy. As a consultant, he has advised numerous operators and manufacturers across Europe, Asia, the Middle East and Africa. In 1999, he joined Siemens Communications in Germany, now Nokia Networks, and has held a number of senior positions in Marketing, Sales, Finance, M&A, Portfolio Management and Managed Services.

Pierre has lived and worked in the UK, France, Malayoia and now lives in Munich, Germany. He holds a Master of Science from Ecole Centrale Paris, France, as well as a Master in Finance from the University of Cambridge, England.

Pierre was prompted to write this book because he could not find any book that deals with the practice of business planning and summarises everything that one needs to know. So he set out to write the book himself...

Business Planning
for Managers and Entrepreneurs

How to write better Business Plans
that set you apart

with 100 illustrations and case studies from the ICT industry

Pierre A. Lurin

INVESTAURA Management Consultants

Published by INVESTAURA Publications – Pierre Lurin
Email: enquiries@investaura-group.com
Web: www.investaura-group.com

Bibliographic information published by Die Deutsche Bibliothek.
Die Deutsche Bibliothek lists this publication in the Deutsche Nationalbibliographie; detailed bibliographic data is available on the Internet at http://dnb.ddb.de

The author is particularly grateful to Manfred Illenberger for his pivotal role in proof-reading this book; Chad Miller, who provided the background cover picture to this book, "The Launch of a NASA Space Shuttle by Night" (see http://flickr.com/chadmiller); Duncan Werner, from Structured Data LLC, for his great support on RiskAMP, the Monte Carlo Add-In for Microsoft Excel spreadsheet software.

Edited by Pierre Lurin
Cover picture (background): Chad Miller
Production: Books on Demand GmbH, Norderstedt
Printed in Germany
ISBN: 978-3-9813734-2-4
www.business-planning-for-managers.com

Table of Contents

Foreword and Introduction   11

Part One: Getting Started

Chapter One: Structuring a Business Plan   21

Chapter Two: Case Study of a UMTS Service Provider   37

Chapter Three: What Can We Learn from the dot.com Crash?   57

Part Two: Financial Statements and Valuation

Chapter Four: Understanding Financial Statements   65

Chapter Five: Valuing Businesses   93

Chapter Six: Checklist of Common Pitfalls   143

Part Three: Forecasting Revenues and Costs

Chapter Seven: Forecasting is an Art   149

Chapter Eight: Forecasting on the Supply Side   165

Chapter Nine: Forecasting Demand   177

Part Four: Advanced Techniques

Chapter Ten: Knowing Your Competitors   227

Chapter Eleven: Value Chain and Business Model   243

Chapter Twelve: Scenario Planning   255

Chapter Thirteen: Valuing Business Opportunities as Real Options 267

Conclusion: Did MNOs Overpay for their UMTS Licence?   299

Annex: A note on Regression   309
Bibliography   315
Index   322

This book is dedicated to my wife, Erika,

for her unconditional love

DISCLAIMER

While the publisher and author maintain that all reasonable care and skill have been used in the preparation of this book, neither the publisher nor author shall be under any liability for loss or damage (including consequential loss) whatsoever or howsoever arising as a result of the use of this book by readers, customers, companies, their agents, or any third party.

The author does not make any representation or warranty as to the accuracy or completeness of the information contained in this book and nothing contained in this book is, or shall be relied on, as a promise or forecast as to the future. Financial and non-financial projections are illustrative only. Any interested party shall rely solely on its own judgment, review and business analysis. The author does not accept any liability whatsoever or howsoever arising to any interested party from advice, recipe, formula or instruction contained in the book, and such party relies on the book, or any part of it, entirely at its own risk.

The opinions expressed in this book are those of the author only and do not necessarily reflect the views of his employers, neither past nor present.

Foreword

This book is the paperback edition of the hardcover book first published in 2010 under the title "Business Planning for Managers" (ISBN 978-3-9813734-3-1). Apart from the new cover, the new title, the use of black and white pictures - rather than colour - in the paperback edition, and this foreword, the present book does not materially differ from the 2010 version. So readers who have not bought the hardcover version will equally benefit from the present book. An accompanying eBook (ISBN 978-3-9813734-4-8) also complements the paperback version.

Four years have passed since 2010. The topic of business planning remains as relevant as ever. Millions of managers worldwide engage in the preparation of business plans, in the three phases of a company's life: at birth when the company is first set-up (start-up phase); then annually during the company's growth and maturation phase, as part of the preparation of the 5-7 year strategic plan; then finally in the 'exit' phase when the company changes owner, typically in a trade-sale transaction (M&A).

Although the use cases and purposes are different in the three phases above, the techniques used are the same. This book will equally serve the needs of readers whether in an 'entrepreneur', 'business owner' or 'manager' role.

Unfortunately the results are not always convincing, or correct! The most common challenges that people involved in the preparation of a business plan face are the following:

- **Business planning is a holistic activity** that requires not only a strong understanding of the business, but also a clear vision of where the company wants to go, and the skills to translate these into robust revenue and cost forecasts. Forecasting costs can be difficult, but forecasting market and revenues is really a lot more so.

- **Finding the right level of detail can be tricky**. Remaining at the high-level renders the plan superficial; but too much detail does not help either.

- **Good templates to help people get started can be hard to find**. So managers re-invent the wheel again and again.

- **The financial statements that are generated often contain mistakes**. Apart from trivial errors or omission in Excel formulae, people often forget to include the impact of taxation in their calculations. Does taxation have an impact on cashflow and value? Certainly it does, so it should be included.

To make things easier, we have set up the web site

www.business-planning-for-managers.com

where templates can be downloaded. The web site builds up on the book and additionally provides useful information on related topics such as entrepreneurship, strategy and pitching to investors.

Writing, calculating and presenting business plans successfully is a never ending learning process, even for long-time practitioners. Reflecting on my recent personal experience, I would like to share with you the following 'big ideas' that are currently influencing the work that we do (and our business plans) in the ICT, IT and Software space:

- **Consolidation yes, but there is no lack of product and market fragmentation**: the IT industry remains extremely fragmented. Although global players and brand names do dominate the industry at the macro level (think Oracle, or Apple, or Google), at the micro level there are hundreds of different 'markets', each with its own competitive landscape, market dynamics, user requirements, pricing model, and tens of products in any of these markets competing for the attention and money of end-users. The good news, in a way, is that beyond the blockbusters, there is still space in the long tail.

- **The competition will keep increasing**: In a global world, where communication and transportation costs keep decreasing, every firm (and even every individual) competes with far-away companies (and workers), and this is not about to stop. Barriers to entry do remain, such as proximity of customers, language and cultural know-how, governmental regulation and licensing. More than ever, companies and employees need to watch out for un-expected competitors that might be eating their lunch tomorrow.

- **Don't get trapped in the middle**. Companies need to decide whether they compete in the low cost or premium segment. Both are usually not possible at the same time or under the same brand. And those stuck in the middle can lose a lot of money.

- **Small can be beautiful.** Large companies have massive amount of resources compared to small ones, but also massive amount of people who don't add much value to their organisation. Small companies have the upper hand at least in two areas: their agility and speed of decision making and execution; and the motivation, engagement and productivity of their staff, who understand that what they do has a direct impact on the bottom line.

- **People and personal relationship matters more than ever.** Even in the modern, digital, virtual world, turning a successful business plan into a successful business is all about people. Starting a business can only happen once a team comes together (starting with two people), and this team manages to convince providers of finance to fund the business. Once a product is commercially launched, the company will only be successful if it sells. Selling is about understanding what other people need, and convincing them that you have the best product for them. And growing the business is about recruiting the right people, keeping the team focused and pushing in one and the same direction...

All the best,

Pierre Lurin

Partner
INVESTAURA Management Consultants

Introduction

This book has been written to help managers turn their theoretical knowledge of business planning into practice. In the last decade many good books have been published that cover business planning and valuation techniques in general, but they tend to remain at the general level and lack practical examples from industry. My ambition here has been to combine the key principles of business planning with concrete applications that can be relevant to your daily business. The book is supported by a rich number of illustrations that make the reading of what is often seen as a dry topic more lively.

Business planning should not remain the preserve of financial managers. Having spent most of my time in the high-tech sector in the last two decades, this book is also an attempt to reconcile, if not marry, commercial skills and technology know-how. Financial and commercial managers require high quality financial plans and valuations to support their investment decisions. But they need much more than this: to perform optimally they must be armed with a strong understanding of how their industry is ticking. The high-tech sector provides a fairly unique combination of permanent innovation, rapid technological development, strong competition and constant changes that have a direct impact on our work and lifestyle. Financial managers must possess a combination of technology know-how, market understanding and business skills. I hope that the synthesis performed in this book will help engineers develop business skills, and conversely, financial managers cultivate an affinity for technology and develop their own gut feeling for innovation adoption and the pace of change in the market.

The book has been written with a practical focus in mind so that the learning can be applied immediately in business. It reviews the fundamental techniques currently available to practitioners, including many recommendations on what works well and what does not work so well in practice. Hopefully this will guide practitioners in avoiding the mistakes made by others.

This book is targeted at professionals active in any kind of fast-changing business, including but not limited to high-tech. Readers will typically be working in Business Development, Strategic Planning or Portfolio Management. However, this book is also targeted at business unit managers wishing to develop a stronger understanding of value management, as well as product line managers working on a product or service business case. The book will also be valuable to financial managers who regularly have to review and evaluate projects and prioritise business opportunities. Finally, students in the area of finance and science at Bachelor's, Master's or MBA level will be able to complement what they are learning at university with concrete and practical cases.

The book is divided into four parts.

- In **Part One** we provide a review of business planning in general. This includes the case study of a mobile network operator looking to acquire a UMTS licence in the year 2000.

- In **Part Two** we review the main ingredients of financial statements and the valuation techniques used to quantify how financially attractive a business opportunity really is. A minimum knowledge of financial accounting is useful, but not strictly necessary.

- In **Part Three** we investigate the tough issue of forecasting, not only on the supply side, but also on the demand side.

- In **Part Four** we present more advanced techniques. We discuss competition and market share, value chain and business models, scenario planning as well as the valuation of options embedded in business plans. Part Four has been written for advanced readers already possessing a good command of the traditional techniques.

The conclusion is an echo to Chapter Two and the UMTS licence auctioning of the year 2000-2001. It provides answers to those who wonder whether mobile network operators overpaid to acquire a UMTS licence at that time. Finally, we have provided a brief note on regression analysis in the Annex. There is also an Index at the end of the book that should help the reader find easy entry into key topics.

Most readers will benefit from reading the book from the beginning to the end. However, each chapter has been written with the objective to be as self-contained as possible, allowing readers familiar with classical business planning topics to jump straight to the issues that interest them most. Each chapter is supported by a short bibliography focussing on key business books, interesting research articles and useful web sites.

As is common in many English-speaking countries, we use the period "." as the decimal separator and the comma "," as the thousands separator throughout the book. In continental Europe the period and the comma are used the other way round, so that 1,234,567.89 in the English world is written 1.234.567,89 in mainland Europe.

This book has been a long journey for me. As I am putting these final words on paper, I would like to wish you good luck in your business undertaking. The success of this book will not be measured by the number of people who have bought it, but the number of markers that have been used to colour its pages and highlight its key messages. If you have any feedback or suggestions for improvement, please write to me at the following address: feedback@investaura-group.com.

So let us get started.

Part One

Getting Started

## Chapter One

Structuring a Business Plan

"Failing to plan is planning to fail"
Chinese Proverb

In this chapter we start by looking into the typical structure of a business plan and then discuss its main components in further detail. The key aspects presented below should be covered one way or another in a business plan, at least at a high level. Depending on the audience and recipients of the plan, the time available for preparation and presentation, and other circumstances, you will have to decide in which area to put more emphasis. Preparing a business plan can be time consuming, but it does not have to end up as a long document: remember that quality is more important than quantity.

Overview of Chapter One

1. Purpose of Business Plans 22
2. Typical Business Plan Structure 23
3. Detailed Review of the Business Plan Components 25
4. Focus on the Right Issues 33
5. Execution is Key 35

1. Purpose of Business Plans

A business plan is a document that presents an idea and explains how this idea can be turned into a profitable venture. It describes a product or a service, the market that it is addressing and the problems that it solves. It also looks into the competitive environment, as well as processes and resources that are required to serve the market successfully.

Business plans are pervasive in business and are prepared for a variety of reasons. One of the key responsibilities of a company's Chief Financial Officer and his team is to prepare and maintain an aggregated company business plan and use it as instrument for capital budgeting, financing as well as communication with the financial community. Business plans are not confined to the realm of the CFO though. Within companies, most business plans are prepared at the individual project or product level by commercial or non-commercial managers who sometimes have limited finance know-how, but a strong technical and operational understanding for the project.

The most common objectives of business planning are:

- Convincing the management of a company to go ahead with a new product or a project. In this case the business plan is an instrument that supports decision-making and sets out the strategic rationale and financial implications of a go/no-go decision.

- Estimating the synergies to be achieved from the acquisition of one company by another or the set-up of a joint venture between two firms. The tangible synergies can be valued in monetary terms and the results be used as price indication for the negotiations between the two partners.

- Convincing providers of finance, in particular venture capitalists and banks, to provide capital in the form of loan or equity stake to fund the launch and development of a new business. In this case the business plan should demonstrate that the venture can be profitable in the medium term and create value in line with the expectations of its share- and debt-holders. The business plan should also create confidence that the management team has the necessary skills to execute the plan and turn the business into success.

Before you can prepare a business plan, you need to find a promising idea, whether a product or a service, that addresses a real market need. There are numerous techniques for stimulating creativity, in particular brainstorming, working with analogies or using lateral thinking. But the idea does not always have to come from inside: you could copy an idea that has already proved itself in another market or another industry, as long as you are respecting Intellectual Property Rights (IPRs) and trademarks.   In all cases, a great business idea is worthless if not executed well.

2. Typical Business Plan Structure

The detailed content of a business plan will depend on the context in which it is generated and the objective to be achieved. At the top level, a business plan can be structured as follows.

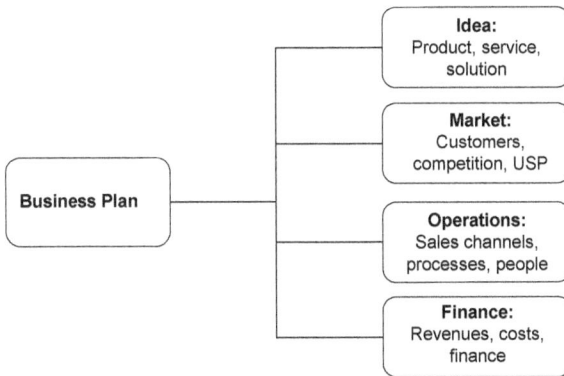

Figure 1.1: Top-level business plan structure [Source: INVESTAURA].

At a minimum a business plan should cover the following aspects:

- An overview of the business idea: this starts with the description of the business idea, whether product, service or solution, and the technology or manufacturing process behind the idea. As pictures are worth a thousand words, a picture of the proposed product or use case for the service will help capture the attention of your audience.

- The market addressed by the business idea: this includes the characteristics and needs of the target customers, alternatives to the product or service, as well as competition analysis. This should also state the differentiating feature of the new business, often called its Unique Selling Proposition (USP).

- The operational aspect of the business, including manufacturing and business processes, people, sales channels, as well as marketing and advertising measures.

- The financial and resource plan, where revenues and costs are summarised into financial statements, in particular the statement of cashflow and the profit and loss account. A scenario analysis with a worst case, base case and optimistic case can be undertaken as well to analyse the sensitivities of the financial plan to various possible futures. In practice, what you have called the worst case often materialised as the actual case. The financial plan should end with a summary of the key risks and key success factors.

These four main parts should be seen as guidelines. The level of detail presented in the business plan should be adapted to circumstances and individual project requirements.

In backup to the plan, supporting and more detailed analysis can be provided, as well as answers to questions that are likely to be raised. If possible, the founding team and their competences are presented there, as well as a detailed execution plan including key milestones or roadmap and a detailed marketing and sales plan to address the customers initially targeted. The backup section might also investigate alternatives to the main business model assumed in the business plan.

Knowing who your customers are might be one of the most difficult issues, and you might not find out before going to market. Understanding target customers is critical to business success because it allows the derivation of the appropriate marketing measures, planning production volume correctly and finding the right price point for the product. Many companies have gone bankrupt for never being clear enough about who their customers are and what they expect and value.

Business plans are not only useful to present and convince others, but also as an execution roadmap with clear targets to be achieved by the management of the new business. A business plan is prepared in a complex set of assumptions about the future. A comprehensive plan forces the management team to think through the whole concept, the business drivers, the prerequisite for success, uncovering gaps and risks and planning for contingency in case the market turns out to behave other than expected – as it most likely will! When the future is particularly uncertain a scenario technique can be used to clarify possible futures and help identify a robust strategy (see Part Four Chapter Twelve).

Business planning is admittedly a complex exercise, drawing on inputs from product development, operations, marketing, sales, finance and human resources. Unfortunately there is a widespread belief that a business plan is nothing more than the financial statements. Although the financial plan certainly is a key component of the business plan, financials are as good as the assumptions they are based on, and unsurprisingly, the 'garbage in, garbage out' principle also applies here. If the other parts of the business plan have been thoroughly thought through and prepared before, the financials should be a fairly straightforward exercise and provides nothing more than a quantitative summary of the business idea. It would be a dangerous mistake to limit a business plan to its financial results and gain false comfort from the numbers if the underlying facts, research and assumptions have not been undertaken properly.

3. Detailed Review of the Business Plan Components

In practice, a business plan will include a minimum of two documents: a presentation as a set of PowerPoint® slides, and a financial calculation prepared in Excel® spreadsheet software. Additionally the plan can be provided in text form as Word document, either as a two-page summary or as a detailed exposure of the business idea. In my experience, the business plan presentation should include 15-20 slides excluding back up and can be broken down as shown in Figure 1.2.

IDEA	1	Executive summary	1 slide
	2	Opportunity, Product & Service offering	1-2 slides
MARKET	3	Target Market	1-2 slides
	4	Competitive environment	1-2 slides
	5	Unique selling proposition	1 slide
OPERATIONS	6	Sales channels and marketing	2 slides
	7	Manufacturing, processes	2 slides
	8	People, resources	2 slides
FINANCE	9	Revenue, Costs & Financial plan	3-4 slides
	10	Risks & opportunities	1 slide
	11	Decision proposal	1 slide
	12	Backup	10-20 slides

TOTAL: 15-20 slides

Figure 1.2: Structure of a business plan presentation [Source: INVESTAURA].

We will now review the individual items in turn.

3.1 Executive summary

Decision makers who will read your business plan might only have five minutes to understand what the topic is about and develop their own opinion. The executive summary is your elevator pitch. It is *the* key slide and demonstrates whether the business idea can be communicated simply and in a convincing manner. Typically the executive summary should set out the business idea, the target market, the USP(s) compared to the competition, the key risks and success factors, and a short summary of its financials.

When presenting to an audience and assuming that sufficient time is available, I do not recommend presenting the executive summary as the first slide, but as conclusion instead. The reason is that the executive summary might raise unnecessary questions that will be answered in the later part of the presentation. These early questions can interrupt the flow of the presentation, undermine confidence in the business idea and make the rest of the exposure more difficult.

3.2 Business opportunity, product and service offering

This slide should briefly and concisely summarise what you want to sell. This might be a product or a service business. Your product might build up on existing technologies and improve on them, or be a totally new concept.

The description of the product should be as simple as possible and without going into much detail. Simplicity is also particularly important for business ideas that are quite complex in themselves. Do focus here on what is essential, and remember that if you can't explain the business idea in a simple way, the end-customers are unlikely to be convinced either. So this slide can be seen as a test to communicate the business opportunity and customer benefits simply. In my experience, the simplest business ideas often had the largest success; so if your concept is too complex, look for something else as it will probably not sell.

If you need two slides, use the second slide to show a picture of the prototype that has already been designed, a high-level product roadmap, or an illustration of the use case and the key benefits for end-users, especially compared to alternative products.

The problem solved or needs addressed from the customer perspective should also be clearly answered, if not on the slide then orally. Ask yourself why the product is valuable to end-users compared to similar products or alternative solutions available on the market. Also, remember that apart from children and teenagers who often act as trend-setters, human beings change their habits rather slowly, especially when they have been doing without your product all their life or the product does not fit with their cultural habits. So make sure that your expectations on end-users are realistic, and read Chapter Nine on the diffusion of innovations if you need to explore this topic further.

3.3 Target Market

Who is your customer?

Developing a strong understanding of who your target customers are provides the key to a successful business. To do this, segment, segment, segment, and talk to potential users. Although your product might be relevant for a broad section of the population, you can probably not afford to address everyone in the early phase as this would only dilute your limited resources, especially your advertising budget. This does not mean that you will not address everybody eventually; it only means that you need to focus in the first instance. So your primary target market and your secondary market should be very clear. Other market segments are not your priority in the immediate future.

Knowing your target market, you can customise your product or solution to the specific needs of this market. For this purpose, use the 'four Ps' of any successful marketing strategy:

- product features, including packaging (e.g. opening hours for a service company) and brands
- price and pricing structure
- placement, in particular sales channel strategy, point of sales, direct sales versus indirect sales via resellers or distributors
- publicity, including the communication concept and key messages, choice of advertising media, and promotion measures.

How large is the market?

The objective of market analysis is also to quantify the size of the business opportunity so that the resource and production plan – stocks, production volume, and people – can be dimensioned accordingly. The current size of the market should be estimated as well as future market growth. This should include as a minimum the number of units sold and revenues. In addition, qualitative statements on market dynamics and the business environment can complement quantitative projections, for instance regulatory and political issues, business cyclicity, and current market trends.

3.4 Competitive environment

Competitive analysis complements the target market analysis above by identifying the key competitors, looking into their offering and estimating how the competitive environment is likely to evolve in the short to medium term. This analysis is often neglected, but is extremely important as the intensity of the competition directly influences the market share that you can aspire to achieve, as well as the price that your product and services can command, so impacting on your profit. After all, it is not the customer who is eating your lunch, but the competition.

A high quality competition analysis should:

- provide an overview of the main competitors or potential competitors when a new and emerging market is being addressed
- analyse their product and sales strategy, business model, and organisation
- review their strengths and weaknesses
- provide quantitative benchmarks in particular revenues, market share, pricing, number of customers, number of units sold.

Remember that if there is a market somewhere your company will not be alone selling to your target market, so don't neglect the analysis of competition. Most company's difficulties have directly or indirectly to do with a fierce competitive environment. If the business opportunity that you are addressing is attractive, competitors will quickly join the party and put pressure on price and profit margins. On the other hand, if you seem to be the only company addressing this market, you might wonder whether there really is a market waiting for you out there and you should ask yourself whether you are not coming to the market too early, and customers are not ready yet. As educating end-users could be very time consuming, it might be a better strategy to let others develop the market for you and do the hard 'awareness' work in the early stage. In this case you would only join later with a second-generation product to address a higher level of demand. This is the upside of coming second to market – and the downside of being a first mover in a new market.

3.5 Unique selling propositions (USPs)

This section should clarify how your business plans to differentiate from the competition and what your unique selling propositions towards end-users are going to be. These aspects are often neglected in a business plan, but doing so is dangerous for the viability of your business. If you do not have a USP, you will find it difficult to communicate to end-users why they should buy your product and not that of the competition. The good news is that there are many ways to differentiate, as we will discuss in Chapter Ten.

USPs might either be tangible like 'a unique product advantage' or 'a great distribution channel', or intangible like 'the coolest company'. When USPs are difficult to identify, it is worth asking yourself whether it is really attractive to follow a 'me-too' strategy, such as perhaps because the market has strong growth potential and is large enough for you to get a portion of it. Alternatively, the business plan might have to be refocused on its core strength, for instance a refocus on a market niche where you do have a USP.

In order to sustain a first-to-market advantage in the long-term, a business needs a lot of cash to grow faster than potential competitors and keep the largest market share. Needless to say, it is also a race against time to remain the innovation leader, maintain a technology leadership and attract best-in-class staffing.

Now that you know your target market, understand the competition and have defined your USP, you can work out your pricing strategy and set a realistic target market share. A low price is usually associated to a low cost strategy; a medium price with differentiated product features, and a high price with high quality or something truly unique. Market share estimation will be discussed in detail in Chapter Ten.

3.6 Sales channels and Marketing

A common mistake in a business plan is to believe that your product will sell on its own. Engineers in particular tend to grossly underestimate the amount of time and money that are necessary to create awareness for the product in the market and sell it. Developing a product might be a very challenging job technically, but only the first step in a successful business, and in some cases only the tip of the iceberg.

You also need to answer the following question: what is the natural place to go for your customers to find and buy your product? Building up your own points of sale takes time and is expensive, so that using existing sales channels might be a better approach. If you address consumers, these will be B2C channels like retailers or door-to-door sales; if you sell to business customers, you will need B2B channels, for instance Value-Added-Resellers or System integrators. Additional channels include the Internet, call centres and franchising systems.

In all cases you will need your own sales force to manage your direct and indirect sales channels, and you need to think carefully about its size and the best way to organise it.

In addition, you will need marketing and advertising budget to advertise in the press, on the street, on radio, on TV, at fairs, via a mailing, on the Internet. You should review the alternatives available to you, their respective advantages and disadvantages, and select your preferred go-to-market model.

3.7 Manufacturing and business processes

Next you need to figure out how your business will operate. The typical issues here are:

- Which activity do you plan to internalise or externalise? Will you manufacture yourself or rely on contract manufacturing? Will you build up an IT team or will you outsource your IT needs to a supplier? Will you build up your own customer care centre, or outsource to a service provider? How will you provide after-sales customer services?

- Where will you locate your headquarters, your R&D, manufacturing, warehouse and sales forces? Will you operate on multiple sites? Should you manufacture from a foreign country? What are the benefits and risks of each option?

- How does the overall business process look like from a customer perspective, from order entry, via manufacturing to delivery? How long is the overall cycle?

When relying on external sourcing, alternative providers should be benchmarked against each other. Also, a roll-out roadmap including key milestones will be helpful as it provides a clear picture of what should be achieved in the short term, as well as later on.

3.8 People and resources plan

Once the business processes and production volumes are clear, they can be translated into resource requirements:

- physical resources: for instance building, land, machines, tools, vehicles, software, warehouse space
- people: in particular skills, responsibilities, targets, compensation package, organisation.

In the early rollout phase, accurately planning for resources is often difficult as demand is often uncertain, but growth rates can be exponential. Plan too low, and you won't be able to meet demand, so risk losing market share; plan too high, and you end-up being burdened with over dimensioned facilities, large inventories and high running costs. In the early phase, the management team should favour a set-up that gives maximum flexibility, minimise fixed costs and rely on variable costs and scalability, even if this approach does not give the lowest cost per unit of goods sold, as the primary objective is to check that the business concept is viable and there is demand for your product. To avoid high fixed costs in an uncertain environment, some activities can be outsourced to partners initially. At a later stage, outsourced activities can be re-internalised to have a better control on cost or quality.

3.9 Revenues, costs and financial plan

This section provides a financial summary of the business plan. Emphasis is on revenues and costs, and how they relate to each other. Revenues will be driven by your market share assumption and unit price. Both can be challenging to forecast, as we will discuss in Part Three. The difference between revenues and costs is the *cashflow*, which is also the most important financial result for a new business. From the cashflow, the total capital requirement, cashflow break-even and payback period can be derived. These are useful indicators for providers of finance.

While aggregating revenues and costs, you should check the consistency of the input data that you have collected from multiple sources. You can for instance build in a number of crosschecks, and run a few simple simulations, for example modify the input assumptions and control whether the outputs behave as you expect. If you do not understand why the financial results are the way they are, then perform a deep dive and crosscheck all relationships until the dynamics of results become clear. To bring transparency into the results, a summary of the economics and main costs factors can greatly help, for instance represented as a waterfall diagram showing how revenues minus costs lead to profit.

The financial summary presented here should be backed up by a solid analysis of every individual cost item. The main cost items that will be incurred by your business are, at a high level:

- investment cost, also called CAPEX for capital expenditure
- direct cost of goods sold, including bill of materials and production costs
- SG&A for Sales, General and Admin. This includes sales, marketing and advertising costs, as well as central function costs such as HR
- other costs, in particular R&D.

The detailed analysis of the cost forecast should be included in back up to the business plan and contain at least a cashflow statement and a profit and loss account. The balance sheet is optional but useful to show how capital intensive the business is and how the business will be funded. Financial statements will be reviewed in detail in Chapter Four.

3.10 Risks and opportunities

To complement the financial plan, a risk analysis can be prepared and summarise the key risks, mitigation plans and contingency measures that would be taken if unfavourable events happen. The mirror image on the opportunity side is that the market might offer more chances than expected. Risks and opportunities can have strong impact on cash burn and capital requirement, so it is important to show that you understand what they are.

In addition, alternative scenarios might be developed to estimate the sensitivity of outputs to changes in key inputs. Scenarios are used to quantify the impact of alternative market development into operational and financial results. Typically, three scenarios are presented: a base case, a best case and worst case. The base case should be your most realistic case, but beware that the worst case can often materialise in practice.

3.11 Decision proposal

Finally, a decision proposal should be provided that summarises what you would like to achieve from the presentation of the business plan. Decision makers should not leave the room without having taken decisions or agreed on the next steps, for instance:

- when the business plan is presented within a company: agreement on the strategy, decision to start a pilot project, decision to invest immediately or undertake further R&D or test marketing, staffing decision and so on
- when talking to providers of finance outside the company: overall agreement with the business concept, readiness to support the new venture, agreement with key milestones and roadmap, provision of equity or debt financing, additional support to the management team.

4. Focus on the Right Issues

A prerequisite for a successful presentation of your business plan is that you have undertaken in-depth research and show that as a result, or based on your personal experience, you understand the business and the industry that you are planning to enter. You should demonstrate that you know what the key drivers for success (and failure) are, and also that you understand the economics of the business underpinning the financial plan. A good business plan is also about generating confidence in an audience, whether it be your management or the financial community, that there is a well-understood business opportunity to be seized.

The preparation of a business plan can be very time consuming and span anywhere between 2 weeks and 2 months. How much to go into details depends on the amount of time that you have for preparing the business plan. However, adding too many details will get you lost and only see trees where it would be more valuable to reflect on the forest as a whole.

As your time and resources will be limited, it is better to spend them wisely from the start and focus on the key aspects and parameters driving your business. This could be the size of the market, or the availability of a key technology, or obtaining a licence from a government body or a private entity. To identify and screen the key issues to focus on, you can organise a brainstorming session with your team to kick-off the business plan activities. In a follow-up meeting, these issues can be positioned on a matrix as shown in Figure 1.3. Let us discuss the four quadrants of the matrix.

Quadrant 1: Less uncertain, More important factors

Most of your time should be dedicated to analysing factors identified in quadrant 1. These are uncertain issues having a strong impact on the business case, but uncertainty can be reduced by market research, the development of a prototype or a pilot project.

More Important

1 --------------------------------- 2

These factors have a strong influence on the business opportunity; uncertainty can be considerably reduced by analysis

These factors will remain very uncertain even after analysis; they have a strong impact on the business opportunity

Less Uncertain ⟶ More Uncertain

These factors have a secondary influence on the business and uncertainty can be reduced by analysis ⚠

These factors will remain very uncertain even after analysis but have a secondary impact on the business opportunity

4   3

Less Important

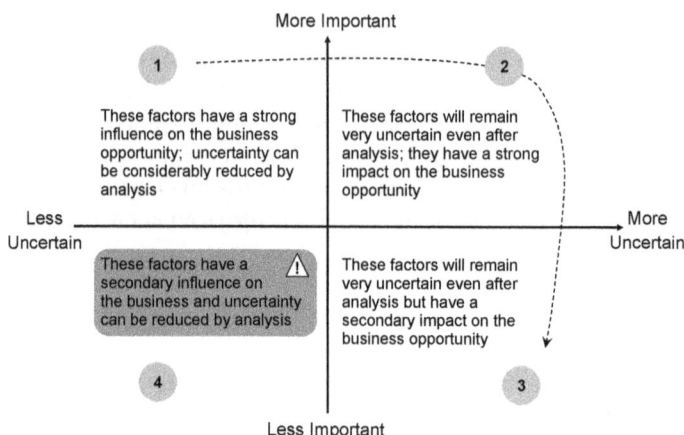

Figure 1.3: Positioning of key issues in an 'Uncertainty' x 'Importance' matrix [Source: INVESTAURA].

Quadrant 2: More uncertain, More important factors

You should also identify those factors that have a strong impact on the business opportunity and will remain very uncertain even after extensive analysis, additional R&D or test marketing. A scenario planning technique, as presented in Chapter Twelve, can be used to clarify the potential 'pictures of the future'. If quadrant 2 is empty then you are lucky, but you should not live in an illusion of certainty either and perhaps you can at least identify one key factor to position in that quadrant.

In most cases you will not address issues located in quadrant 2 in the main body of the business plan but reserve them for back-up and risk analysis, as those issues signal major uncertainties and are unlikely to help you achieve your objective (usually: getting funding). However, if the issues arise, you will be well prepared and can provide answers. This will create credibility towards your audience.

Quadrant 3: More uncertain, Less important factors

If you have any time left, then you might as well invest it in quadrant 3, which contains issues that have a secondary impact on the overall case but remain very uncertain. Here, after making assumptions on how these factors might turn out, you can estimate the size of the impact on the business case and confirm that they have a secondary importance indeed. If not, then they probably belong to quadrant 2, not quadrant 3.

Quadrant 4: Less uncertain, Less important factors

You should spend as little time as possible in the last quadrant. These are issues that have a secondary impact on the case and whose uncertainty can be reduced by analysis and research. Unfortunately, this is the quadrant where most people working on business plan tend to lose their valuable time, leading to low quality results. Don't get lost into details here. By not addressing the factors in this quadrant, you can tremendously simplify your business plans and increase their impact, because you will automatically have more time to think about the key issues identified in quadrant 1 and 2.

If you have difficulty positioning the business plan drivers in the four quadrants, remember that things are relative so try to compare issues against each other and decide if one is more important than the other or more uncertain than the other.

5. Execution is Key

Last but not least, remember that a good idea and a good business plan is only as good as the team that is going to implement it. The best thought-through business plan can turn sour if not properly executed. The team that has prepared the business plan needs to think carefully and openly whether all competences are available on board to turn the business into success. Some people are great innovators but poor executors, or vice-versa poor innovators but great executors, and people who are great at both are few. So be careful to select the right people in the management team of the new business. These are not necessarily the same people who brought up the idea first.

Having explained the main ingredients of a business plan, we now turn to a case study in the following chapter.

Case Study of a UMTS Service Provider

"Money never starts an idea, it is the idea that starts the money"
W. J. Cameron, the Ford Motor Company

In this chapter, we go through a case study to illustrate how a business plan can be prepared in practice. As UMTS has been a much-debated topic in recent years, we take the perspective of a mobile network operator in late 1999 planning to bid for a UMTS licence in the following year. We take a narrative style to describe the course of events that might have happened at that time. The company Xiliom and the people referred to are imaginary, and any resemblance to actual companies and people would be purely coincidental.

Overview of Chapter Two

1. Setting the Scene 38
2. Strategic Options..39
3. Target Market and Market Forecast................................42
4. Mobile Data Applications..45
5. Traffic Forecast 46
6. Network Infrastructure 47
7. IT Platform 48
8. Cost of Content..48
9. Cost Model..49
10. Financial Results...50
11. Scenarios...54

1. Setting the Scene

We are in October 1999. John Smith works in corporate strategy for Xiliom, a European tier 1 mobile network operator. Xiliom was founded in 1992 and received a GSM licence in the same year. The company rolled out its network between 1992 and 1996 and initially focused on business customers. Since 1997, Xiliom has experienced considerable growth in the consumer segment, in particular due to its low entry cost pre-paid packages that have sold extremely well. In 1999, the telecom regulator has indicated its intention to award UMTS licences to existing operators and new entrants during the course of 2000, using an auction process that it regards as economically efficient. The objective is also to encourage new entrants to enter the mobile market, which is expected to reach 25% population penetration in December 1999, but still has considerable growth potential. Some analysts go as far as thinking that a 100% penetration level and more is achievable in the long term.

Within corporate strategy, John's area of expertise lies in the preparation of decision proposals for the executive board. John has been appointed by the CEO of Xiliom to set-up a task force and to investigate the business opportunity that UMTS represents. At top management and board level, there is a unanimous opinion that UMTS is the way ahead to catapult Xiliom one step further. The current subscriber growth at Xiliom has been primarily driven by voice services, but with high double-digit annual increase in customer numbers, growth is likely to tail off in the next 3 to 5 years. On the other hand, the Internet is booming in the fixed network, so the mobile Internet looks like the next big thing. GPRS is expected to come to market in 2000, however its bit rate is similar to current analogue Internet access rates. UMTS on the other hand promises rate of up to 384kbps. This makes it the mobile equivalent of a new technology called ADSL, which promises rates 10 times higher than current fixed-line analogue rates.

John decides to set up a project staffed with a team of experts, and keeps it deliberately small to ensure rapid progress. The team will be assigned 50% of its time on the UMTS business plan project. John contacts the head of Marketing who appoints Anna Barns to supporting the team. Anna is an expert in market forecasting; she will consolidate industry opinion on the UMTS potential but also generate an internal company forecast based on interviews with current mobile users. John also contacts the head of Network Planning within the network division, who nominates Andrew McGeer. Andrew, a middle-aged radio planning expert, will estimate the volume of equipment and investment necessary to set up a UMTS network, which is thought to be strongly driven by the number of base stations, called

NodeBs in UMTS networks, required to achieve a certain coverage in the roll-out phase, as well as the long term capacity necessary to transport end-user traffic.

Michael will also be part of the team. In corporate finance, he is responsible for maintaining the current GSM business plan of Xiliom on a monthly basis and for monitoring Xiliom's business performance compared to plan. In recent years, Xiliom has systematically exceeded its own expectations. Michael will be responsible for setting up the financial forecast for the UMTS business and perform the business valuation. This includes estimating the annual cashflow and total capital requirement, and providing recommendations on how to best finance the business. Finally, Jim from the IT department will advise the team on IT issues. Data applications in UMTS are expected to be predominantly 'server-to-person' and therefore the business is expected to require an IT platform similar to that currently used by ISPs and on-line Web portals.

John will act as project manager, keeping the team on track and consolidating results for a final presentation to the board shortly before Christmas. The team has almost three months until then, which does not seem much though considering the low level of knowledge currently available in the company on UMTS. In addition John would like most of the work to be completed by early December so that there is enough time for a round of discussion with key stakeholders ahead of the board meeting. Workshops with key suppliers are also planned in order to learn from their experience with UMTS and collect valuable data.

2. Strategic Options

The team quickly realises that two strategic options are actually available to Xiliom: either acquire a UMTS licence and participate in the data opportunity; or do not participate and get the most out of the GSM network. In the second option, a GPRS upgrade would certainly make sense and enable the provisioning of low to medium rate data services. However, as Xiliom is already facing spectrum constraints in some dense urban areas, the present spectrum situation would not allow high volume of GPRS traffic to be transmitted, so bandwidth per user would remain low and this could create disappointment. Although a limited amount of additional GSM spectrum still remains to be allocated by the national regulatory body, the team quickly comes to the conclusion that this GSM spectrum would only help Xiliom address further growth in voice traffic for existing and new subscribers. EDGE is also ruled out as option because it is rather uncertain whether the technology will ever come to market as it currently lacks industry momentum.   Although EDGE would alleviate the spectrum scarcity by offering better spectrum efficiency than GPRS, it is thought to be a stopgap solution that is inadequate to capture the full data opportunity.

If Xiliom does not participate in the UMTS spectrum auctioning, the team has reason to believe that the company will not only lose market share to the new entrant(s), but also put its GSM business at risk in the long term.   From a current 35% market share, Xiliom would continuously lose market share to UMTS players as it would not be recognised as an innovation leader any longer.   Xiliom's GSM licence has a finite duration of 18 years, and the renewal conditions in 2010 are highly uncertain.

The team around John believes that the benefits provided by the UMTS licence are first to ensure the long-term viability of the current GSM-based voice business, and second to open the right to play in the nascent but promising mobile data space.   From his current GSM business plan, Michael runs a simulation assuming that the GSM business would continue until 2010 only and compares results with the case where the voice business would run to perpetuity.   Comparing discounted cashflows, including terminal value between beyond 2010 in the scenario with a UMTS licence, he evaluates that a UMTS licence as insurance for the GSM voice business would be worth the considerable amount of €10.4bn.   With a forecast subscriber number of 7m at the end of December 1999, the current GSM (voice) business is also valued at €2190 per 1999 subscriber, and €650 per 2010 subscriber.   A summary of results and the financial calculation are provided in Figure 2.1 and 2.2.

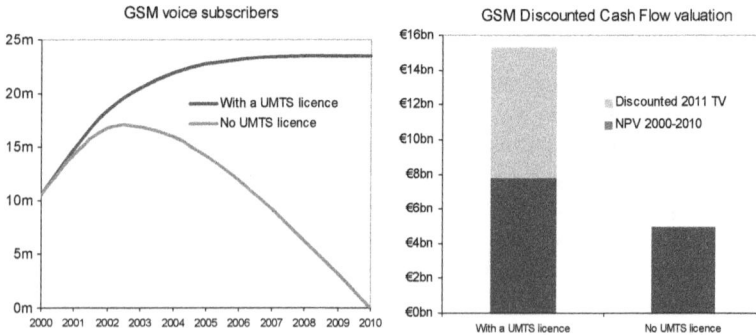

Figure 2.1: GSM business with and without a UMTS licence (NPV and TV are explained in Chapter Five) [Source: INVESTAURA].

Assumptions

ARPU per month	€30	average revenue per user
EBIT margin	25%	
Tax rate	35%	
NOPAT margin	16%	FCF (Free Cash Flow) assumed same as NOPAT (Net Operating Profit After Tax)
FCF growth per sub	2%	Due to voice traffic increase, SMS increase, ROIC improvement, but after pricing erosion
WACC	10%	Nominal term

Scenario 1: GSM+GPRS assuming UMTS licence

	2000	2001	2002	2003	2004	2005	2006	2007	2008	2009	2010	2011
Total subs	30m	42m	53m	60m	66m	71m	75m	77m	78m	78m	78m	78m
growth	50%	40%	25%	15%	10%	7%	5%	3%	2%	0%	0%	0%
Market share	35%	35%	35%	34%	33%	32%	31%	31%	30%	30%	30%	30%
Mobilex Subs	10.5m	14.7m	18.4m	20.5m	21.9m	22.7m	23.1m	23.4m	23.5m	23.5m	23.5m	23.5m
FCF (€/sub/year)	€59	€60	€61	€62	€63	€65	€66	€67	€69	€70	€71	€73
Annual FCF	€0.6bn	€0.8bn	€1.0bn	€1.2bn	€1.3bn	€1.4bn	€1.5bn	€1.6bn	€1.6bn	€1.6bn	€1.7bn	€1.7bn
Discount factor	91%	83%	75%	68%	62%	56%	51%	47%	42%	39%	35%	32%
Discounted FCF	€558m	€621m	€756m	€825m	€834m	€814m	€775m	€730m	€682m	€634m	€588m	€545m

NPV 2000-2010	€7.8bn
TV 2011, discounted	€7.5bn
Total	€15.3bn

Scenario 2: GSM+GPRS assuming no UMTS licence

	2000	2001	2002	2003	2004	2005	2006	2007	2008	2009	2010	2011
Total subs	30m	42m	53m	60m	66m	71m	75m	77m	78m	78m	78m	78m
growth	50%	40%	25%	15%	10%	7%	5%	3%	2%	0%	0%	0%
Market share	35%	34%	32%	28%	24%	20%	16%	12%	8%	4%	0%	0%
Mobilex Subs	10.5m	14.3m	16.8m	16.9m	15.9m	14.2m	11.9m	9.2m	6.3m	3.1m	0.0m	0.0m
FCF (€/sub/year)	€59	€60	€61	€62	€63	€65	€66	€67	€69	€70	€71	€73
Annual FCF	€0.6bn	€0.7bn	€0.9bn	€1.0bn	€1.0bn	€1.0bn	€0.9bn	€0.7bn	€0.5bn	€0.3bn	€0.1bn	€0.0bn
Discount factor	91%	83%	75%	68%	62%	56%	51%	47%	42%	39%	35%	32%
Discounted FCF	€558m	€611m	€711m	€715m	€646m	€550m	€442m	€332m	€225m	€127m	€39m	€0m

NPV 2000-2010	€5.0bn
TV 2011, discounted	€0.0bn
Total	€5.0bn

Value of voice	€10.4bn

Figure 2.2: Calculation details (subscriber numbers are end-of-year values) [Source: INVESTAURA].

The team agrees to model UMTS as incremental to the existing voice-dominated GSM business, as considerable economies of scope can be expected in reutilising GSM sites for UMTS NodeBs, as well as using the same teams for network maintenance, network operations, sales and customer care. For other costs position e.g. advertising, IT platform and content costs, no significant economies of scale are expected because UMTS will be used to provide brand new mobile data applications.

Before moving on, the team organises a brainstorming session to identify the key uncertainties in the business plan. Andrew mentions that UMTS is a new technology and he only has a vague idea of the number of NodeBs required for coverage; in addition, infrastructure pricing is very uncertain, and so are terminal costs. Anna adds that the largest uncertainty in her opinion in the take-up of UMTS subscribers as well as the ARPU that could be generated for data services. Jim also believes that the investment required in the IT platform, as well as the cost of content, will vary enormously depending on the type of data services provided. The cost of the UMTS licence is also unknown, but the amount that Xiliom should be prepared to pay is one of the expected outputs of the business plan. Beyond the initial coverage, the additional network investment could be estimated from traffic assumptions and the cost per additional Mbit/s of capacity, both of which need to be estimated. At the end of the brainstorming session, the team agrees to the following classification of uncertainties and their relative importance.

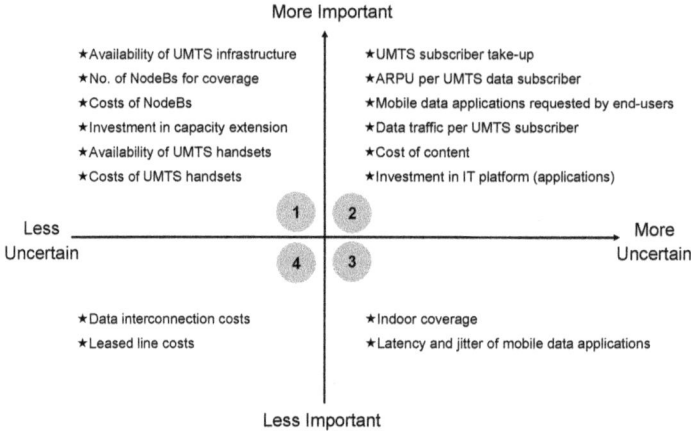

More Important

★ Availability of UMTS infrastructure   ★ UMTS subscriber take-up
★ No. of NodeBs for coverage   ★ ARPU per UMTS data subscriber
★ Costs of NodeBs   ★ Mobile data applications requested by end-users
★ Investment in capacity extension   ★ Data traffic per UMTS subscriber
★ Availability of UMTS handsets   ★ Cost of content
★ Costs of UMTS handsets   ★ Investment in IT platform (applications)

                                    1   2

Less ─── More
Uncertain   Uncertain

                                    4   3

★ Data interconnection costs   ★ Indoor coverage
★ Leased line costs   ★ Latency and jitter of mobile data applications

Less Important

Figure 2.3: Key drivers for the UMTS business plan [Source: INVESTAURA].

Issues in quadrant 1 have a large impact on the business plan, but can be clarified to a large extent, in particular via discussions with suppliers. On the other hand, the uncertainty of issues in quadrant 2 cannot be reduced in the short term – they relate mostly to unknowns on the demand side and customer acceptance of UMTS applications. Issues in quadrant 3 and 4 are felt to have a secondary impact on the overall business plan outcome so that no time should be unnecessarily lost here.

3. Target Market and Market Forecast

After two weeks of data collection from various analyst reports and industry fora, Anna comes back to the team with an industry estimate of the market potential, starting with data ARPU (average revenue per user).

As Figure 2.4 shows there is no industry consensus for the UMTS data ARPU and no clear pattern emerges as to whether the ARPU would be increasing or decreasing over time. Most industry analysts seem to believe in an ARPU range of €20 to €50 between 2005 and 2010. Anna's expectation is that if Xiliom starts addressing business customer first as it did at launch of the GSM network, then it should be able to generate a data ARPU of about €70 in the first 2 years by providing access to the Internet and corporate

Intranet from anywhere. However, the addressable market for this service is thought to be fairly limited and estimated at 20% of the business customer base, or 5% of Xiliom's current customers. This would only be one part of the total market opportunity. Additional UMTS services like email access from mobile handset are thought to have good potential as well. In addition, the residential market makes up 75% of all Xiliom customers and could be addressed with various types of services. Consumer willingness to pay for UMTS data service is estimated at only €20-€30 per month. Therefore, Anna believes that ARPU is likely to witness a period of 'dilution' from 2003 to 2005 as a shift in the UMTS customer base takes place from business customers only to a mix of business and consumers.

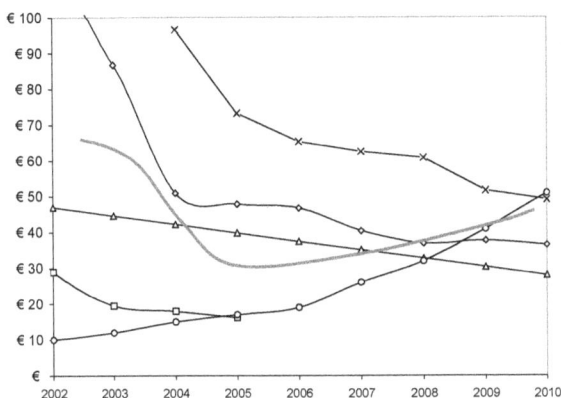

Figure 2.4: Monthly UMTS data ARPU (in red, the team's estimate of the likely ARPU development) [Source: INVESTAURA].

Beyond 2005, ARPU could grow again at a rate of about 10% per annum as the number of UMTS applications rapidly increases. As a point of comparison, the current ARPU per sub for Xiliom (mainly voice) is €40 per month, and is expected to decrease to €30 per month in year 2000. The team recognises that the ARPU forecast is very uncertain though, so that this should be one of the key variables in the scenario analysis to follow.

Regarding the UMTS subscriber numbers, Anna expects a low take-up phase in year 2002, the launch year, as well as 2003. The team shares the same opinion; in particular it is questionable whether UMTS networks would be up and running as early as January 2002. A launch towards the end of 2002 is more likely, but the issue should be further discussed with network manufacturers and suppliers of terminals. For the market forecast Anna suggests a simple segmentation between business and consumer on one hand

and in addition between low rate (up to 20kbit/s), medium rate (typically 64kbit/s) and high rate (typically 384kbit/s) data services. Low rate applications can also be provided over the GPRS network in the launch phase, but medium and high bit rate applications can only be provided over UMTS.

Anna decides to adapt the forecast generated by the UMTS Forum (Report Number 8 has just been published) to Xiliom and its early market entry strategy, and prepares the market take-up estimation shown in Figure 2.5. Only the subscribers shown in orange will be modelled in the UMTS business plan, for the following reasons:

•   the GSM network will further be used for voice in the foreseeable future and the economics of UMTS for voice are expected to be similar to that of GSM

•   low speed data services will be predominantly transported over the GPRS network.

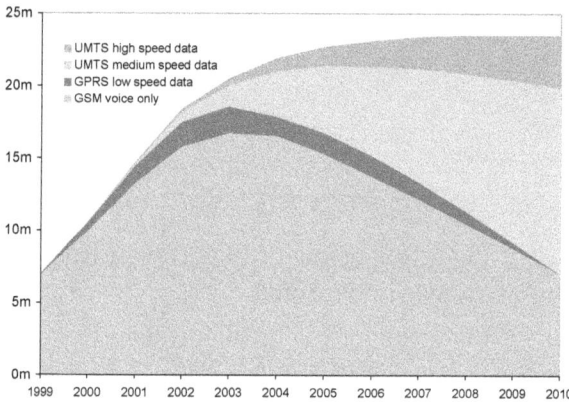

Figure 2.5: Forecast of the number of subscribers to Xiliom data services [Source: UMTS Forum Report No. 8, INVESTAURA].

The team, consistent with most industry forecasts, believes that a penetration close to 100% is achievable in the long term. This would almost quadruple the current customer base in the country where Xiliom is operating. As a new entrant is expected to enter the market, Xiliom believes that it can triple its current customer level in the long term, from 7m in 1999 to 23m in 2010. This would be consistent with a market share lost of 5% point, from today's 35% to 30% in the long term.

Xiliom, as an incumbent operator, will base its differentiation strategy on being first to market with the UMTS launch and offering the best possible coverage. In addition, Xiliom's ambition is to develop its brand further to be recognised as a leading content player.

Anna suggests validating the subscriber and ARPU forecast with customer interviews undertaken by telephone. A market research firm will be contracted for that purposes. But before doing so, a questionnaire should be prepared and the team first needs clarification of the potential UMTS services to be provided.

4. Mobile Data Applications

To help stimulate the discussion further and estimate network infrastructure and IT platform costs, the team agrees that applications should be split between:

- 'content poor' (from an operator perspective): this means that content is generated by end-users themselves or their organisations and is transparent to the mobile operator. For this type of content the operator network is mostly used as 'bit pipe'.
- 'content rich': premium content is downloaded from a mobile operator portal and billed to the end-users.

The mobile data applications expected to come to market are mapped on Figure 2.6.

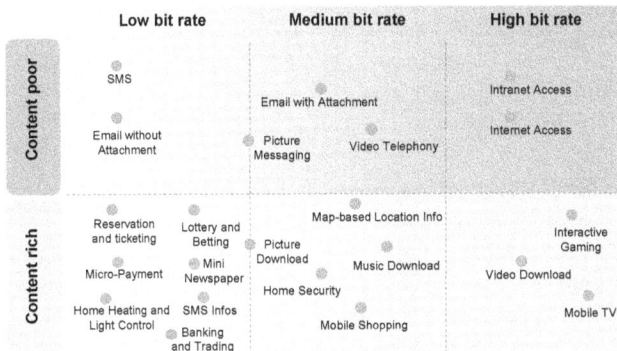

Figure 2.6: Mapping of possible mobile data applications across the 'content' and 'bit rate' dimensions [Source: INVESTAURA].

5. Traffic Forecast

A key issue for the dimensioning of the UMTS network, both on the base station side and on the core network side, is how much traffic subscribers will generate. This can be captured as the bandwidth that has to be reserved in the network per subscriber, expressed in bits per second (bps), and then be translated in Mbytes per subscriber per month if a certain user traffic profile is assumed. For example, if 10% of the daily traffic falls into the peak time (also called Busy Hour) and 25 days per month with a peak time are assumed (excluding Sundays), then 1 kbps of reserved bandwidth is equivalent to

$$\frac{1024\,\text{bits}\,/\,8\,/\,(1024 \times 1024)}{10\%} \times 25\,\text{days} = 110\,\text{Mbytes per month}$$

To generate a traffic forecast, Anna uses various sources in particular discussions with suppliers and industry market forecasts from the UMTS Forum. She also models the individual UMTS applications identified above, including the bandwidth required per application, its take-up rate and usage per month.

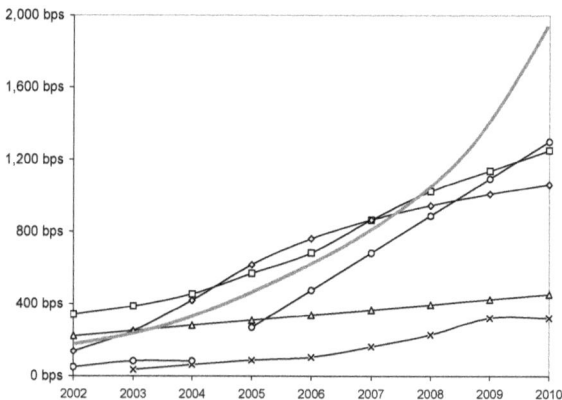

Figure 2.7: Busy Hour data bandwidth per subscriber in bits per second (Network Average) [Source: INVESTAURA].

Her model indicates that the average traffic per sub in 2002 would be about BH 200bps i.e. about 20Mbytes per month, and grow ten-fold to about BH 2000bps in 2010, i.e. 2000Mbytes per month. These are average values over all subscribers – some subscribers are expected to generate a lot more traffic and others will have a lower bandwidth requirement.

6. Network Infrastructure

The CEO of Xiliom has been very concerned that a new 'overlay' network will have to be rolled-out for UMTS services in addition to the UMTS licence costs. Andrew and Jim have just returned from a workshop with a supplier and confirm to the team that this is indeed the case. The UMTS radio interface has just been standardised by 3GPP, the Third Generation Partnership Project. Two alternative modes are available, called respectively FDD (Frequency Division Duplex) and TDD (Time Division Duplex). As a larger amount of FDD spectrum has been allocated to UMTS in the World Radio Conference in 1999 and FDD has received the strong backing of the leading GSM vendors Nokia, Siemens, Ericsson and Alcatel, Andrew expects that FDD will become the dominant technology in the short to medium term.

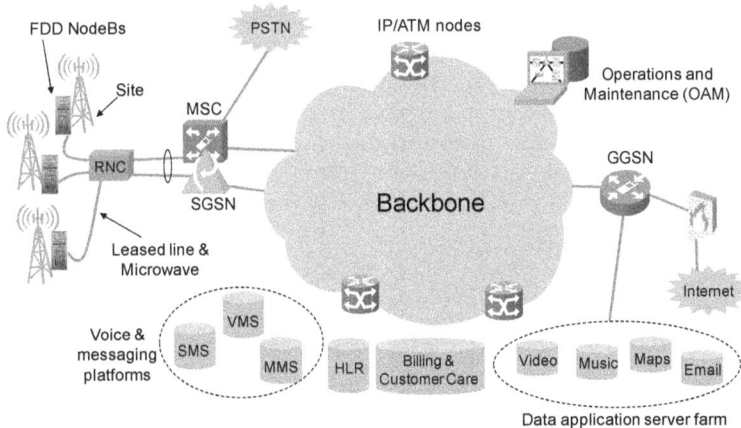

Figure 2.8: Architecture of a typical UMTS network [Source: INVESTAURA].

Separate UMTS base stations called 'NodeBs' must be rolled out to transmit radio signals in the 1.9-2.1 MHz band back and forth from the core network to mobile handsets. In addition, for data transport, a core data network based on Serving GPRS Support Nodes (SGSN) and Gateway GPRS Support Nodes (GGSN) will have to be set up, connected by high capacity links (typically STM1). Additional backhaul transmission bandwidth will also have to be installed in the radio network between NodeBs and RNCs (Radio Network Controllers), between RNCs and MSCs (Mobile Switching Centre) for voice and video circuit switched traffic as well as between RNCs and SGSNs. To facilitate discussions about the UMTS network and the investment associated, Andrew has prepared a summary network picture shown in Figure 2.8.

7. IT Platform

Jim thinks that this makes a lot of sense and on his side, develops a concept and architecture for the IT application platform that will be necessary to deliver the services above.

Video telephony will initially be provided in circuit switched mode over the UMTS MSCs. If the called party is not available, a video message will be recorded and stored in a 'Video Messaging Centre' (VMC). For Internet / Intranet access an existing ISP platform will provide a good benchmark. For content rich applications like maps download and video streaming, a server-based application logic, a content server as well as an application client on the handset will be required. Jim performs a simple network dimensioning based on Anna's traffic model and benchmarks that he has collected from fixed network operators. Overall he estimates that an investment budget of €5-€10 per sub and application would be necessary, with a reinvestment period of 3 years. Although the budget is somewhat sensitive to the number of sessions generated in the peak period by end-users, the team believes that the economies of scale and application price decrease in this area is likely to more than compensate the additional investment required due to the increasing traffic load. In the business case, the IT platform costs will be modelled as a percentage of content related ARPU to simplify the cost estimation. Assuming 5% of a €15 monthly content ARPU gives a platform investment cost of €9 per sub per year, or €27 over three years. This would be enough for 3-6 applications per user on average.

8. Cost of Content

In addition to the cost of the IT platform, one of the major cost component for 'content rich' UMTS services will be for the content itself. Access to content will need to be secured from content providers, in particular music, video, and maps. Content will be adapted to various handset models and mobile phone limitations, especially small screen size and network bandwidth constraints – for instance by reducing the video frame rate. The cost of content will come in addition to the IT platform costs already budgeted. For video content, the team decides to use benchmarks derived from the CATV industry for video content, where content providers typically receive 30% of the total revenues collected from end-users. Also, to crosscheck those benchmarks, Anna will get in touch with well-known content providers and engage first informal discussion on that topic to better understand their expectations. Based on desk research and a number of external and internal contacts, 20% to 40% of end-user revenues from content rich services is expected to be passed on to content providers. As this will have a major impact on the business case results, the cost of content is also selected as critical factor for the scenario analysis.

9. Cost Model

To simplify the cost model, the team agrees to take a shortcut. Rather than modelling every single cost component in detail, the team identifies the key cost items, the driving volumes as well as cost benchmarks. This information is derived from multiple sources: the team's current experience with the GSM business, discussions with suppliers, benchmarking from fixed network and CATV businesses as well as the team assumptions.

Fixed costs	Cost drivers	Volume benchmarks	Cost benchmarks in 2001
Upgrade of existing site to UMTS	Current site reuse ratio	70% reuse	€20000 / site
Acquisition of new sites	# New site required	3000 sites	€70000 / site
NodeB for coverage	Surface, Cell Range	10000 NodeBs	€40000 / NodeB
Core network costs	# of NodeBs	10000 NodeBs	€3000 / NodeB
Billing and CRM	# of GSM subscribers	10m	€20 per sub
Marketing cost for launch	% of today's turnover	5%	€200m over 3 years
Other launch costs	# staff in launch team	200 staff	€150k / staff

Variable costs	Cost drivers	Volume benchmarks	Cost benchmarks in 2001
Radio capacity CAPEX	Data traffic in Busy Hour	200bps in 2002, 2kbps in 2010	€60 / BH kbps
Core capacity CAPEX (RNC, xGSN)	Data traffic in Busy Hour	200bps in 2002, 2kbps in 2010	€30 / BH kbps
IT platform CAPEX	Content ARPU	€15 content ARPU	5% of content ARPU
Network OPEX (OAM, leased line)	Transport ARPU	€35 per sub per month	15% of transport ARPU
Data peering costs	Transport ARPU	€35 per sub per month	5% of transport ARPU
Service OPEX (Adv., Sales, Billing)	Total data ARPU	€50 per sub per month	30% of data ARPU
UMTS Handset subsidies	Gross incremental subs	Subs growth + 20% churn	€150 every 2 years
Content costs	Content ARPU	€15 content ARPU	20%-40% of content ARPU

Figure 2.9: Main cost items and cost drivers [Source: INVESTAURA].

Costs are split between fixed and variable costs. Fixed costs are incurred upfront and are mostly independent of the UMTS subscriber evolution. They are driven by the geographical coverage of the network, as well as the size of the current GSM operations. Variable costs are driven by the number of UMTS subscribers, the UMTS data ARPU as well as the data traffic generated by subscribers. The team is careful to specify a validity date for cost benchmarks as some cost items change rapidly over time.

A major investment is expected in infrastructure in particular UMTS sites and NodeBs for coverage. A substantial investment will also have to be undertaken in NodeB capacity when the traffic increases. Reinvestment is estimated to take place 6 years after the initial rollout expected to start in the second half of 2001. Infrastructure costs are assumed to decrease at a rate of -10% per annum, so that reinvestment will be lower than the initial investment. Finally, on the CAPEX side, an IT platform for data services will have to be installed especially for content rich applications.

On the OPEX side, the main cost items are the launch cost in 2001-2003 including a major marketing campaign (TV, print, billboards) to create awareness for UMTS services; network OPEX and Internet-peering connectivity; sales, billing and marketing OPEX; handset subsidies; cost of licensing content from content providers.

10. Financial Results

The team decides to run a first scenario based on the forecasts and cost benchmarks discussed previously. To estimate the cost of content, the end-user ARPU is split between transport ARPU (for transporting Mbytes over the mobile wireless network) and content ARPU (for accessing rich content). This does not necessarily imply that end-users will be billed separately for transport and content, as both could be bundled and charged as a lump sum, for example per application usage. To split the total ARPU, an additional assumption has to be made. At launch, with a focus on business subscribers, services will be predominantly fast Internet and email access so that content ARPU will be close to nil. In the long term, additional content rich services will be provided to the consumer market: the team believes than in 2010, 80% of the ARPU could come from premium content, the remaining 20% from transport.

A price per Mbyte of traffic transport will also be set in relationship to the pricing for Internet access from fixed networks, in particular over analogue PSTN lines, ISDN as well as ADSL, which is being rolled out in a number of European countries in the second part of 1999. In 1999, Internet access costs on average €0.06 per Mbyte, but this is expected to decrease to €0.01 in the long term. Once the ARPU for data transport and the price per Mbyte is known, the traffic per sub can be derived and its value and pattern can be crosschecked. Vice-versa, knowing the ARPU for transport and the traffic per sub, a price per Mbyte can be derived and compared with the fixed-line Internet access price.

Two other crosschecks are performed. Firstly, the UMTS ARPU and penetration take-up curve is compared with the business and consumer willingness-to-pay obtained in interviews with customers. This helps check whether the assumptions are broadly consistent. Secondly, the tariff per Mbyte for transport is compared with the network infrastructure cost per

Mbyte. The latter is obtained by dividing the annual network depreciation costs by the total annual traffic transported measured at the handset point.

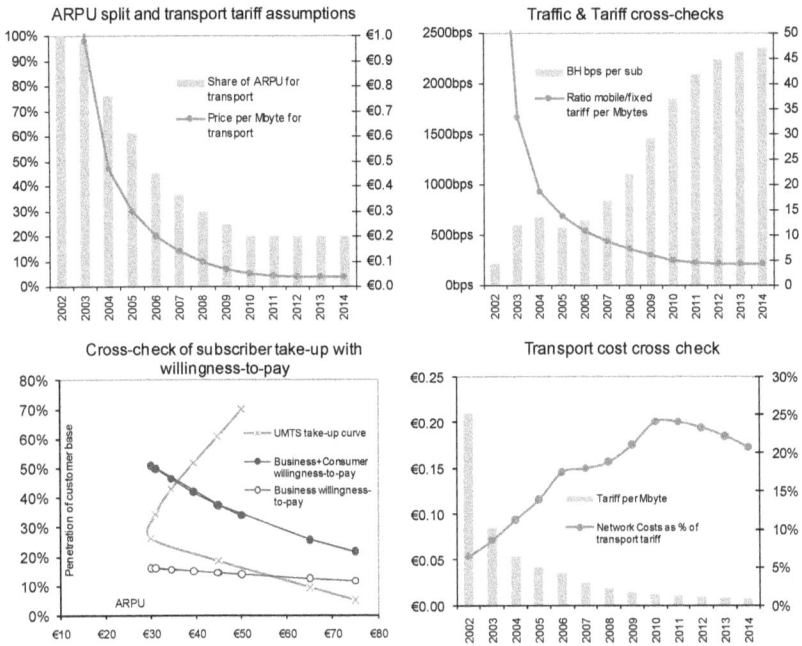

Figure 2.10: ARPU split and transport tariff assumptions, as well as three crosschecks [Source: INVESTAURA].

We can now review the financial results shown in Figure 2.11.

	2001	2002	2003	2004	2005	2006	2007	2008	2009	2010
Subcribers (m)	0.0	0.9	1.9	4.1	6.0	8.0	10.0	12.2	14.3	16.5
Turnover (€m)	0	420	1,122	1,618	1,802	2,587	3,715	5,251	7,112	9,232
EBITDA (€m)	-65	-46	354	438	486	745	1,243	1,929	2,803	3,796
in % of turnover		-11%	32%	27%	27%	29%	33%	37%	39%	41%
Annual OPEX/sub		€499	€395	€291	€221	€232	€246	€273	€301	€330
Depreciation (€m)	22	51	88	136	184	257	328	431	562	709
in % of turnover		12%	8%	8%	10%	10%	9%	8%	8%	8%
Cumulative Net CAPEX/sub		€228	€201	€148	€121	€108	€109	€120	€135	€146
EBIT (€m)	-87	-97	266	302	302	489	915	1,499	2,241	3,087
in % of turnover		-23%	24%	19%	17%	19%	25%	29%	32%	33%
Free Cash Flow (€m)	-177	-266	27	13	104	128	318	571	943	1,481
Cum. DFCF (€m)	-167	-388	-368	-360	-300	-235	-91	137	471	935
EVA (€m)	-99	-131	177	112	99	196	437	764	1,180	1,662
ROIC	-195%	-56%	65%	35%	28%	38%	55%	69%	78%	84%
NPV 2001-2020 (€m)	6,020									

Figure 2.11: Financial results 2001-2010 [Source: INVESTAURA].

Note that originally the model only covered the period 2001 to 2010. However, as the team realised that the business had not reached maturity in 2010 in terms of subscriber growth and traffic per sub, the modelling horizon was extended to cover the period 2001-2014, and the Free Cashflow was extrapolated beyond 2014 in order to calculate the Net Present Value (NPV).

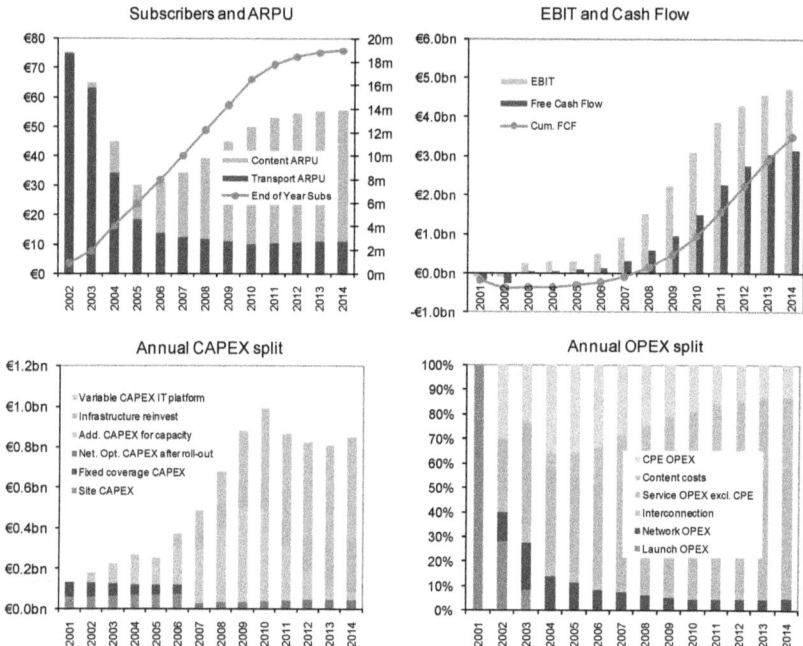

Figure 2.12: Financial results 2001-2014 [Source: INVESTAURA].

Due to the important synergies with the existing GSM business, limited UMTS investment costs in the early phase as well as strong subscriber growth, the business turns cashflow positive as early as 2003, and in 2008 in cumulative terms. The investment requirement increases strongly between 2006 and 2010 due to traffic increase as well as the necessary investment in IT applications. The impact is that the Free Cashflow FCF remains limited until 2008 when it breaks the €500m line. Beyond 2008, the business generates strong Free Cashflow supported by healthy EBITDA and EBIT margins.

The key financial results are summarised in Figure 2.13.

Key results	Value
NPV 2001-2020 (€m)	€6,020m
NPV per 2010 UMTS sub	€365
Cum. Capex 2001-2010	€4.4bn
Cum. IT Capex 2001-2010	€1.1bn
Net Cum. Capex / sub in 2010	€146
BH kbps per sub in 2010	2.0kbps
EBIT > 0 in	2003
FCF > 0 in	2005
2010 EBITDA margin	41%
2010 EBIT margin	33%

Figure 2.13: Key Financial results [Source: INVESTAURA].

As the cost of content is in the low range, the EBIT margin on the content business is actually higher than on the transport business, as confirmed by Figure 2.14.

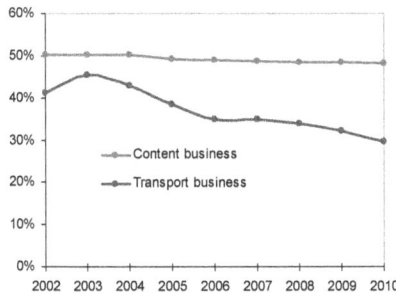

Figure 2.14: EBIT margins for the content and transport businesses, excluding the costs of handset subsidies [Source: INVESTAURA].

Note that the EBIT margin on transport is decreasing over time, an indication that the data transport tariff is decreasing more rapidly than the infrastructure cost per unit of capacity. This is confirmed by the transport cost crosscheck on Figure 2.10: network costs increase from 6% of transport revenues in 2002 to 24% in 2010. A trend reversal happens beyond 2010 as the decrease in tariff per Mbyte slows down, so that network costs stabilise around 20% of transport revenues.

Overall, the UMTS data business is valued at about €6bn over the period 2001-2020 before licence costs. The value per 2010 sub is €365, whereas the GSM business was valued at €650 per 2010 sub.

The difference is due to a number of factors:

- in line with the higher risk involved, a project WACC (Weighted Average Cost of Capital) of 13% was used for the UMTS valuation, and 10% only for the GSM valuation
- GSM is already a mature business generating strong cashflows, whereas UMTS is a new business still to be developed, and will consume a lot of cash in the initial phase
- the valuation period is different for the two businesses. GSM has been valued until perpetuity, whereas UMTS is valued over the period 2001-2020 only.

11. Scenarios

Having recognised that the UMTS data business has substantial uncertainties that cannot be resolved in the near future, the team decides to run a number of scenarios and quantify the impact of changes in key assumptions on the valuation results. Three main parameters are used to define the scenarios.

Parameter 1: Data ARPU level

The long term ARPU level is uncertain. Some analysts believe that €50 per month per sub is too high in the long term, and €30 more realistic. On the one hand new UMTS data applications should drive ARPU up but on the other hand, the GSM business has shown that a strong ARPU dilution takes place as subscribers with lower budget are being addressed, for example with prepaid packages.

Parameter 2: Tariff per Mbyte

On the upside, tariff per Mbyte might not fall as low as €0.05 in the long term, and remain substantially higher than the Internet fixed line tariff. After all, the number of Internet Service Providers is much higher than the number of mobile network operators, so competition intensity is high, for the benefit of end-users. SMS is also priced at €1,000 per Mbytes and this has not prevented its success. In addition, GSM voice tariffs show that end-users are ready to pay €0.50 per minute for calls that would cost only €0.03-€0.05 per minute when generated from a fixed network phone. Therefore, a price of €0.20 per Mbyte might be achievable in the long term with UMTS, especially if 'content rich' applications turn out to be less successful than envisaged in the base scenario, as Internet users expect content to be mostly free, so why should it be any different with the mobile Internet? As the total ARPU is held constant, the impact of a higher tariff for data transport is to increase the transport ARPU and to lower the content ARPU. As IT investments are assumed proportional to the content ARPU, IT costs are reduced in the same proportion.

Parameter 3: Cost of content

On the downside premium content might turn out to be a lot more expensive than assumed in the base scenario – 20% of content ARPU. Due to the limited number of large international content firms (e.g. Music labels, Hollywood studios), the bargaining power between content providers and mobile operators could favour the former at the expense of the latter. In this case, content costs could be as high as 40% of content ARPU.

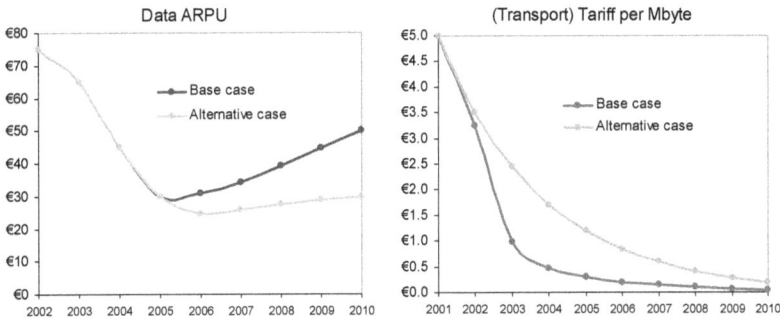

Figure 2.15: Data ARPU and tariff per Mbyte forecast for alternative scenarios [Source: INVESTAURA].

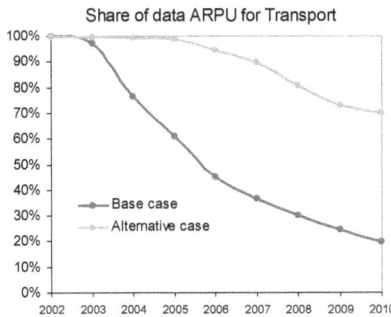

Figure 2.16: Share of ARPU for transport versus content for the data tariff scenarios depicted in Figure 2.15 [Source: INVESTAURA].

These alternative assumptions give rise to a total of 2x2x2=8 scenarios. The results of the eight scenarios are shown in Figure 2.17. They show that the UMTS business will require cumulated investment between €2.6bn and €4.4bn, while the investment in the IT application platform will range from €200m (€12 per 2010 sub) to €1.1bn (€66 per 2010 sub). In the long term, the traffic per sub should be in the range of 1-2 kbps in the busy hour. Three scenarios out of eight value the UMTS business between €5.5bn and €6.5bn, however four scenarios come to a valuation range of €2.5bn to €3.1bn only. In the worst case, the UMTS business would be valued at only €700m. This is regarded as very pessimistic though.

	Base case	Best case with high transport tariff	Expensive content	Expensive content but low data tariff	Low ARPU but high data tariff	Low ARPU and low data tariff	Low ARPU and high content fees	Worse case
ARPU	€ 50	€ 50	€ 50	€ 50	€ 30	€ 30	€ 30	€ 30
Content cost	20%	20%	40%	40%	20%	20%	40%	40%
Transport pricing	€0.05	€0.20	€0.20	€0.05	€0.20	€0.05	€0.20	€0.05
NPV 2001-2020 (€m)	€6,020m	€6,583m	€5,487m	€2,790m	€3,118m	€2,731m	€2,472m	€766m
NPV per 2010 UMTS sub	€365	€400	€333	€169	€189	€166	€150	€46
Cum. Capex 2001-2010	€4.4bn	€3.6bn	€3.6bn	€4.4bn	€2.6bn	€3.3bn	€2.6bn	€3.3bn
Cum. IT Capex 2001-2010	€1.1bn	€0.3bn	€0.3bn	€1.1bn	€0.2bn	€0.7bn	€0.2bn	€0.7bn
Net Cum. Capex / sub in 2010	€146	€143	€143	€146	€91	€94	€91	€94
BH kbps per sub in 2010	2.0kbps	1.8kbps	1.8kbps	2.0kbps	1.1kbps	1.2kbps	1.1kbps	1.2kbps
EBIT > 0 in	2003	2003	2003	2003	2003	2003	2003	2003
FCF > 0 in	2005	2005	2005	2007	2005	2005	2005	2009
2010 EBITDA margin	41%	42%	36%	25%	34%	34%	28%	18%
2010 EBIT margin	33%	36%	30%	17%	28%	25%	22%	9%
Comment	high margins on content, high IT costs, low transport tariff	high transport and content margins. Lower IT costs	low content margins but lower IT costs	low content margins but high IT costs	lower network investment but lower margins	high IT costs	low IT investment but high content costs	low ARPU, low tariff, high content cost, high IT invest

Figure 2.17: Key scenario results [Source: INVESTAURA].

Overall, the team believes that a valuation of €3bn to €6bn for the UMTS business is realistic, equivalent to €180 to €360 per 2010 sub. A licence price in the order of €1bn would therefore make sense. When adding the value created by the UMTS licence in securing the voice business in the long term, UMTS could be valued in total at €13bn to €16bn. This would justify bidding for a higher licence price than €1bn if necessary.

Having reached this point, it is high time for the team to start working on the presentation to the board along the structure presented in Chapter One. In March 2000, Xiliom successfully bids for a UMTS licence for a price of €4bn.

## Chapter Three

What Can We Learn from the dot.com Crash?

"The only people who never fail are those who never try"
Ilka Chase, American actress and novelist

Business plans have been invented to help us make the right investment decisions at the right time. In Part Two we will learn how to use key investment criteria, especially the Net Present Value as a measure of the value created by a business. Before moving on, let us catch our breath for a couple of pages to digest the previous chapters and reflect on some learning from the recent past.

Do you remember the roaring years of the 'New Economy'? The dot.com bubble that marked the end of the 20ᵗʰ century, followed by the dot.com crash at the dawn of the new one? Did this really happen? As I look back, events seem so unreal and both so close and so far at the same time.

I can remember the extraordinary excitement of a period that was apparently reinventing the rules of business, the hundreds of start-ups that mushroomed every year, the IPO's and their founders who were celebrated as the new pop stars of the era, the great hope for a better and easier world where stocks only knew one direction, where taxi drivers and secretaries alike had turned into daily stock traders. Then followed some tough years where trillions of dollars evaporated into thin air and hundreds of thousands of jobs were slashed in the wake of the dot.com collapse. As hard as the downturn might have been, I miss the buzz, the dynamic and glory of the time.

As private individuals, venture capitalists or business managers, were we simply too naïve, greedy and blinded by this new Eldorado? Or were we misled by start-up managers and their great skills at selling good-looking stories that eventually turned out to have no market at all? Probably a mix of both. Although we might not have noticed at the time, we were acting like bad venture capitalists, making very risky bets and selecting shares fairly randomly, as long as it had something to do with the Internet. As any good venture capitalist knows, from any ten well-selected investments, one on average turns out to be a jewel, three end up as semi-precious stones, and the remaining six will turn out to be castles built on sand. So we should not be surprised if our not so well selected investments have turned sour.

What can we learn from the dot.com crash? Each of us will have learnt their personal lessons. Having worked in the area of forecasting and business planning since the early 1990s, my lessons learnt are summarised below and might coincide with some of yours. A lot of this sounds like common sense today, and so it should be, but in the heat of the New Economy growth this was not always the case.

Here are ten rules that you can follow before investing your or someone else's money in any business opportunity.

1. *"You shall strive to get money from end-users for the value that you deliver to them"*.

   There is no such thing as a free lunch. Beware of business models that are free for end-users and financed by advertising only, usually the numbers do not add up. Also, be aware that for an advertiser, your business is just another space in the ocean of options at their disposal and not necessarily the better one.

2. *"You shall not expect customer habits to change overnight"*.

   If change is the only constant in life, end-user's behaviour and beliefs need time to evolve. When looking into market and demand projections, ask yourself whether the forecast requires customers to change their habits. Put yourself in the customer's shoes: would you ever be likely to use the service and product of this company? If yes, when? Do you regard yourself as an 'early adopter' or rather a 'laggard'?

3. *"You shall not believe without questioning the optimistic forecasts that people put before you"*.

   Over-optimism is a common pattern in financial forecasting, whether you are a stock analyst or a business unit head. You might ask, without being sarcastic: "Are projects presented to me because they have positive NPV, or have projects positive NPV because they are presented to me?". It seems to be a human trait that project leaders are either blinded by the excitement of their business proposal, or (and this is worse) deliberately overestimate business potential to secure a better future for themselves – far away from the business opportunity that they once recommended.

The solution for you as decision maker is to encourage a culture of trust where uncertainties are not hidden, but discussed openly to find out what can go wrong with the idea and identify preventive and corrective actions if things turn wrong; finally to create a controlling and reward system that motivates managers to achieve targets aligned with the business plan.

4. *"You shall not come too early to market".*

Is the timing right? Is the market ready? Are the key technologies required in place? Being too early has been a problem for many mobile data applications since UMTS has been launched. For instance, Location Based Services on mobile phone could never really take off because most business models required location-positioning technologies that were never rolled out by mobile network operators in the first place.

5. *"You shall not mourn over sunk costs".*

When a lot of money has already been spent on a bad project, don't believe that more money will turn it into a good one. That money has already been spent, is already lost and should not influence your decision either to plough more money into the business or to exit the business now. Drive your current investment decision by looking purely into the future value potential. Free yourself from wrong decisions made in the past. Accept and get over previous mistakes. This is easier said than done when personal egos, careers and historical reasons weigh so heavily on the present.

6. *"You shall not make it complex".*

Avoid complex business models that are difficult to explain or place too many requirements on demand and supply. They are doomed to fail. The simpler your idea is to sell to others and implement, the better its chances of success are.

7. *"You shall not invest in businesses that you do not understand".*

Inquire about the problem that the product is going to solve and the value that it will bring to customers. If you do not understand the product or the value, or none of both, then keep your money away. This recommendation applies also to any complex financial instrument like option, swap and future. If you do not understand how they work, then hands off, or you will get burnt.

8. *"You shall not invest without knowing when you will need your money back".*

Be clear about your investment horizon, your exit opportunities and whether they fit together. Don't invest in businesses when they do not bring you the exit opportunity that you may need. If your investment turns out to be a success, can you cash out at the time you want to?

9. *"You shall not underestimate the competition".*

What can you do better or different than your competitors? This might be a timing advantage; a technology breakthrough that will take your competitors years to catch up; a process innovation that gives you cost leadership and translates into higher profit, lower price or both; having a charismatic leader with a unique ability to motivate your staff, and so on. Be honest with yourself, clear about the strength of your team and build on your advantages.

10. *"You shall not invent new and fanciful investment criteria".*

Don't believe that the financial rules are different this time. The objective of business has always been to generate profit. If you take a long-term investment perspective, the source of value creation will always be the same: the ability for a company to generate positive cashflows. In Chapter Five we will see that the NPV already provides the decision criteria that we need.

Coming back to the 'New Economy', had the principles of business valuation really changed at the time? Up to the year 2001, many people argued that even with Price Earning (P/E) ratios of 40 on average, the market was fairly valued because the rules had changed. Some of the arguments were as follows:

- New technologies were thought to have a massive impact on productivity and growth, although this was difficult to quantify and hardly visible in macroeconomic data.

- Historically, academics were struggling to understand why the equity risk premium had been so high at about 5-6% per annum, and recommended that a value of 0%-2.5% per annum would be more appropriate for the future. Our readiness to take risk had increased, and we were ready to receive lower compensation for the same or higher risks. So the cost of capital should decrease, pushing the price of shares up.

These two factors were repeatedly used to explain a change in valuation patterns and high P/E ratios. Today, as we have emerged from the dot.com crash and still recovering from the financial crisis of 2007-2009, P/E ratios are back in ranges between 13 and 17 where they historically resided. In hindsight we believe that the market in 2000 was indeed overvalued. And maybe we have another explanation along the following lines:

- The market is certainly very risky, and even if we forget about it in times of low volatility, we are always reminded once in a while. On 19. October 1987, the Dow Jones fell by 29% in one single day, but fortunately quickly recovered without much damage apart for our nerves. If the market was well behaved, with returns following a normal distribution, the probability that such a shock would happen would be 1 to 10^{50}. If this does not sound unlikely enough, remember that in the last 15 billion years since the big bang, we only had 5.5×10^{12} days so far.

- Human beings have a huge aversion for losses – which hurt them 2.5 times as much as wins. We want and need to be rewarded for risks and the losses that accompany investment decisions.

So next time someone comes around and tells you that the rules have changed, remember that historically speaking, the odds are against it. And don't forget that anything you could sell in the old economy, you can still sell in the new one, only with a new sales channel called the Internet.

## Part Two

Financial Statements and Valuation

## Chapter Four

Understanding Financial Statements

"If you owe the bank $100 that's your problem. If you owe the bank $100 million, that's the bank's problem"
J.P. Getty, American business executive

If one component of a business plan attracts more attention that any other, this is certainly the financial plan. The financial plan is a forecast of the business financial statements and includes a minimum of a profit and loss account and a cashflow statement, over multiple years. Before we can generate a financial forecast we need to develop a good understanding of one year's financial statements.

In this chapter we therefore perform a deep dive into financial statements and review what their rationale is, how they are structured, and how cashflows, profits and balance sheets are calculated. If you keep with us until the end of this chapter, you will acquire a good understanding of financial statements on the journey. This knowledge will prove invaluable later on when preparing a financial plan – or evaluating an investment proposal as a decision maker. In Chapter Five, we will then show how you can estimate the business value from the financial plan. Finally, in Chapter Six, we will close Part Two with a list of common pitfalls relating to financial forecasting.

Overview of Chapter Four

1. The Rationale behind Financial Statements.......................................66
2. The Statement of Cashflow...70
3. The Profit and Loss Account..73
4. The Balance Sheet..76
5. Key Ratios...81
6. Generating a Financial Statement Forecast 90

1. The Rationale behind Financial Statements

Financial statements comprise three financial accounts called the Cashflow statement (CF), the profit & loss account (P&L) and the Balance Sheet (BS). From these statements, key ratios can be derived and provide useful measures to managers and providers of finance on the profitability of the business, its operational performance, its short-term liquidity and its longer-term stability.

Financial statements are traditionally prepared in the context of financial reporting and can be found in every company annual report. Reading annual reports is the best way to learn about a business before investing into it, however annual reports focus on the immediate past and only cover the last year or two or a few quarters. In a business plan, we will need to generate financial statements that are looking into the future and span a number of years. The time horizon must be at least as long as the product, service or project full lifecycle in order to be meaningful. For instance, for a fast-moving consumer good product like a mobile phone the forecast horizon might be as short as 2-3 years, including a period of 12 months when the product is marketed and an additional period of 2 years to cover after-sales service. For an infrastructure product like a UMTS base station, a horizon of 5 to 10 years will be common.

Financial statements can get extremely complex in the context of financial reporting. As an accountant or auditor you have to be very precise, above all because of issues of revenue recognition, the amortization of intangible assets as well as taxation issues. Annual reports must be prepared in conformity with certain accounting standards and the local accounting practice, which both vary from country to country and also change over time. Even within the Generally Agreed Accounting Principles (GAAP), issued by the American Financial Accounting Standards Board (FASB), there are considerable differences between countries. For instance US GAAP is not the same as UK GAAP: the latter allows the amortization of purchased goodwill, the former not any more. In addition, in some countries like Germany, the same set of financial statements is used to report to shareholders and tax authorities, whereas in other countries like the UK and the USA, two sets of books are required. In the latter countries, accelerated asset depreciation can be used when reporting to the tax authorities; the direct impact is to lower short-term tax payment and postpone tax to a future period. Taxation rules are often complex in their application and change all the time, so that we will not enter into much detail here.

On the other hand, the guiding principles behind financial statements are simple to understand and resistant to the passing of time. At a high level, the calculation of the main items is straightforward and remains the same in all accounting standards. This will be sufficient in almost all business plans. If you need very accurate and audit-proof figures, for instance in an M&A context, then you will have to draw on the expertise of accountants and other financial advisers. As the saying goes, the devil lies in the detail (are accountants devils?).

But to start with, why are there three statements? Each financial statement looks at the business from a different perspective and with different objectives, so that the three statements complement each other nicely.

1.1 The Cashflow statement

The Cashflow statement deals with *flows* over a certain time period (usually a year or a quarter) and shows how the revenues generated and collected by the business during that period ('cash in') have been used to cover costs ('cash out'). Costs comprise:

- operating costs, also called running costs or operating expenditure (OPEX) and cover in particular the direct cost of goods sold (COGS), salaries, research and development (R&D) and marketing costs
- capital costs (CAPEX) are incurred to purchase medium to long-term assets, for instance machines
- other cost categories such as interest payments to providers of finance (interest paid) and tax to the state (tax paid).

The difference between 'cash in' and 'cash out' forms the cashflow before financing, also called 'capital requirement', and is either a cash surplus or a cash deficit. A positive capital requirement can be used to pay dividends to shareholders or reimburse debt, and the remainder increases the cash position of the business. A negative capital requirement needs to be covered by raising additional debt or equity capital.

The beauty of cashflow is that cash is 'real money' and independent of accounting standards. We will also see that the value created by a business is ultimately related to its ability to generate a surplus of cash in the medium to long term, which exceeds the cash invested in the early phase.

The cashflow statement is particularly useful to providers of finance like venture capitalists, debt holders and equity holders. It shows:

- how much cash is required to fund the business in its launch and growth phase
- when the business will reach cash-flow break-even i.e. positive cashflow
- whether an established business is generating or consuming cash. In the maturity phase, the business will be expected to be cashflow-positive and self-financing.

A negative cashflow is not necessarily bad news as it might relate to an investment in a major growth opportunity for the business.

Note that the capital requirement can be quite volatile from one year to the next, in particular due to the lumpiness of the large capital investments that are sometimes required. Therefore, it is neither easy nor possible to derive, from historical cashflow statements, whether the business is running in a profitable manner and has enough short-term liquidity. For that purpose, we need the Profit and Loss account and the Balance Sheet.

1.2 The Profit and Loss account

The profit and loss account shows, from the point of view of the shareholders, the performance of the year's activities. Its key bottom line results are the operating profit for the year also called EBIT for Earnings Before Interest and Tax, and the Net Profit (after tax) attributable to shareholders, from which dividends can be distributed.

Profit is a flow, but unlike cashflows that deal with 'real money', profit is measured in 'accounting money' as defined by the *accruals* principles. These state that revenues and costs are recognised as they are earned and incurred respectively (in practice when they are invoiced or recognised as such), and not as they are received from customers or paid to suppliers. So revenues (sales) in the P&L is not the same as cash received ('cash-in'), because most sales are credit sales: customers pay for services and goods sold a number of days after the invoicing date. This implies that customers are debtors to the business. Similarly on the cost side, companies pay their suppliers some time after the invoicing date, so suppliers are creditors to the company.

In addition, the accruals principles state that revenues and costs are matched as far as their relationship can be justified. One important implication is the concept of *depreciation* for fixed assets. These are assets that have a durable life longer than the reporting period, which is typically one year. As those assets will be participating in the generation of revenues over a period longer that the reporting period, their costs are not deducted from the P&L revenues in full, but pro-rata of their expected lifetime. Fixed assets are capitalised on the asset side of the balance sheet and written-off in the P&L statement over their depreciation lifetime.

Whereas cashflows can be quite volatile following the decision to buy new business assets, the P&L smoothes out the capital expenditure spikes and is a more appropriate instrument to measure the intrinsic profitability and viability of the business.

The P&L results are also used to calculate taxation in some countries, for instance Germany, but not in those where differing depreciation lifetimes are usually used for financial reporting and taxation purposes, in particular the USA and the UK. In some countries also, a dividend distribution when no profit has been generated during the year might not be allowed, so that being profitable is a prerequisite to paying dividends to shareholders. Profits that are not distributed as dividend are called retained profits and go into the balance sheet to increase the total shareholder equity on the liability side.

1.3 The Balance Sheet

The Balance Sheet gives a picture of the business at a particular point in time: the end of the reporting period, usually the 31 December of the year. Unlike the CF or P&L, it does not report on a flow but reflects the state of the company at the reporting date. The Balance Sheet provides details about:

- on one side, the assets owned by the business: tangible goods such as machinery or buildings; intangible assets like patents; inventories, debtors and cash
- on the other side, the liabilities it has towards its long-term providers of finance and short-term creditors.

As the Balance Sheet shows how the liabilities and shareholder equity have been used to invest in assets, it should be no surprise that the Balance Sheet always balances: the total assets value must be equal to the sum of the liabilities plus equity. From the Balance Sheet, liquidity and stability ratios can be derived and provide an indication of the company's ability to serve its short-term and long-term debts. This will be of particular interest to debt-holders like banks financing the business via loans, but also suppliers to evaluate the risk of doing business with this company.

For business planning purposes, and as long as we are not trying to answer how the business will be financed, the Balance Sheet is optional, so that we can focus on profit and cashflows. However, if a business valuation has to be prepared using the EVA® (Economic Value Added) approach, then key financial ratios such as the ROIC (Return On Invested Capital) must be calculated, which will require a Balance Sheet forecast, or a least an estimation of the net fixed assets as well as the working capital – the difference between inventories plus debtors and creditors – and their change over time.

Note that the CF, P&L and BS statements are not fully independent. On the asset side of the Balance Sheet, changes between the opening and closing positions will reflect increases in fixed assets as a result of investments, additional depreciation falling due, increase in the cash balance during the period, and change in working capital. These are all items appearing in the CF statement as well as the P&L account.

We now review the structure of each financial statement in more detail, starting with the statement of Cashflow.

2. The Statement of Cashflow

2.1 Overview

The statement of cashflow reports on the cash receipts and cash payments of a business during a certain period, typically one year. It details the causes for changes in the cash position of the business by providing information about operating, investing and financing activities:

- operating activities include collections from customers, cash payments to employees and suppliers, interest payment to debt holders and tax payment to the state
- investing activities are purchase of property, plant, and equipment, but also purchase of intangible assets such as licenses when these are recognised as investments
- financing activities cover borrowing of cash from debtors and shareholders, or reimbursement to providers of finance when required by the terms of the loan.

R&D as well as marketing and advertising expenditures, although providing benefits over multiple years, are usually treated as operating activities, not investing activities – a deviation from the accruals rule, and a reflection that accountants feel uncomfortable with intangible assets that have a fairly arbitrary lifetime.

The operating, investing and financing activities give rise to three cashflows in the CF statement: the 'cashflow from operations' also called 'cashflow before investment', the 'cashflow before financing' which is the cashflow after investment, and the 'cashflow after financing', which is the same the change in the Balance Sheet cash balance during the period.

2.2 Cashflow calculation

The calculation logic for the various cashflows discussed above is shown in Figure 4.1.

	Revenues
-	OPEX
-	Change in Working Capital excluding cash (Inventories + Debtors- Creditors)
-	Interest Paid
-	Tax Paid
=	**Cashflow from Operations**

Alternatively, the calculation starting from the P&L provides the same result:

	Pre-Tax Profit
+	Depreciation & Amortisation
-	Change in Working Capital excluding cash
-	Tax Paid
=	**Cashflow from Operations**

The derivation of the two other cashflows goes as follows:

	Cashflow from Operations
-	Capital Expenditure (tangible and intangible)
=	**Cashflow before Financing**
+	Change in interest-bearing debt (loans, bank overdraft)
+	Change in Share Capital (issue of equity, share repurchase)
-	Dividends Paid
=	**Cashflow after Financing**
=	Change in Cash during the period

Figure 4.1: Main items and derivation of the cashflow statement [Source: INVESTAURA].

The cashflow statement is a great instrument to diagnose the health of a business, its ability to be self-sustaining and generate cash from its operations, to cover investment and reimburse its debt as it falls due. Also, from a valuation perspective a positive cashflow sustained over time is a much better driver of value than profit (EBIT), in particular because the former deals with real money and you cannot fake cash, whereas EBIT levels are influenced by accounting rules, which can change over time and unfortunately be somewhat misleading or even manipulated.

2.3 Free Cashflow (FCF)

Another cashflow often talked about in the context of valuation is the Free Cashflow. This is the Cashflow before Financing that is generated by the business excluding Interest payment and not considering how the business is financed. Note that the Free Cashflow is always after tax. It is derived from the Cashflow before Financing after adding back the Interest Paid and recalculating Tax Paid as if there had been no interest payment. To put it another way, the Free Cashflow excludes the tax shield provided by debt financing as interest payments are tax deductible.

The cash is said to be 'free' because this is the cashflow after investment that is available for distribution to the providers of finance. It is also 'freed' from any financing consideration.

2.4 Treatment of tax-credit for loss in a business plan

The issue sometimes arises as to whether tax should be included in a business plan. The answer is a definite YES. Tax is a cost to businesses and projects, and has a real, material impact on cashflows and business value.

At the project level, when profit before tax is negative, it is possible to consider that the specific project has generated a tax reduction for the rest of the business (if it has made an overall profit) and to include this accordingly in the valuation of the project as a tax credit, a positive cash inflow. This is the approach that you should follow if you are looking at a project, but not as a whole stand-alone company. At the company level, when the company has a made a loss in one year, no tax is due and it is usually allowed to carry the loss forward for a number of years. When the company makes a profit in the following years, the tax expenses will be reduced by the amount of the loss carried forward.

Beyond these general rules, as tax issues are very country- and company-specific, you will need the support of a tax specialist if you need a precise, auditor-proof result.

3. The Profit and Loss Account

3.1 P&L structure

The P&L account sets out the profitability of a business from the point of view of its shareholders. A typical P&L structure is provided in Figure 4.2 below.

	Revenue (Sales, Turnover)
-	OPEX (Operating Expenditures, Running costs)
=	**EBITDA** (Earnings Before Interest, Tax, Depreciation and Amortisation)
-	Depreciation of tangible assets
-	Amortisation of intangible assets
=	**EBIT** (Earnings Before Interest and Tax; also called Operating Profit)
-	Interest Expenses
=	**Pre-Tax Profit**
-	Tax Declared
=	**Net Profit**
-	Dividends Declared
=	**Retained Profit** (Retained Earnings)

Figure 4.2: P&L structure [Source: INVESTAURA].

Revenues represent the amount invoiced to external customers excluding VAT and other sales tax. VAT on customer sales is collected by the company and forwarded to the tax authorities after deduction of VAT payments incurred by the business. Acting as a collector of VAT, at any moment the business might owe VAT to the state or vice-versa, so that VAT, except for timing of collection and payments, has a neutral impact on the P&L, so should not be accounted for here. On the other hand, VAT has an impact on liquidity, so its impact on the cashflow and balance sheet are real and should be included in business planning when the amounts involved are substantial compared to other items.

Sometimes OPEX is broken-down into more detail as shown in Figure 4.3. The costs of Sales, General and Admin are often abbreviated as 'SG&A' when aggregated in one lump sum.

	Revenues
-	Cost of Goods Sold (CoGS)
=	**Gross Profit**
-	R&D costs
-	Cost of Sales (including marketing and advertising)
-	General & Admin costs
=	**EBITDA**

Figure 4.3: Alternative P&L structure up to EBITDA [Source: INVESTAURA].

3.2 Depreciation and amortisation

Depreciating an asset means spreading its cost over its estimated useful lifetime, in line with the accounting principle of matching costs to revenues. The acquisition costs of long-lived assets are allocated to the P&L in those periods that benefit from the use of the assets. The assets can be either tangible, for instance physical assets such as buildings, machines, equipment, office furniture; or intangible assets like licences, patents, trademarks, copyrights, franchises owned by the entity, in which case the term 'amortisation' is used instead of 'depreciation'. Intangible assets are a class of long-lived assets that are not physical in nature. Both tangible and intangible assets are said to be 'fixed' as they contribute to the ongoing operation of the business over multiple time periods, to contrast them with current assets that are expected to be turned into cash within less than one year.

The depreciation period varies considerably according to the asset type and the accounting standards in use. Buildings tend to have a very long depreciation period e.g. 40 years, whereas plant and infrastructure are typically depreciated over 3-10 years.

The most common form of depreciation is the straight-line depreciation, whereby the acquisition value of the asset is depreciated linearly over the useful life of the asset, and each year an equal amount is passed on to the P&L. The useful life of an asset is determined as the shorter of the physical life of the asset before it wears out and the economic life of the asset before it is obsolete.

Note that US GAAP and IFRS, the International Financial Reporting Standards, do not allow the amortisation of goodwill any longer, an intangible asset arising in the context of merger and acquisitions. Also, some intangible assets such as land are recognised to have an indefinite lifetime and should not be amortised either. For both categories of intangible assets, an impairment test should be performed annually and a possible de-valuation be written off against reserves in the Balance Sheet. More on this later when we turn to the Balance Sheet.

3.3 Taxation revisited

Unlike depreciation periods for accounting purposes, the depreciation periods used for tax purposes are defined with precision by the tax authorities and are binding. In the UK and the USA they are shorter than the depreciation periods used for financial accounting purposes, which provide more flexibility as the financial accounting standards only recommend ranges. In addition, assets are usually depreciated using the accelerated depreciation method for tax purposes, and linear depreciation for financial reporting. This has the effect of increasing tax shields from depreciation in the short term, and postponing tax payments. In cumulative terms, taxation charge remains the same, but the accelerated depreciation has a positive impact on NPV and value compared to a linear depreciation.

Even within GAAP, there are substantial differences in depreciation periods between countries. German companies tend to use shorter depreciation periods than in the UK and the USA because the depreciation periods are specified for tax purposes and German legislation requires that the same periods must be used in the preparation of the financial accounts.

Note also the subjective nature of profit measurement that not only depends on the depreciation period, but also on the way inventories are accounted for in the balance sheet using historical cost or current cost accounting, and First-In-First-Out or Last-In-First-Out. More on this in the next section.

4. The Balance Sheet

From the three financial statements, the balance sheet is the most extensively affected by the accounting standards used for financial reporting purposes, whether this be US GAAP, UK GAAP, IFRS, French, Dutch, German or any other national accounting system. The impact of the standards on the valuation and depreciation of assets is significant. Whereas cash is cash and can't be mistaken, traditionally considerable room was left open to interpretation in the standards regarding the balance sheet, and indirectly the P&L account. In the future, increasing internationalisation, opening-up of financial markets as well as globalisation of companies should lead to the convergence of local accounting practices towards international standards. This has already started, but this will still take time.

4.1 Balance Sheet structure

The balance sheet as at a certain date shows what the assets of the business are at that date ('the Assets') and who the assets are owed to ('the Liabilities'), either shareholders, or lenders and other creditors.

Closing Balance Sheet as at 31. December of Year 2009	
Assets	**Liabilities**
Fixed assets	**Equity capital = shareholders' funds**
1. tangible assets (e.g. land, building, plant) 2. intangible assets (e.g. patent, licence, brands, goodwill)	1. share capital 2. cumulated retained profit (reserve) 3. annual retained profit (surplus or deficit)
	Liabilities
Current assets	1. long-term liabilities (e.g. loans, financial lease)
1. inventories (stocks) 2. debtors 3. cash or cash equivalent	2. current (short-term) liabilities (e.g. trade creditors, bank overdraft, tax payable, dividend payable)
Total Assets	**Total Liabilities & Equity**

Figure 4.4: Typical balance sheet structure [Source: INVESTAURA].

On the asset side, assets can be split between fixed and current assets. Fixed assets are 'fixed' in the concrete sense that they might not be movable, or in the figurative sense that they contribute to the long-term success of the business and are not expected to be turned into cash in the short term, contrary to current assets.

The liabilities side comprises shareholders funds on one hand and other sources of finance provided by and owed to debt holders on the other. Debt liabilities are split between current liabilities, which are due within one year, and long-term liabilities. Debt can also be split between interest-bearing debt like short-term overdraft and long-term bank loans, and non-interest-bearing debt like trade creditors and pension funds.

Current liabilities, once deducted from current assets gives 'net current assets'. The 'working capital' is the difference between non-cash current assets and non-interest-bearing current liabilities. In many cases, tax payable and interest payable are low or nil because tax and interest due have already been paid, so that working capital is approximated as the difference between debtors plus inventories and creditors. Unlike working capital, net current assets include cash from which short-term interest-bearing liabilities like bank overdraft are subtracted.

The balance sheet creates a valuation problem for the assets that it contains, and to a lesser extent for its liabilities. On the asset side, the main issues are: the use of current cost or historical cost accounting for fixed asset valuation; the valuation of inventories using FIFO or LIFO; the valuation of intangible assets like brands and goodwill. We will briefly review these issues now.

4.2 Current cost versus historical cost

Traditionally, companies used historical cost accounting to value assets in their balance sheet. Some practitioners take the view that the balance sheet should be seen as a historical record, in which historical cost is the best approach and has the advantage of being objective and verifiable by independent parties. Other accountants believe that a balance sheet that does not show how much the assets are worth is of little use to shareholders, and historical costs can be considerably misleading in high inflation periods.

To alleviate the problem, historical costs are sometimes re-valued to account for inflation as a measure of change in general price level. This is called Current Purchasing Power (CPP) accounting. This was mandatory in the USA until 1985. On the other hand, Current Cost Accounting (CCA) was developed to adjust asset values to changes in specific prices and introduced the notion of Current Cost. Current costs are the lowest of replacement costs and the 'recoverable value', the latter being the higher of the realisable market value in a transaction and the economic value from the further use of the assets in the business (i.e. the NPV of future cashflow from the assets).

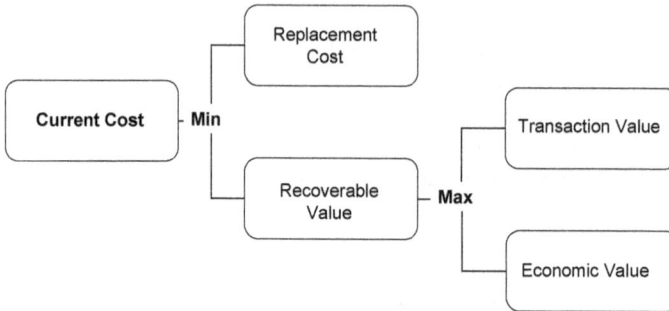

Figure 4.5: Current Cost definition [Source: INVESTAURA].

US GAAP and IFRS are increasingly requesting companies to report their assets and liabilities in the balance sheet at 'fair value'. Fair value is defined as the amount for which an asset could be exchanged between knowledgeable, willing parties in an arm's length transaction. Where there is a market for the asset, fair value is equal to the market value of the asset. Note that companies listed on European stock exchanges had to migrate to IFRS by the end of 2005.

In practice today, a mixture of historical cost, current replacement cost and fair (market) value is used by companies. In high inflation countries, or for buildings and land held over very long period, it is not uncommon to revalue assets so that they come more into line with their current market value. This leads to an increase in reserves to shareholders on the liability side of the balance sheet.

4.3 LIFO versus FIFO valuation of inventories

The accounting standards historically give ample freedom regarding the valuation method that should be used for valuing inventories. Inventories are usually valued at cost or at the lowest of cost and net realisable value. When the cost of inputs such as raw material varies over time, the issue becomes whether Last-In-First-Out or First-In-First-Out should be used. The former has been popular in the USA while the latter is mainstream in Europe. Last-In-First-Out refers to the assumption that inventories produced last are first used or sold. In period of inflation, LIFO leads to lower profit, so lower tax, but higher after-tax cashflows. FIFO on the other hands leads to higher profits, but lower after-tax cashflows. There is also some evidence that a switch from LIFO to FIFO leads to a decrease in share price on the stock market.

IFRS has ruled through IAS2 that inventories should be valued using FIFO or a weighted average cost formula.

4.4 Valuation of brands and other intangible assets

Intangible assets such as brands, Intellectual Property Rights (IPR) and licences are increasingly the most important assets of companies, and we can expect them to attract even greater attention in future financial reports.

Historically, intangible assets were valued at historical costs and amortised over their estimated useful lifetime, usually no longer than 40 years. This is now changing. In particular, IFRS has issued IAS 38 on intangible assets in 2004, and intangible assets are now recognised as either having a definite or an indefinite useful lifetime and are valued using either cost accounting (including amortisation), or re-valued annually. Intangible assets with indefinite useful lifetime cannot be amortised, but must be tested annually for impairment. An asset is said to be impaired if the value at which it is recognised in the balance sheet exceeds it recoverable value, which is the higher of its selling price and its current value in use.

In addition, IFRS 3 is also mandating that acquired brands be valued on the balance sheet of the acquiring company, and distinguished from goodwill that might arise when an M&A transaction is taking place. An indefinite life is applied to brands and therefore brand value should not be amortised, but tested for impairment annually.

Beyond these accounting aspects, valuing intangible assets is also increasingly regarded as important for portfolio management. Valuing brands allow managers to better understand the source of the value creation in their businesses, and provide useful insight when brands and other intangible assets are considered for sale or lease to third parties.

4.5 Valuation of goodwill

Goodwill results from the acquisition of assets at a cost higher than their book value. This mainly arises in the context of merger and acquisition. Historically, an M&A transaction would take place either as a 'purchase' for accounting purposes (with potential creation of goodwill) or as a 'pooling-of-interest' in the case of a merger (with no goodwill creation and the merger of two balance sheets). These were also respectively called 'acquisition accounting' and 'merger accounting'. Under 'acquisition accounting', companies could either capitalise and amortise goodwill or eliminate it against reserves in one step, with most companies choosing the latter approach, as goodwill amortisation would not reduce future profits and capital employed would be lower in the balance sheet, so ROIC would be increased.

According to US GAAP since 2001 and IFRS since 2004, 'merger accounting' is not allowed anymore. This means that 'acquisition accounting' is compulsory in an M&A, even in the case of a merger. In addition, purchased goodwill cannot be amortised any longer, but has to be tested for impairment annually. In practice, this implies that goodwill will play an increasingly important role in companies' balance sheet in the future, and companies' net assets be higher than under the past accounting standards.

4.6 Why does the balance sheet balance?

Although probably not straightforward at first sight, the difference between the closing and opening balance sheet for the year is equal to the movements of cashflows from the cashflow statement and the retained profit for the year as bottom-line of the P&L.

Figure 4.6 provides a restatement of Figure 4.1 above. It shows that changes on the asset side of the balance sheet during the year equal to changes on the liabilities side of the balance sheet. As the balance sheet at time zero balances (cash as asset has been provided by shareholders and debt holders), the balance sheet in all subsequent time period remains balanced.

	Change in cash during the period
+	Change in debtors
+	Change in inventories
+	CAPEX
-	Depreciation
=	
	Change in long-term debt
+	Change in short-term creditors (trade creditors, short-term debt)
+	Change in tax payable ('tax declared'- 'tax paid')
+	Change in dividend payable ('dividend declared' – 'dividend paid')
+	Change in Share Capital
+	Retained profit for the year (from the P&L)

Figure 4.6: Restatement of the cashflow calculation [Source: INVESTAURA].

After this long exposition, we will now review the main key ratios used in business. This will be useful for two reasons: firstly, managers reviewing business plans will use these ratios to benchmark the business plan against their own expectation and alternative investment opportunities; secondly, key ratios are often useful to forecast some of the items appearing in the financial statements beyond the explicit modelling horizon. Therefore understanding key ratios will also help us generate financial forecast for the financial plan

5. Key Ratios

From the three financial statements, we can calculate financial ratios and draw implication on the profitability, liquidity, stability and overall operational performance of the business.

Ratios used in isolation are rarely useful, but on the other hand, some ratios are strongly correlated with each other, so ideally a small, but meaningful number of ratios should be calculated for performance analysis. Financial ratios are used by the management, shareholders, debt holders and financial analysts to estimate business performance, highlight areas of concern and benchmark the current situation with past historical performance and with other companies on the market. Benchmarking can be challenging as the accounting methods used can change over time for one company, but also not remain consistent across a peer group of comparable companies within one country or across countries, so that considerable care is required here.

5.1 Profitability metrics

The most important profitability metrics are the EBIT and EBITDA margin, as well as the Return of Invested Capital ROIC (entity perspective) and the Return on Equity (shareholder perspective):

The EBIT and EBITDA margins express profit as percentages of revenues:

$$EBIT\,margin = \frac{EBIT}{Revenues}$$

$$EBITDA\,margin = \frac{EBITDA}{Revenues}$$

The EBITDA margin provides an indication on how well operating costs are managed and controlled. The EBITDA margin is to be preferred to the EBIT margin when making cross-company comparison, as companies often use differing depreciation and amortisation schemes.

Figure 4.7 provides typical EBITDA and EBIT margin for various types of player at maturity in the telecom value chain.

Company type	EBITDA margin	EBIT margin
Mobile Network Operators	25%-50%	15%-30%
Fixed Network Operators	25%-35%	10%-20%
MVNO and Resellers	4%-10%	3%-8%
CATV operators	40%-60%	10%-20%
Internet Service Providers	5%-15%	3%-10%
Infrastructure suppliers	5%-20%	0%-15%
Handset suppliers	10%-30%	5%-20%
TV broadcasters	10%-25%	5%-20%

Figure 4.7: EBITDA and EBIT margins for various telecom players [Source: company annual reports, INVESTAURA].

Note that the more capital intensive a business is, the higher its EBITDA margin will have to be in order to achieve a ROIC higher than its cost of capital, the weighted average cost of capital WACC.

The Invested Capital is the Total Assets from the balance sheet net of non-interest-bearing liabilities like trade creditors. The Invested Capital is also equal to Total Liabilities minus non-interest-bearing liabilities. Note that the Invested Capital is not exactly the same as Capital Employed, which is Total Assets net of Current Liabilities, including interest-bearing short-term debt, so that Capital Employed is lower than Invested Capital.

The ROIC is the ratio of NOPAT to Invested Capital. NOPAT is the Net Operating Profit minus Adjusted Tax. Tax is adjusted as in the calculation of the Free Cashflow in Section 2.3, as if the business did not pay any interest charge.

$$\text{Return on Invested Capital (ROIC)} = \frac{\text{NOPAT}}{\text{Invested Capital}}$$

The ROIC can be compared with the WACC and provides a useful indicator whether the business has created value during the year or not. The ROIC takes the perspective of the overall entity, and therefore uses values in the numerator and denominator that do not depend on the way the business is financed.

When a business carries goodwill on its balance sheet, ROIC should be calculated with goodwill included in the Invested Capital. On the other hand, goodwill should be excluded from amortisation in the calculation of NOPAT. The rationale is not so much that according to US GAAP and IFRS, goodwill should not be amortised anymore, but rather that unlike other assets, goodwill does not wear out and is not replaced. The overall impact will be to decrease ROIC values, so an acquisition generating substantial goodwill for the acquiring company will only be value-creating if the NOPAT of the acquired entity after integration is high enough to cover the capital charge relating to goodwill recognition. This should place a higher hurdle on the acquisition of companies, which can only be motivated if additional value is created on top of the intangible value acquired and recognised in the balance sheet as goodwill.

The Return on Equity takes a shareholder perspective only and is the ratio of the after tax profit generated by the business during the year to the equity capital:

$$\text{Return on Equity (ROE)} = \frac{\text{Net Profit}}{\text{Equity Capital}}$$

The Return on Equity shows how much profit is earned by the business from a shareholder perspective in proportion to the own engaged capital. Equity investors can use this indicator for a comparison with alternative investment possibilities. ROE of 10%-20% are common in practice for mature businesses.

Finally, there is the concept of Return on Investment (ROI) and Return on Assets (ROA), which we do not recommend using because they are ambivalent. In practice, ROI either takes a shareholder perspective in which case ROI is the same as ROE, or takes an entity perspective in which case ROI means ROIC. The ROA is often used instead of the ROIC, but is actually an inconsistent ratio, as Net Profit (after interest, tax: equity approach) is divided by Assets (entity approach!). It is better to use ROIC instead. If you are really keen to use total Assets rather than Invested Capital in the denominator, then take NOPAT in the numerator, so that at least your ratio is consistent.

Note that a company's profit can be low but ROIC high when capital employed is low. In capital-intensive industries like utilities, profit margins have to be high to lead to acceptable ROIC.

ROE and ROIC can be restated as follows.

$$ROIC = \frac{NOPAT}{Sales} \times \frac{Sales}{Invested\ Capital} \qquad \text{(entity perspective)}$$

$$ROE = \frac{Net\ Profit}{Sales} \times \frac{Sales}{Assets} \times \frac{Assets}{Equity} \qquad \text{(equity perspective)}$$

The ROE expression states that ROE is the product of the net profit margin, the asset turnover and the financial leverage. Profit margins and capital turnover tend to vary inversely: the lower the profit margin, the higher the capital turnover has to be to generate acceptable ROE level. Think about a supermarket for instance. The third term, the leverage, can be restated as (1+Liabilities/Equity). The more stable and the higher a business cashflow is, the higher it can borrow to increase its financial leverage, and the higher it can increase its ROE for shareholders.

Figure 4.8 shows how the ROIC is related to other key operational performance metrics. The two key levers to achieve a high ROIC are the profit (EBIT) margin and the capital turnover (Sales / Invested Capital). Improvement of the EBIT margin can be achieved by setting and implementing OPEX cost management measures, whereas increasing Capital Turnover requires active management measures for all items on the assets side of the Balance Sheet: fixed asset, inventories and debtors management. Note that the third lever, financial leverage, does not appear here as we are looking at the overall entity and not taking a shareholder perspective.

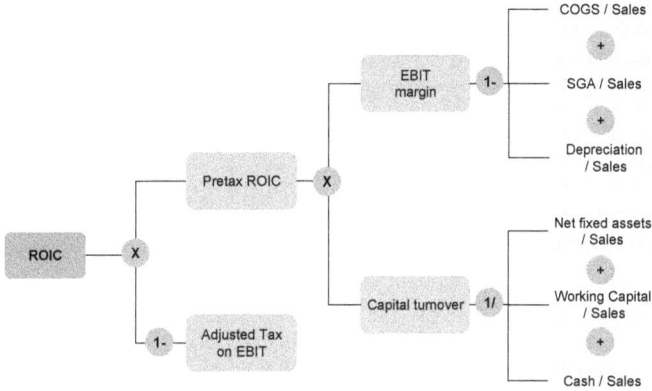

Figure 4.8: ROIC driver tree [Source: INVESTAURA].

5.2 Liquidity metrics

In the short term, there is an aspect that is more important than anything else for a company: remaining liquid, as otherwise it cannot pay its short-term creditors and the interest on its debt, and might be declared bankrupt. Once in bankruptcy (Chapter 11 in the USA), a company either manages to restructure its debt, or it will be driven into liquidation and its assets sold to reimburse creditors. Shareholders get the rest once creditors have been served, but in practice usually get nothing from the proceeds – certainly an undesirable outcome. So remaining liquid is very important.

Liquidity is the degree to which a firm's potential access to cash can cover its debt, seen in a short-term perspective, but in the large sense i.e. including current liabilities like tax payable and not only short-term interest-bearing debt and trade creditors. Liquidity ratios therefore compare current liabilities with current assets. For instance, the current ratio is defined as:

$$\text{current ratio} = \frac{\text{current assets}}{\text{current liabilities}}$$

This ratio is sometimes called the 'extended' current ratio as it includes all currents assets in the numerator.

The current ratio should be larger than one i.e. cash in hand and other current assets that can be expected to be turned in cash in the near term are sufficient to cover the short-term liabilities. When the current ratio is too low, this could signal a liquidity crisis. On the other hand, a high current ratio signals that there is room for improvement: either the company has too much inventory (inventory turnover can be improved), or collects its receivables too slowly from customers (collection period should be reduced), or has too much cash idle (which might be a transitory situation to finance an imminent investment). For most companies, the current ratio should be around two.

So a high and increasing current ratio is certainly not a good sign. The curse for a typical high-growth company is that current assets grow faster than current liabilities. When this happens, working capital is high and the current ratio increases. Cash is invested in inventories and receivables at high speed, which can lead to a cash liquidity crisis in case cash cannot be raised from shareholders or banks. A very active cash and current asset management is critical in this growth phase.

As some current assets are more liquid than others, managers often focus on cash (including marketable securities) and invoices that customers have not paid yet, and exclude inventories from the current ratio, so as to derive a more conservative ratio called the 'liquid ratio', the 'quick ratio' or the 'acid-test'.

$$\text{liquid ratio} = \frac{\text{cash} + \text{receivables}}{\text{current liabilities}}$$

Indeed inventories and work-in-progress must continue to be held by the company if it is to remain in business, so often cannot be sold to reimburse short-term liabilities. The advantage of the liquid ratio compared to the current ratio is that it does not depend on the inventory valuation method: as it is not uncommon that inventories have to be written off for obsolescence, the value of inventories in the balance sheet might not be able to be turned into cash.

Some managers go one step further and define an even more conservative form of current ratio called the 'cash ratio', which as its name indicates, only includes cash (and marketable securities) in the numerator:

$$\text{cash ratio} = \frac{\text{cash}}{\text{current liabilities}}$$

Shortly before failure, companies typically have very low cash ratio, low inventories, high receivables and comparatively low current ratios.

Note however that the cash ratio does not take into account the fact that the business might be able to borrow cash at short notice if it has a line of credit that it can draw on from a bank, so a low cash ratio is not necessarily bad news.

The conclusion here is that abnormal values for current, liquid or cash ratios should lead you to look deeper into the business to clarify why values are out of range.

5.3 Stability metrics

Stability is the long-term counterpart of liquidity. Stability analysis investigates how much debt can be supported by the company and whether debt and equity are balanced. The most common stability ratios are the Debt-to-Equity ratio and gearing (also called leverage).

$$\text{Debt-to-Equity ratio} = \frac{\text{Net Debt}}{\text{Shareholder's Equity}}$$

$$\text{gearing} = \frac{\text{Net Debt}}{\text{Net Debt} + \text{Shareholder's Equity}}$$

$$\text{Net Debt} = \text{Interest-bearing debt} - \text{Excess cash}$$

Net debt is defined as interest-bearing long-term and short-term debt less excess cash in the business. Note that only interest-bearing net debt is included here, and other current liabilities are excluded as they are short-term and can impact on liquidity, but not stability. Excess cash is the cash held on the balance sheet that is not needed and exceeds the normal cash level required for business operations (usually 3%-5% of annual sales).

Both Equity and Net Debt should be taken at market value as far as possible, otherwise book value should be used. Book values mostly record historical costs only and not 'fair value'. For debt, unless the company has a high credit risk or interest rates have changed considerably, the difference between book and market value will be small. For equity, market values are usually considerably higher, at least when the company is operating as a going concern and is not in liquidation.

Note that while the cost of debt is usually lower than the cost of equity, and a company attempts to minimize its cost of capital by using debt, it is unwise and often disastrous to put a company in a situation where it cannot pay its interest and meet its redemption payments as they fall due. So gearing is all about using the right mix of debt and equity to finance the business in the long term.

Different levels of gearing are regarded as normal across various industries, in particular depending on the ability of the business to generate a high level of cash and therefore bring protection from a risk of default, thereby reducing risk to debt holders. Even within one industry, some companies are more geared than others, especially those with stable profit and assets like land and buildings who are unlikely to fall in value quickly over time and therefore provide good security. When a company's gearing is outside of the usual industry range, its debt can be expected to be downgraded, thereby increasing the cost of debt.

Gearing also varies with time and might temporarily differ from a target gearing. For instance, in the early 1990s an average gearing of 25% was typical for fixed network telecom operators in Western countries, whereas in 2005, gearing of 30%-40% was common for integrated all-purpose operators, reflecting the stronger acceptance in the industry for higher level of debt as well as the high debt level of operators that had engaged in expensive M&A and UMTS licence acquisition. Ofcom, the UK telecom regulator, uses a range of 10% to 30% as the optimal gearing for a UK mobile network operator, with 10% being considered as low gearing and 30% high gearing. Currently, mobile operators are seen as more risky than fixed-line or integrated telecom businesses as they are more specialised than integrated operators, and consume more cash, whereas the market dominance of most incumbent fixed-network operators, especially in voice, is seen as a cash cow and stabilizing factor. This might change though with the emergence of Voice over IP and increasing price competition.

According to Michael Pomerleano, a World Bank economist, gearing also varies by geographic zone, with gearing being typically lower in Latin Americas, which have often less access to debt in their own capital markets, but higher in Asian countries, where governments have encouraged state-owned banks to lend to companies without being too strict on their creditworthiness.

Other useful ratios here from a debt holder perspective are the interest cover ratio (also called times interest earned), the times burdened covered and the debt cover ratio.

$$\text{times interest earned} = \text{interest cover ratio} = \frac{\text{EBIT(DA)}}{\text{Net Interest payable}}$$

$$\text{times burden covered} = \frac{\text{EBIT}}{\text{Net Interest payable} + \dfrac{\text{Principal Repayment}}{1 - \text{Tax}}}$$

$$\text{debt cover ratio (long - term)} = \frac{\text{Net Debt}}{\text{EBITDA}}$$

The interest cover ratio indicates by how much profit would have to fall until the company is unable to pay its interest. EBIT and EBITDA are taken from the Profit & Loss account and can be seen as proxy for respectively Cashflow from operations and Cashflow after investment. Sometimes interest cover is calculated using cashflows from the Cashflow statement.

Times burden covered not only includes interest on debt, but also one year of principal repayment, grossed up to account that principal repayment, unlike interest payment, is not tax deductible (principle repayment does not appear in the P&L). When a company can roll-over its maturing obligations and refinance maturing bonds with new bonds, then times burden covered is somewhat irrelevant and times interest earned ratio is the more important.

Finally, the debt cover ratio shows how many years of EBITDA would be necessary to reimburse company debt (principal) in full. For telecom network operators, a ratio lower than 2 is regarded as acceptable.

5.4 Other operational performance indicators

In Section 5.1 above, we have briefly reviewed profitability ratios and the related key financial performance indicators. Additional key operational figures can enhance these purely financial indicators and provide insight on operational performance. Operational performance indicators are very industry-specific and also vary with a company's business model and its role in the value chain.

Among the few ratios that probably apply to all industries, we can cite the revenue per staff ratio, although benchmarks here will vary widely from capital-intensive industries to manpower intensive ones, such as services.

In telecom businesses, the following key operational figures are commonly used:

- subscribers per staff (service provider)
- average revenue per user ARPU (service provider)
- CAPEX per subscriber (network operator), CAPEX per cell site (mobile operator), CAPEX per building passed (CATV network operator)
- CAPEX percentage of revenues (network operator)
- R&D percentage of revenues (equipment manufacturer)
- subscriber acquisition cost per new subscriber (service provider)
- churn level: this is percentage of customers lost over a certain time period (service provider)
- average selling price (consumer goods manufacturer).

Additional qualitative factors can be taken into account in a balanced scored card approach and linked to quantitative indicators – as the saying goes, only what gets measured gets done.

After this review of financial statements, we now turn to the issue of valuing a business.

6. Generating a Financial Statement Forecast

One of the major tasks in business planning involves the preparation of financial statements not only for one year, but for multiple years beyond the initial year. This set of financial statements is essentially a forecast of how revenues and costs will change over time and what the impact of these changes will be on the accounts, in particular profitability and liquidity. A set of financial statements will be useful for two reasons:

- From the financial statements we can derive an estimate of the value of the business, using in particular the Net Present Value (NPV) or the Economic Value Added (EVA®).

- The financial statements can be used as a roadmap by the company management as they translate the strategy and long-term vision for the business into a set of numerical figures that can be acted upon. For example, the annual company budget will have to be consistent with the overall business plan. Once the budget for the year is set, actual financial results can be compared, typically on a monthly basis, with the initial forecast (the budget) and the source of variance between *actuals* and *budgeted* can be analysed.

Most people preparing a financial business plan will be using Microsoft Excel spreadsheet software. Alternatively, there are other software packages on the market, for example Implied Logic STEM® (Strategic Telecoms Evaluation Model) for the telecom industry. If you use spreadsheet software, the preparation of a financial statements forecast will mostly involve two steps:

- Generating forecasts for revenues and cost items. This is where the real challenge is. We will cover this topic extensively in Part Three of the book, where we will show how to forecast demand and revenues (this is the harder part) on one side, and costs such as CAPEX and OPEX on the other side (this tends to be easier). Typically the overall financial attractiveness of the business plan is most sensitive to the revenue forecast and the estimated profit margins.

- Replicating the financial statements structure and generating a 'standard' P&L, a Balance Sheet and a Cashflow statement. To a large extent this is mechanical if you understand the logic of financial statements well, however this can become tricky in some cases, in particular when calculations have to be undertaken in months and aggregated in quarters and years, on a rolling basis. This is one area where specialised software can is a real advantage.

To produce forecasts for demand, revenues and costs, we will often rely on models. Models are an approximation of reality and describe dependencies between multiple variables, in particular how explained (also called dependent) variables can be expressed as functions of explanatory (also called independent) variables. If the explanatory variables are easier to forecast, then they provide a way to estimate the dependent variables. In the jargon of econometrics, there are 2 main classes of models:

- Cross-sectional model, where at every point in time the explained variable is function of other variables $Y = F(X, Z, \ldots)$. The function F formulates a behavioural relationship. For example, the level of demand might be function of price, the level of market awareness for the product and the number of points of sale.

- Time-series model, where the value of the variable Y_t is explained solely in terms of its own past $Y_t = F(Y_{t-1}, Y_{t-2}, \ldots)$. For example, the cost of manpower at time t will usually be expressed as a function of the cost of manpower at time t-1, using a growth coefficient capturing the impact of inflation and real-term salary increases.

In Excel, the formulae used in a cell will either state that the cell value should be derived from values in other cells at the same point in time (cross-sectional calculation: Revenues = Price x Volume of Sale), or from the value of the same variable at a previous point in time (time-series calculation: $ManpowerCost_t = ManpowerCost_{t-1} \times (1+5\%)$).

But before entering into the details of forecasting revenues and costs, we need to talk about *valuation* first, as this is one of the cornerstones of business planning. This is the topic of our next chapter.

Valuing Businesses

"When it is a question of money, everyone is of the same religion"
Voltaire, French Enlightenment writer

In the previous chapter, we have discussed how to generate cashflow and profit forecasts for a business opportunity. In this chapter we will learn how to derive an estimate of the business value from these forecasts. For a new business, valuation is an important exercise telling us whether it is worth undertaking the project or not, and if it is, how much value the project will be creating for those who are funding it (shareholders, debt holders) on top of what they typically expect considering the risk involved (dividends, capital gains, interests). Valuation can also help us prioritise projects when funding is limited.

After reading this chapter you will be able to value all sorts of companies and businesses. However, beware that a valuation will never be precise, it will only be as good or as bad as the quality of the assumptions it is based on and the correct application of valuation methods. Valuation involves substantial judgment on how the future is likely to unfold and as to whether the managers can influence this future. Therefore, valuation will always be relative to the party undertaking the valuation.

We will start by reviewing the meaning of value and valuation. We will then turn to the allegedly simpler valuation methods based on Sales and EBITDA multiples, and explain their limitation. Asset-based methods are not discussed as they play a marginal role in high tech as innovation and price decreases are high and existing assets depreciate quickly. We will then review the Net Present Value (NPV) method and the Economic Value Added (EVA®) approach, and explain their equivalence. Both methods provide better valuation as they capture the growth and profitability of the business explicitly rather than implicitly: a good valuation should be primarily bottom-up, based on deep understanding of the business dynamics. Finally, we will discuss the estimation of the cost of capital.

Overview of Chapter Five

1. A Holistic View on Value and Valuation 95
2. 'Multiples' Valuation based on Key P&L Figures.. 102
3. The Net Present Value (NPV) 108
4. The Economic Value Added (EVA®) 116
5. The NPV Terminal value, or the Multiples Method Revisited.................. 120
6. Estimating the Weighted Average Cost of Capital (WACC) 124
7. Estimating the Cost of Debt 127
8. Estimating the Cost of Equity.. 131
9. Don't Use the Internal Rate of Return (IRR)............................... 138

1. A Holistic View on Value and Valuation

Before diving into the various valuation methods, we will first take a holistic approach on value and discuss some of its key characteristics.

1.1 What is value?

Financial value is the maximum amount of money that a buyer would be willing to spend to acquire an entity, and the minimum amount of money that a seller would demand in exchange for this entity. This definition implies that value is relative and personal. A transaction between buyer and seller can only take place if the value to the buyer is higher than the value to the seller. At transaction price, both buyer and seller realise a surplus: the buyer gains a surplus for acquiring a good at a price less than the value to him; the seller obtains a surplus for selling a good at a price higher than the value to him.

1.2 Why value businesses?

In general, businesses are valued for various purposes:

- Companies quoted on the stock market are valued by share analysts who calculate the 'fair value' or target price for a share of equity, and place recommendations on whether to 'hold', 'buy' or 'sell' the share.

- In a transaction perspective, business units or companies are valued to derive a transaction price estimate used as base for negotiations in the perspective of a merger, acquisition, joint venture or divestment.

- Within companies, new ventures or projects are valued to check that they are worth being undertaken. Valuation is typically done as part (or as result) of a business plan.

It is this third aspect that will be of most interest to us here. Project valuations, although not the sole purpose of a business plan, are usually undertaken to check that the project or venture can create value to the parent company, and if any, how much. Valuation of projects is also undertaken to help rank projects and identify the most promising business opportunities.

Project values will often be used as one of multiple ranking criteria to select between projects when budget and resources are scarce and not all projects can be undertaken. Alternative or additional key financial results can be used to complement the project valuation in this selection process. Although the Internal Rate of Return (IRR) is sometimes used, we strongly recommend not using it because it is difficult to interpret and rare are those who precisely understand what it means. More on this in Section 9. Instead, we recommend looking at the peak cash requirement to fund the business, which will be a constraint in all companies as cash and budget have to be fought for. In addition, the payback period should be in line with expectations and acceptable to financial managers and providers of finance.

1.3 Valuation is future-based, subjective and often biased

At the outset, you should be very clear that valuation itself, although based on mathematical formulae and fairly accurate methodologies, is more an art than a science.

Firstly, a valuation will always be based on a forecast, whether it is explicit as in the NPV approach or implicit as in the Multiples approach. A forecast will always remain subjective, although it should be based on the best possible information available at the time. It is in human nature to overestimate revenues and underestimate costs, therefore cashflow forecasts are usually positively biased.

Secondly, projects have various risks so should in principle use various costs of capital to reflect the nature of the risks. As this is usually difficult or impossible, the same cost of capital is applied to all projects within a company, creating additional bias.

Finally, even assuming that cashflows are not positively biased and the correct cost of capital has been used, the traditional valuation methods do not capture the fact that the business plan will be executed dynamically and flexibly according to changing circumstances, and not in a static manner, as if everything had been decided on day one. To put it another way, the classical valuation methods do not consider that most decisions will not be taken today but tomorrow: they miss the value of day-to-day management as well as the learning effects. Therefore the standard valuation methods systematically underestimate value – a negative bias, maybe compensating the positive bias discussed above. In Part Four, we will show how business opportunities can be interpreted or structured as 'options' and how this approach provides more accurate estimation of value, as well as a recommendation on the timing of investment.

1.4 Valuation and 'Make or Buy' issues

Generally, a new business can either be built up from scratch or bought from a player who is already on the market. As no one would spend more money than necessary, from an acquirer's perspective, value is the minimum of the replication costs required to build the business up yourself and the acquisition value. Moreover, an existing business can either be run as-is, or transformed to leverage synergies with another business, or liquidated with its assets sold to the highest bidder. This tells us that when looking into a business, the alternative options should be analysed and some options might provide substantially more value than others. Note that liquidation is usually the option of last resort and the worst one: a forced sale often does not even reach book value, as many assets are specific and cannot be reallocated to other usage. This is particularly the case in high tech where equipment experiences sharp price decreases over time.

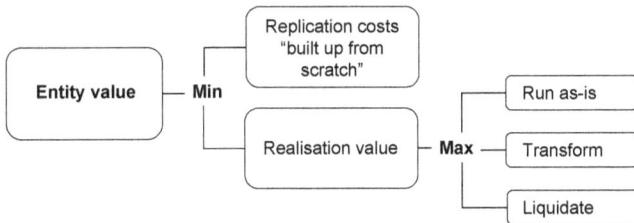

Figure 5.1: Company value is the lower of replication costs and the higher of the value as a going concern and the liquidation value [Source: INVESTAURA].

The 'Keep as-is' and 'Transform' options also show that the same business might be valued differently by interested parties depending on the synergies that they believe can be achieved with other businesses and depending on their execution skills. As a result, it might be worth selling a business to a company that is better able than you to create value from it.

1.5 Value changes over time

The fact that value fluctuates over time should also come as no surprise as the market if full of surprises that cannot be anticipated. New information permanently becomes available and has an influence on value, for instance an unexpected competitive entry, a demand higher than expected for a product, or external macroeconomics changes. The best proof for changing value is provided by the stock exchange itself, which provides a market for ownership change in companies' equity. Price for shares fluctuate on a minute-by-minute basis depending of the latest information made available and how it is interpreted by buyers and sellers.

Figure 5.2: Value of Siemens share 2000-2010 [Source: Cortal Consors].

So remember that a valuation can quickly become out of date, and you should always mention the date when the valuation was carried out in the business plan.

1.6 Value is relative to the valuer

This brings us to the following point: why value companies when they are quoted on the stock market and therefore already valued there, with the stock-market value representing a market consensus between buyers and sellers?

Firstly, you might have differing beliefs about the future of the company or you might know something that others don't know. A substantial value gap might show that there is a strong discrepancy between market expectations and your own view of the company. In an undervalued company, improved communication with the financial market should lead to realignment between both views.

Secondly, if you are thinking of acquiring a company, the value to you might be different from the stock-market value, especially if you believe that you can better manage the business or create substantial synergies with another business that you already own.

Thirdly, most business plans that you will make will look at a single project or a business unit, not a whole company quoted on a stock exchange, so you do not have the luxury of simply checking the project value on a stock exchange in that case.

1.7 Value in a transaction context

Occasionally, your business plan will not be based on building-up a company from scratch, which is time-consuming and requires tremendous effort, but on acquiring an existing business and transforming it. If this is your case, this paragraph is relevant to you.

Generally, the total business (entity) value is the sum of the value of debt and the value of equity, so that the equity value of a project or company (its market capitalization on the stock market) is derived from the entity valuation after deducting the market value of debt, if the business has any debt at all.

From an acquisition perspective, remember that the transaction will only take place in case the business has more value to the acquirer than to the seller. In the opposite case, buyer and seller cannot agree on a price and the transaction does not materialise – or it takes place with a different buyer.

Transaction value is not the same as stock-market capitalisation as it includes a premium for control and some of the synergies are expected to be paid out to the previous owner. Premium for control relates to the difference between the valuation of company for financial investment purposes (with a minority share) and for strategic purposes: ownership of the company implies that you obtain one or more seats on the management board and can actively participate in decision making, change the value of the company with superior management skills, and create of synergies.

When full control is assumed, the control and synergy premium typically cumulate to 30%-40% of the market value. This mark-up should be applied on the equity value, not on the firm value, as debt remains debt and does not attract premium. In some cases though, the acquisition battle can lead to a much higher premium. Academic research has shown ample evidence that one acquisition in two can be regarded as a failure from a financial point of view as it led to a high value transfer from the buyer to the seller which could never be recovered by the new owner later on. In total value was created, but predominantly for the previous owner.

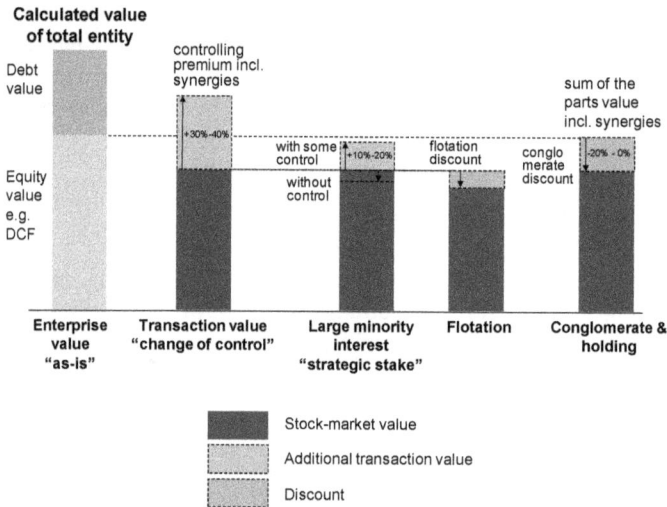

Figure 5.3: The value of an entity depends on the perspective taken and whether it assumes control or not [Source: INVESTAURA].

A large investment in a company should attract a lower premium that depends on the size of the minority interest:

- if the stake brings some form of control, then a 10%-20% premium might apply over stock-market investment value
- if the stake is substantial but brings low or no control, the transaction might be valued at less than the stock-market investment value because its disposal on the stock market would put pressure on the share price
- if the transaction is a flotation of a business on the stock market, the flotation often takes place at a price lower than what the market would command in order to attract buyers (new shareholders).

When the business is a conglomerate, it can be valued using a 'sum of the parts' approach, valuing the various entities individually and adding the value of synergies at the end. These companies are usually valued on the stock market at a discount of about 20%. This might be an indication that the market does not really believe in synergies between the individual units, or even worse that limited freedom and the fight for capital resources at the conglomerate level prevents some business units to achieve their full potential.

An equity valuation using NPV assumes a controlling stake and will usually lead to a level comparable to the large minority-interest perspective as shown in Figure 5.3 above. The 'full-control' perspective can be expected to be higher than the equity value 'as-is' as it embodies synergies, some of which are passed on to the previous owner.

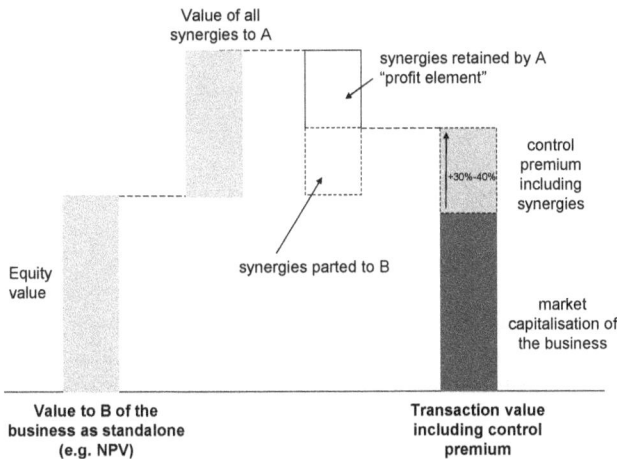

Figure 5.4: Transaction value: split of synergies between buyer 'A' and seller 'B' [Source: INVESTAURA].

When planning to acquire a company, some practitioners set a higher hurdle rate and increase the cost of capital (WACC) that they use for internal purposes to capture the buyer's 'profit' element of the transaction. As the increase in the WACC is fairly arbitrary, we recommend valuing the company as standalone and then add the potential synergies to the buyer. This will include a premium for both control and synergies and sets an absolute maximum price level before entering negotiations.

In practice, the respective bargaining power will decide on how the value of those synergies is shared between both parties in the negotiation phase. The share of the synergies retained by the seller is equivalent to an increase in the WACC, and reflects the increased risk as to whether the synergies will really materialize or not.

By now it should be clear that there is no such thing as a 'true, unique, timeless' value but that value changes with time and with the perspective of the person or company performing the valuation, as well as the context of the valuation.

2. 'Multiples' Valuation based on Key P&L Figures

Although there is ample evidence in the literature that enterprise value has low correlation with earnings or sales, and strong correlation with cashflows, multiples methods are still widely used in the industry. Their main advantage is the 'beauty of simplicity', so that if you are under time pressure or have to generate many valuations in a short time frame, this is the method to choose. Their main inconvenience is that they require substantial experience that only (good) investment bankers or security analysts can have, otherwise they lead to grossly wrong results.

2.1 A bit of theory: the rationale behind P&L multiples

It can be shown that under very special circumstances, multiples-based methods generate the same results as cashflow-based methods. When sales growth is constant and both EBITDA and EBIT margins remain constant in the future – conditions that in practice will never be met – the entity value of a business as calculated by the NPV method can be expressed as follows:

$$\text{Entity Value} = \frac{\text{NOPAT} \times (1 - g/r)}{\text{WACC} - g} \qquad (1)$$

where:

- *NOPAT* is the Net Operating Profit minus Adjusted Tax
- *g* is the growth rate in sales (or cashflow or earnings), assumed constant
- *r* is the after-tax rate of return on net new investment i.e. new investment after deduction of depreciation in the year
- *WACC* is the cost of capital.

A prerequisite for formula (1) to hold true is that the rate of return of future investment *r* be constant over time. *r* is calculated as the ratio of the additional after-tax EBIT generated divided by the value of the new investment, so it is the ROIC of future investments. When *r* is equal to the present rate of return on existing investment, it can be replaced by the current ROIC.

As EBIT and EBITDA margins are constant, NOPAT is simply derived from EBIT:

$$NOPAT = EBIT \times (1 - TaxRate)$$
$$EBIT = Sales \times EBITMargin$$
$$EBITDA = EBIT \times (1 + DA/Sales)$$

Expression (1) above can be transformed to give (2):

$$Entity\ Value = \frac{(1 - g/ROIC) \times (1 - TaxRate)}{WACC - g} \cdot EBIT$$

$$Entity\ Value = \frac{(1 - g/ROIC) \times (1 - TaxRate)}{(WACC - g) \times (1 + DA/Sales)} \cdot EBITDA \quad\quad (2)$$

$$Entity\ Value = \frac{(1 - g/ROIC) \times EBITMargin \times (1 - TaxRate)}{WACC - g} \cdot Sales$$

These three formulae simply state that the Entity Value is proportional to EBIT, EBITDA and Sales, and provide relationships for the respective multiples.

The (apparent) advantage of these formulae is that they do not require a detailed forecast of the future of the business: the value of the business today can be derived from its current accounting results, which is a great simplification indeed. The disadvantage of this approach is that it is misleadingly simple and a dangerous short cut: the underlying assumptions are rarely met in practice, in particular the idea that growth is constant into perpetuity. In addition, the Multiples approach does not apply to a new business that has no Sales, or has Sales but negative EBIT or EBITDA. The formulae above also assume that the business remains in operation in perpetuity, which is not the case of projects with limited lifetime.

2.2 A four-step approach to valuation

Formulae (1) and (2) above are rarely applied as such in a Multiples valuation, but provide a useful crosscheck to the approach used by most people in practice. The method follows a four-step approach as illustrated in Figure 5.5.

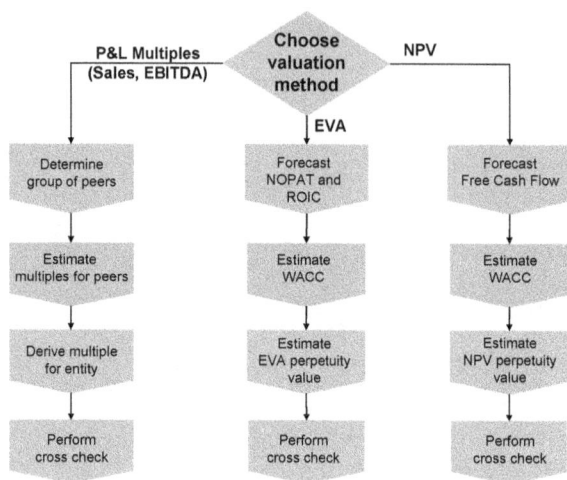

Figure 5.5: P&L Multiples, EVA, NPV methods with their respective steps [Source: INVESTAURA].

In the first step of a multiples valuation, a group of peer companies is selected, typically made of 3-4 firms. These companies will be used as proxy to the entity being valued. Peers should be sufficiently comparable to the entity, be active in the same industry, address similar customers in similar geographic regions, perform the same type of activity, and ideally demonstrate similar growth pattern and margins as the entity itself. In addition, peers should be either quoted on a stock exchange so that their market value is observable, or transaction data should be available for these companies. This methodology only makes sense when a group of peers exists for the entity being valued. Although no one expects that all assumptions mentioned above will be met in the strict sense, the peers are representative enough of the entity so that P&L multiples for the target can be inferred from the peer multiples. Also peers should have similar business models.

For example, let's assume that you are valuing a new Mobile Virtual Network Operator (MVNO) in Europe. As peers, you might first think of using established mobile network operators in the European market. However, these would not be good peers because as incumbents, they have large market shares and benefit from tremendous economies of scale (so try to find peers with similar market share), and in addition they follow a different business model as they invest and operate networks whereas MVNOs only own very limited network assets and are predominantly acting as resellers. Therefore, their profit margin might be expected to be very different. A better group of peer might be pure service providers who do not own network and focus on marketing and sales, making their business model more comparable to that of MVNOs.

In the second step, financial data about the peers are collected and multiples derived, whether Sales, EBITDA or EBIT. Beware to calculate multiples from the total entity value (including debt) and not only the equity value, as Sales, EBITDA and EBIT are financial figures before interest payment (the cost of debt) and refer to the overall entity. For consistency both the numerator and the denominator in the multiples calculation should refer to the whole entity rather than the value to shareholders only. Also, be careful to use financial results applying to the same year on the numerator and denominator, otherwise the multiples are meaningless. Finally, EBITDA multiples are to be preferred to EBIT multiples as companies depreciate their assets using varying methods, so that the EBITDA multiples of companies in the same industry are less biased than EBIT multiples.

In the third step, the multiple to be applied to the entity is derived from those obtained for the peer companies. The simplest approach is to calculate the Sales and EBITDA multiples for the peers, and use the results to derive two enterprise values for the entity. A weighted average using entity values as weight can also be used to take the respective company size into account. Beware to average only same-year multiples for the peers, not multiples applying in different years. Often, when two valuations have been made based on Sales multiples and EBITDA multiples, the results of the two valuations are averaged out to generate an estimation of the entity value. From these results, debt value can be subtracted to get the equity value. In many cases, the multiple applied to the target company will be derived after adjusting the average upwards or downwards to account for additional elements, in particular different growth assumptions or different risk profiles and higher financial leverage. Substantial experience is required here, or this might result in a bad valuation. Differences in capital structure between peers can be somewhat dealt with, but there is no 'scientific' way to deal with differences in growth.

In the last step, put the valuation results in perspective with other benchmarks that you might have. If the entity is a mobile operator, the benchmark might be the value of the entity per subscriber. If the entity is a cable TV operator, this might be the entity value per house passed. If the entity is an equipment manufacturer, this might be the entity value per unit of goods sold. If results depart markedly from your expectation or benchmarks, then question why.

In addition, if the business that you are valuing already generates Sales, you can use formula (2) above to reverse engineer the EBIT margin, ROIC and sales growth in perpetuity that would be consistent with the peer group-based valuation.

Figure 5.6 shows an example of valuation for a hypothetical firm called 'TheIProuter' active in the IP Routing business and held in private hands.

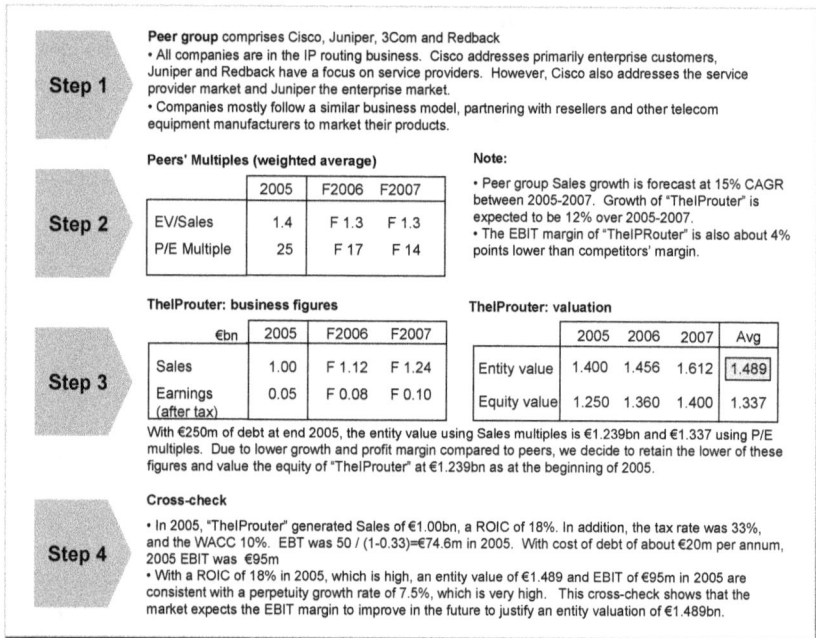

Step 1

Peer group comprises Cisco, Juniper, 3Com and Redback
• All companies are in the IP routing business. Cisco addresses primarily enterprise customers, Juniper and Redback have a focus on service providers. However, Cisco also addresses the service provider market and Juniper the enterprise market.
• Companies mostly follow a similar business model, partnering with resellers and other telecom equipment manufacturers to market their products.

Step 2

Peers' Multiples (weighted average)

	2005	F2006	F2007
EV/Sales	1.4	F 1.3	F 1.3
P/E Multiple	25	F 17	F 14

Note:
• Peer group Sales growth is forecast at 15% CAGR between 2005-2007. Growth of 'TheIProuter' is expected to be 12% over 2005-2007.
• The EBIT margin of 'TheIPRouter' is also about 4% points lower than competitors' margin.

Step 3

TheIProuter: business figures

€bn	2005	F2006	F2007
Sales	1.00	F 1.12	F 1.24
Earnings (after tax)	0.05	F 0.08	F 0.10

TheIProuter: valuation

	2005	2006	2007	Avg
Entity value	1.400	1.456	1.612	1.489
Equity value	1.250	1.360	1.400	1.337

With €250m of debt at end 2005, the entity value using Sales multiples is €1.239bn and €1.337 using P/E multiples. Due to lower growth and profit margin compared to peers, we decide to retain the lower of these figures and value the equity of 'TheIProuter' at €1.239bn as at the beginning of 2005.

Step 4

Cross-check

• In 2005, 'TheIProuter' generated Sales of €1.00bn, a ROIC of 18%. In addition, the tax rate was 33%, and the WACC 10%. EBT was 50 / (1-0.33)=€74.6m in 2005. With cost of debt of about €20m per annum, 2005 EBIT was €95m
• With a ROIC of 18% in 2005, which is high, an entity value of €1.489 and EBIT of €95m in 2005 are consistent with a perpetuity growth rate of 7.5%, which is very high. This cross-check shows that the market expects the EBIT margin to improve in the future to justify an entity valuation of €1.489bn.

Figure 5.6: Valuation of 'TheIProuter' using Sales and P/E multiples. The numerical values are dummy data [Source: INVESTAURA].

2.3 Be even more careful when using P/E multiples

Price / Earnings ratio (P/E) is the ratio of the equity value to earnings (usually after tax), and after interest in all cases for consistency with the numerator. Note that it is important that the numerator and denominator of multiples be consistent, for instance a market capitalization (equity value) to turnover multiple does not make much sense. P/E ratios are functions of interest rates and gearing, so they change over time. The average P/E ratio of US equities was 14 in the 20th century.

Sales, EBITDA and EBIT multiples are not geared because they are not affected by the level of debt of the company. When using geared multiples like P/Es, remember that differences in debt level (interest payments), accounting treatment (depreciation, goodwill) and corporate taxation can make after-tax earnings comparisons difficult at best, and meaningless at worst. An average P/E derived from multiple firms should not be applied to a business that uses other depreciation schedules or tax assumptions. In principle, it is possible to un-lever P/E ratios, although most analysts don't even bother. As P/E ratios are also influenced by changing growth and interest rate over time, P/E ratios are not time-independent. This means that averaging P/E ratios calculated at different points in time is meaningless, and explains our overall preference for Sales and EBITDA multiples.

2.4 Summary of main drawbacks of multiples

All in all, the main problem with multiples is that they contain a large number of embedded assumptions that are not explicit, in particular profit margins, growth prospects, financial leverage, tax and depreciation schedules. In essence, methods based on multiples are attempts to reduce very complex issues to a single factor. Sales and EBITDA multiple can alleviate the fact that depreciation schemes can change from one year to the next, from one company to the next, from one country to the next, but they don't solve all difficulties.

A valuation based on multiples is most appropriate when performing a valuation from outside, with no or limited access to detailed financial information about the business beyond revenue or profit. When substantial information about the business is available, an NPV approach is always preferable as it models growth and margin explicitly and forces the valuer to ask himself the right questions about the business, its dynamics, its economics, its competitive environment and many other important issues that are necessary to generate a cashflow forecast. Sales, EBITDA and P/E multiples might be valid approaches in stable businesses like foodstuffs but are best used as a cross-check to NPV valuations in high-tech industries.

We leave the discussion of multiples for now and turn to the second valuation method, based on cashflow and the concept of Net Present Value. We will get back to Multiples at a later stage when we discuss the Terminal Value component of the NPV in Section 5.

3. The Net Present Value (NPV)

In this section and the next we will review the NPV method based on Discounted Cashflow (DCF), as well as the Economic Value Added (EVA®) method based on P&L and Balance Sheet data. We will also show that both methods are equivalent and lead to the same result. Both require forecasts of financial statements for the business. The EVA method is an operationalisation of the NPV: it has the advantage that value creation is not measured for the total project only, but also year by year. As a result, EVA provides a measure of the annual financial performance and can be linked to management incentives. In comparison, the NPV focuses on capital budgeting and helps managers decide whether to invest in new business opportunities.

3.1 The rationale behind the NPV

The NPV method is based on the idea that the value created by a business comes from the cashflow after investment that this business generates, which can be used for distribution to entity holders and the rest kept on the Balance Sheet as cash. Future cashflows are discounted to the present to take the time-value of money and risk into account: a Euro next year is not worth the same as a Euro this year, and a risky Euro is not the same as a risk-free Euro. As the cashflow considered is an entity cashflow, the valuation result is an entity value as well. From the entity value, the value of net debt can be deducted to derive the equity value. The latter can be compared to the stock-market value if the business is quoted on a stock market.

The NPV takes the point of view that other non-cash assets in the business such as fixed assets and operating current assets are necessary to pursue ongoing operations to perpetuity, so they are resources required to generate cashflows, and adding the value of these resources to the NPV calculation would be double counting. If the company has cash on its balance sheet that is not necessary to support future operation, the excess cash on the asset side can be deducted from the interest-bearing debt on the liability side to calculate the net value of debt. If the company has no debt, but current short-term liquidities beyond the normal cash level necessary for operation, then net debt is actually negative, so that the equity value becomes the sum of the NPV and the (positive) excess cash.

The Present Value in the NPV is said to be 'Net' because the cashflows are net of initial investment necessary to start the project like start-up costs and other investment costs required in the early phase, and net of any continuing investment required beyond the initial phase.

The beauty of using the entity cashflow rather than a cashflow to shareholders (an equity cashflow) is that the investment decision can be separated from the financing decision, and operating managers do not need to get concerned with the mechanism and alternatives available to raise capital and debt – these issues can be delegated to the financial officer. In principle, using an NPV based on cashflow to shareholders is also possible, but then an equity cost of capital should be used to discount future cashflows, and the NPV result is the value of shareholders' equity, not the value of the whole entity. However, the entity approach is usually preferred as it is less prone to error.

Another way to think about the value of a business is to say that from an entity point of view, the value of the business today is equal to the cashflow that is generated during the year (the cash remaining after operating and investment costs are covered, including tax but before financing) plus the value of the business at the end of the year. If one repeats this approach for the following year, the value now is the sum of the cashflows discounted to reflect the time value of money and risk, plus the value of the business in n years from now. Now the value n years from now is certainly a high number, but when extrapolated to infinity, this value won't be necessarily be growing as fast as the cost of capital WACC, so the business value in year n discounted by the factor WACC will tend toward zero in the long term.

3.2 Calculating the NPV

Mathematically, the NPV of the business as of today, the beginning of year 1 becomes:

$$NPV = \sum_{i=1}^{\infty} \frac{FCF_i}{(1+WACC)^i} \qquad (3)$$

FCF_i is the *expected* Free Cashflow in year i, i.e. the cashflow after investment but excluding interest payment tax shield (see also Chapter Four Section 2.3). We are excluding here the impact of interest expenses because we are taking an entity approach, and the question of how the business is financed in practice is already reflected in the Weighted Average Cost of Capital WACC, so including interest tax shield in the numerator would be double counting.

Note that expression (3) also assumes that WACC remains constant over time, which is not always the case. The calculation of the WACC will be discussed in Section 6 below.

Often the cashflow forecast is split in two parts: a first phase where the business is being established and growing up fast, and a second phase where the business has reached maturity, stable growth and profit margins. Therefore, the NPV formula is often expressed as follows:

$$NPV = \sum_{i=1}^{n} \frac{FCF_i}{(1 + WACC)^i} + \frac{1}{(1 + WACC)^n} \times TV_{n+1}^{\infty} \quad (4)$$

TV_{n+1}^{∞} is the terminal value at the beginning of year $n+1$, and is equal to the discounted cashflow generated by the business in the maturity phase. It is also often called the Continuing Value. TV_{n+1}^{∞} is expressed in money at the beginning of year $n+1$, so don't forget to discount it to the valuation date, the beginning of year 1, by using the cost of capital as shown in the previous expression. After discounting, the terminal value is expressed in today's money.

3.3 Selecting a forecast horizon

The forecast horizon should depend on the business life cycle and duration required to reach maturity. At the end of the detailed forecasting horizon, it is important that the business has reached stability, so that simplifying assumptions can be made about the financials of the continuing venture.

Don't make the forecast horizon too long either. Seven to ten years should be sufficient in most cases, as it is very difficult for anyone to forecast beyond such a long period. For a telecom service provider business like a UMTS operator, take a forecast horizon as long as the time necessary to reach market saturation. For a product business case, take a forecast horizon no shorter than the full product life cycle, including an after-sales service period. A product business should generate profit over the product life cycle, unless there are cross-subsidies from other products, or profits are expected to be generated by future generations of the product only.

If the business has not reached maturity at the end of the forecast horizon where a terminal value can be calculated, then you should either extend the forecast horizon or use a two-stage formula as shown in Section 5.4 below.

3.4 Calculating the Terminal Value

If the cashflow is growing at a constant rate in the maturity phase, then it can be shown that the Terminal Value can be calculated as follows:

$$TV_{n+1}^{\infty} = \frac{FCF_{n+1}}{WACC - g} \qquad (5)$$

g is the (constant) growth rate in the Free Cashflow.

In expression (5) considerable care is required to estimate FCF_{n+1}. If growth in the continuing value period is lower than growth between year n and $n+1$, then the business needs to invest less in CAPEX, working capital and inventories in year $n+1$ so that FCF_{n+1} cannot simply be extrapolated from FCF_n by applying the perpetuity growth rate. This is a very common mistake in the NPV calculation. Due to a lower growth, additional cashflow is released, so that FCF_{n+1} is higher than what would be obtained after applying the perpetuity growth rate on FCF_n. Not considering this will underestimate continuing value. To avoid this mistake, make sure to calculate FCF_{n+1} explicitly using the same bottom-up logic as between year 1 and n, and do not extrapolate FCF_{n+1} from FCF_n. An example is provided in Figure 5.7 below.

In addition, if the growth in Revenues, the EBIT margin and the ROIC are constant in the maturity phase, then the cashflow and revenue growth rates are the same, and (5) can be rewritten as follows, also called the 'value driver' formula:

$$TV_{n+1}^{\infty} = \frac{NOPAT_{n+1} \times \left(1 - \dfrac{g}{ROIC}\right)}{WACC - g} \qquad (6)$$

Note that this expression is only valid when g < WACC and g < ROIC.

The value-driver formula (6) is often preferred to (5) as it relates the terminal value to three important value drivers: the perpetuity growth g, the long term ROIC and $NOPAT_{n+1}$. This forces us to estimate whether ROIC will come down to WACC or remain above WACC in the maturity phase. Economic theory suggests that ROIC should return to WACC in the long term, so the spread between ROIC and WACC should be small.

We also prefer using (6) because it is less prone to error. In the value driver formula, $NOPAT_{n+1}$ still has to be estimated, and this should be best done using a bottom-up and detailed calculation as was done between year 1 and n.

However, even if $NOPAT_{n+1}$ is extrapolated from $NOPAT_n$, the calculation error will not be as large as deriving FCF_{n+1} from FCF_n, as NOPAT, being a P&L item, is not directly and as quickly affected by a release of cash from working capital or changing investment needs due to the lower growth rate. In addition, the value-driver formula does not put all the uncertainty in the terminal-value calculation on FCF_{n+1} only, but spread it over $NOPAT_{n+1}$ and the return on invested capital ROIC.

Note that when the business or project has a finite lifetime, then the terminal value might be low or nil. In this case, the Terminal Value can be approximated by the net value of assets in the balance sheet and is similar to a scrap value.

3.5 Crosschecking a valuation based on NPV

Once a valuation has been prepared it makes sense to check how the business' current operational results would have to change in the future in terms of growth, profit level or increase in capital turnover so that the estimated valuation level materialises in practice. This crosscheck can only be undertaken for businesses that already generate Sales and positive NOPAT. When the business is traded on a stock exchange, this can also be used to check what you would have to believe to match the market consensus on the equity value of the company.

For this sanity check, proceed as follows:

- Calculate the ratio of today's NOPAT to the cost of capital, WACC. This gives you the value of the entity if the business financial performance were to remain as it is indefinitely into the future, with no growth. We call this the value 'as-is'.

- Subtract the value 'as-is' from the entity value, either obtained from a previous NPV (or EVA) valuation, or from the market capitalisation on the stock market after adding the net value of debt. We call this result the Future Improvement Value (FIV). The FIV can be compared to the total entity value. The ratio indicates how much value of the entity resides in future growth and improved operating performance as opposed to current performance. This can also help understand what the stock market consensus on the future business improvement is, and whether the stock-market expectation appears as overestimated or underestimated in your eyes. Growth businesses might have an FIV / NPV ratio above 80%.

On the other hand, negative values for FIV indicate that the stock market believes current NOPAT level will deteriorate.

- Finally, use the perpetuity formula (6) above and calculate any set of parameters (g, NOPAT, ROIC) that lead to the entity value. Improvement could come from growth in the Free Cashflow, which might be triggered by growth in Sales, or improvement in NOPAT margin, or improvement in ROIC via a higher capital turnover and better utilisation of assets.

If the Entity Value (EV), NOPAT and ROIC are given, then g is obtained from the following relationship:

$$g = ROIC \times \frac{EV \times WACC - NOPAT}{EV \times ROIC - NOPAT}$$

Let us take a numerical example. Suppose you have a business with an entity value of €5bn, last year NOPAT was €100m, WACC is 10% and ROIC is equal to 20%. Then the value 'as-is' is €100m / 10% = €1bn, so that FIV = €5bn - €1bn = €4bn.

Case 1

Assuming that the NOPAT margin on sales and capital turnover remain constant, then ROIC remains constant in the future, and a growth value of 20% x (5x10%-0.1) / (5x20%-0.1) = 8.9% would have to be assumed into perpetuity, which is a very high rate if you are in a low inflation country. Unless the business is currently growing at very high level (probably above 20%), then the stock might be currently overvalued by the market – or the market simply does not expect that the profit margin and capital turnover will remain constant.

Case 2

Now let us assume that the NOPAT margin can be doubled, so that NOPAT is now €200m instead. If the capital turnover remains constant, the ROIC will also double. Then the current entity value could be justified with a perpetuity growth rate of 40% x (5x10%-0.2) / (5x40%-0.2) = 6.6%. This perpetuity growth value remains very high considering the high value for ROIC (40%).

Case 3

Let us assume that the capital turnover now doubles whereas NOPAT remains equal to €100m. Then a growth rate of 40% x (5x10%-0.1) / (5x40%-0.1) = 8.4% would be necessary. This is marginally smaller than the 8.9% growth rate from Case 1.

All in all, it appears that the entity valuation can only be justified on the belief of an impressive growth rate into perpetuity as well as very high value of ROIC into perpetuity. This is no surprise as FIV is 80% of EV.

3.6 NPV valuation example

We get back to the valuation of our dummy company 'TheIProuter' and show in Figure 5.7 and 5.8 how an NPV valuation can be performed. In the calculation of the Free Cashflow below, EBIT Tax is the tax calculated from EBIT rather than EBT, i.e. as if no interest were incurred in the period (see also Section 2.3 in Chapter Four).

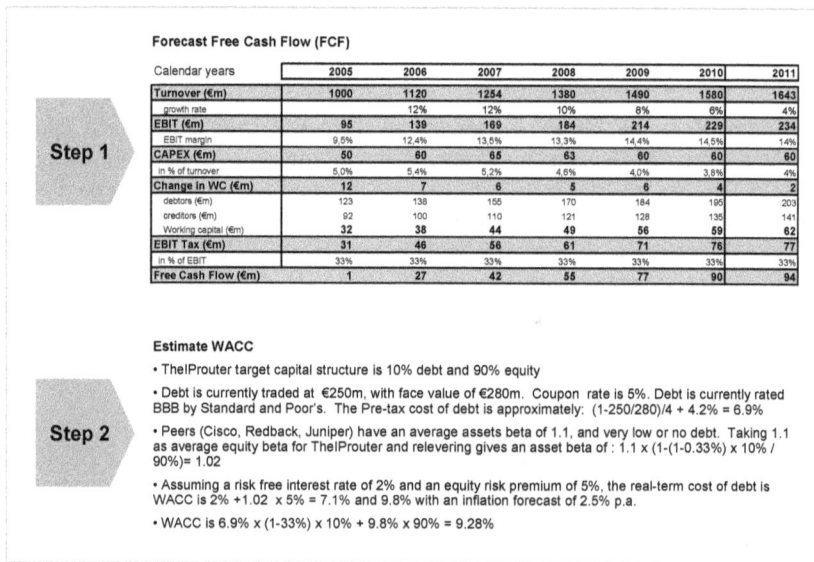

Forecast Free Cash Flow (FCF)

Calendar years	2005	2006	2007	2008	2009	2010	2011
Turnover (€m)	1000	1120	1254	1380	1490	1580	1643
growth rate		12%	12%	10%	8%	6%	4%
EBIT (€m)	95	139	169	184	214	229	234
EBIT margin	9,5%	12,4%	13,5%	13,3%	14,4%	14,5%	14%
CAPEX (€m)	50	60	65	63	60	60	60
in % of turnover	5,0%	5,4%	5,2%	4,6%	4,0%	3,8%	4%
Change in WC (€m)	12	7	6	5	6	4	2
debtors (€m)	123	138	155	170	184	195	203
creditors (€m)	92	100	110	121	128	135	141
Working capital (€m)	32	38	44	49	56	59	62
EBIT Tax (€m)	31	46	56	61	71	76	77
in % of EBIT	33%	33%	33%	33%	33%	33%	33%
Free Cash Flow (€m)	1	27	42	55	77	90	94

Step 1

Estimate WACC

Step 2

- TheIProuter target capital structure is 10% debt and 90% equity
- Debt is currently traded at €250m, with face value of €280m. Coupon rate is 5%. Debt is currently rated BBB by Standard and Poor's. The Pre-tax cost of debt is approximately: (1-250/280)/4 + 4.2% = 6.9%
- Peers (Cisco, Redback, Juniper) have an average assets beta of 1.1, and very low or no debt. Taking 1.1 as average equity beta for TheIProuter and relevering gives an asset beta of : 1.1 x (1-(1-0.33%) x 10% / 90%)= 1.02
- Assuming a risk free interest rate of 2% and an equity risk premium of 5%, the real-term cost of debt is WACC is 2% +1.02 x 5% = 7.1% and 9.8% with an inflation forecast of 2.5% p.a.
- WACC is 6.9% x (1-33%) x 10% + 9.8% x 90% = 9.28%

Figure 5.7: Valuation of 'TheIProuter' using the NPV approach, Step 1 and 2. The numerical values are dummy data [Source: INVESTAURA].

Step 3

Calculating the terminal value (TV)

• We calculate the terminal value as the ratio of FCF in year 2011 over (WACC-g), where g is the perpetuity growth rate. The terminal value is then discounted to the beginning of year 2006.

• With an inflation rate of 2.5% p.a., and strong price decrease acting on the IP router market, we assume a real-term growth to perpetuity of 0.5% only, giving a nominal growth of 3% to perpetuity. This is lower than the growth rate in Sales assumed between 2010 and 2011.

• Due to uncertainty around the WACC as well as the growth to perpetuity, we perform sensitivity analysis around the estimated WACC value.

WACC	NPV 2005-2010	Discounted Terminal value Perpetuity growth rate			Total entity value Perpetuity growth rate		
		2%	3%	4%	2%	3%	4%
9,0%	217	805	939	1127	1022	1156	1344
9,3%	215	759	880	1046	974	1095	1261
10,0%	211	667	762	889	877	973	1100

The entity value of TheIProuter is €1095m. With a market value of debt of €250m, this results in an equity value of ~€845m as at 31. December 2005

Step 4

Cross check

• 2005 NOPAT is €57m. Divided by the WACC, this gives the value of the business as is: €594m.
• The future improvement value is FIV = 1095 – 594 = €501m, or 45% of the entity value.
• The FIV is expected to come from:
    • growth in sales: 9.6% over 2005-2010 (CAGR), and 3% to perpetuity
    • improvement in EBIT margin from 8% in 2005 to 14% in 2010
    • improvement in the capital turnover are less likely as the ratio of sales to invested capital was already high in 2005 (3.35, derived from ROIC = 18% and EBIT = 8%).

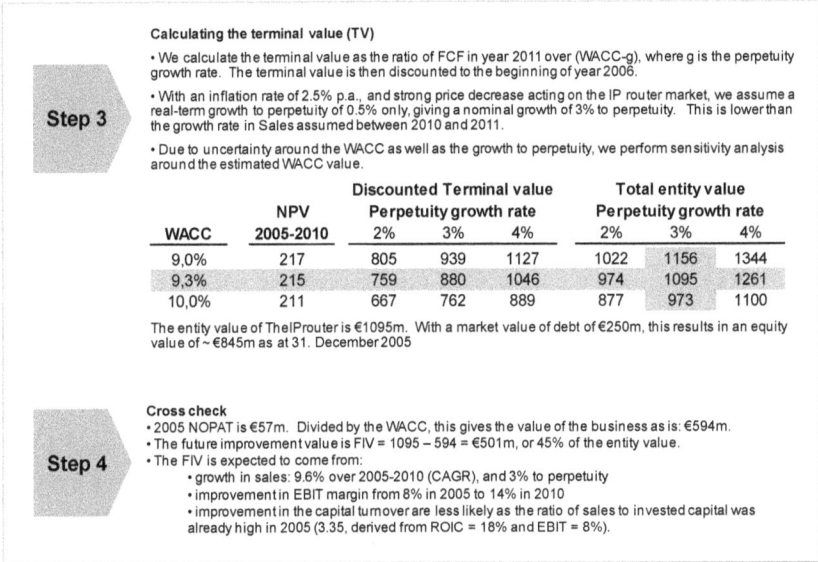

Figure 5.8: Step 3 and 4 of the NPV calculation of 'TheIProuter'. The numerical values are dummy data [Source: INVESTAURA].

A final point about NPV before turning to the EVA approach: the fact that a project has a positive NPV does not mean that it is optimal to start the project now. It might be more valuable if you delay the launch, in particular because a number of remaining uncertainties can be resolved in the mean time, either on their own (e.g. regulation), or via market testing (e.g. level of demand and price expectation), or with additional R&D (e.g. technology). If you can postpone the investment decision without losing substantial cashflows (which should be the case in the early start-up phase) and without fearing competitive entry causing irreparable damage to future market share, then you should do so. Think of yourself as a gardener growing and watering tomatoes from early spring until late in the season: as any point of time, some of your tomatoes will be partially ripe and edible, but probably not particularly savoury, so that you face the alternative of either picking those tomatoes now for consumption, or letting them ripen some more days at the risk that birds might make a feast out of your future crop.

Delaying launch in high-tech businesses will not be a viable approach in most cases as competition is extremely fierce, products quickly become obsolete and innovation is a race against time. However, if delaying is possible without substantial damages, then you should do so. Thus, any project with positive NPV has two mutually exclusive alternatives: do it now, or wait and invest later. We will come back to this point in Part Four when we look at investments as Real Options.

4. The Economic Value Added (EVA®)

4.1 The rationale behind EVA

The EVA approach defines value as that which is left from profit once the capital charge has been deducted. Capital charge amounts to what providers of capital expect to get as return on their investment. The advantage of this method is that value creation (or destruction) can be measured year-by-year based on the financial statements and linked to management compensation. Once the EVA calculation has been made for each year, the annual EVA values are then discounted and summed, using the WACC as the cost of capital to reflect the time value of money and risk. Finally, the value of net assets taken from the balance sheet at the date of valuation is added to the present value of the EVA stream, and this provides an entity valuation for the business.

The EVA method is based on accounting money i.e. it is P&L and Balance Sheet-based, and not cash-based. However, it can be shown that an EVA valuation leads to the same result as an NPV valuation if the accounting rules remain the same over time.

4.2 Calculating EVA

EVA is the operating profit (before interest but after tax) after a capital charge on business assets has been deducted:

$$EVA_i = NOPAT_i - CapitalCharge_i$$

The capital charges can be calculated as follows:

$$CapitalCharge_i = WACC \times InvestedCapital_{i-1}$$

so that EVA_i becomes:

$$EVA_i = InvestedCapital_{i-1} \times \left(\frac{NOPAT_i}{InvestedCapital_{i-1}} - WACC \right)$$

which is the same as:

$$EVA_i = InvestedCapital_{i-1} \times (ROIC_i - WACC)$$

The calculation of EVA says that a business can only create value when its ROIC is higher than the WACC. EVA itself can be seen as 'excess profit' on top of and above capital charge, the profit level expected by providers of finance.

Finally the total value of the entity is obtained by discounting future EVAs to the valuation date and adding the value of the invested capital at the valuation date.

$$Entity\,Value = InvestedCapital_0 + \sum_{i=1}^{\infty} \frac{EVA_i}{(1 + WACC)^i}$$

The logic is simple: if a company exactly earns its cost of capital in every period, then EVA is nil in each period, so no value is created, and the company is worth its net assets i.e. that which was originally invested.

4.3 The Invested Capital

The Invested Capital can be defined as balance sheet total after interest-free liabilities have been deducted, in particular supplier credit, deferred taxes and dividends payable. This is the same as the Net Assets of the business. Often the average of net assets between the beginning and the end of the year is used, rather than the beginning-of-year values, to get a more precise estimate of the business assets.

When the company has substantial goodwill on the balance sheet, this should be included in the Invested Capital after adding back any amortization that might have been passed to the P&L, as goodwill, unlike fixed assets, does not wear out. With this approach, EVA measures the value created by investing not only in tangible assets, but also in intangible ones, in particular following an M&A transaction.

4.4 EVA Terminal Value

As in the NPV approach, the forecasting period for the NOPAT, Invested Capital and EVA calculation can be split into a first phase where a detailed bottom-up calculation is undertaken, and a perpetuity phase where the business is assumed to have reached maturity.

Therefore, the discounted EVA sum is split in two, with the second term being the EFA terminal value:

$$\sum_{i=1}^{\infty} \frac{EVA_i}{(1+WACC)^i} = \sum_{i=1}^{n} \frac{EVA_i}{(1+WACC)^i} + \frac{1}{(1+WACC)^n} \times TV_{n+1}^{\infty}$$

Be careful here not to confuse the NPV Terminal Value, which is based on cash, and the EVA Terminal Value, which is based on accounting items. The values of the two terminal value will be different in practice.

Assuming constant growth in NOPAT in the long term, and constant ROIC, the EVA Terminal Value can be expressed as follows:

$$TV_{n+1}^{\infty} = \frac{EVA_{n+1}}{WACC} + \frac{NOPAT_{n+1} \times \left(\dfrac{g}{ROIC}\right) \times (ROIC - WACC)}{WACC \times (WACC - g)}$$

Here also, do not forget to discount the Terminal Value to express it in today's money.

4.5 NPV and EVA valuations are equivalent

The equivalence between the NPV and EVA valuation can best be understood from the following relationships:

$$EVA_i = NOPAT_i - IC_{i-1} \times WACC$$
$$FCF_i = NOPAT_i - (IC_i - IC_{i-1})$$

EVA allocates a charge to NOPAT based on the invested capital from the balance sheet, whereas FCF allocates a charge to NOPAT corresponding to the increase in invested capital necessary to sustain the growth of the business. When discounting FCF in the NPV expression, the change in Invested Capital from one year to the next cumulates to become equal to the growth in Invested Capital between now and year n, which is the same as the discounted EVA plus the value of Invested Capital at the end of year zero.

4.6 How to choose between the NPV and the EVA method?

The EVA method looks more complex than the NPV method, and indeed it is: it requires estimating the net invested capital over time, so producing a balance sheet. The depreciation of assets becomes necessary and not only a cashflow calculation. When a business plan is prepared for a new project and not an existing business, an NPV approach is more straightforward, and FCF is more appropriate due to the emphasis on cash and cashflow break-even in new ventures. For an existing business or when looking at a multi-business company, the EVA approach is usually a more appropriate method as it shows value creation year after year, which an NPV approach does not.

The NPV approach has some disadvantages though, in its calculation as well as its interpretation. In the NPV approach, a high portion of the value will usually be captured in the Terminal Value, so that results become very sensitive to a correct estimate of the Terminal Value. Also, this creates an illusion that in the early year of the business, value is destroyed because cashflows are negative, and value is only created in the long term. This is a wrong interpretation, and based on confusion between cashflow and value, which are not the same. The misunderstanding would be like believing that "negative Free Cashflow is value destroying, positive Free Cashflow is value creating". This is not quite right. A negative FCF due a high investment can be value creating when the profit generated in the same year from that investment is higher than the capital charge of the investment. Also, later positive Free Cashflows are only possible because invested capital has been built up in the first place, including intangible capital such as brands and patents.

EVA is very good at showing the timing of value creation in the short to medium term, and the EVA Terminal value term should be lower than the NPV terminal value, especially for existing businesses.

It is also an illusion that the NPV method is simpler to apply on the base that a cashflow statement is enough and no balance sheet is necessary. A correct cashflow forecast has to include change in working capital, so working capital has to be estimated in any case. Cashflow is also more volatile than NOPAT. Although in principle a cashflow estimate does not need asset depreciation to be calculated, it requires a good estimation of annual capital investment including replacement of past depreciated assets, so calculating depreciation will be helpful in any case. A good capital investment estimate will be a very important cost item in all capital-intensive high-tech businesses.

Whether you go for the NPV or EVA valuation approach, you should always estimate the ROIC and compare it with the WACC as a crosscheck. It is worth asking yourself whether the ROIC should be decreasing over time. If the capital turnover remains stable or increases due to new processes and lower technology costs, then ROIC might be maintained at a high level above WACC, unless the competition puts pressure on Sales and EBITDA margins that more than compensate for the gains in capital turnover.

In all cases, do prepare a bottom-up forecast including the year $n+1$. Don't derive FCF_{n+1}, $NOPAT_{n+1}$ or $ROIC_{n+1}$ values from year n values and the growth rate g, as this is usually incorrect (see Section 3.4).

5. The NPV Terminal Value, or the Multiples Method Revisited

You might have noticed that expressions (1) and (6) above are one and the same. This is where P&L multiples and NPV valuations give the same results so multiples can be used to estimate the Terminal Value of a project. In the maturity phase to perpetuity, the simplifying assumptions required for a multiple valuation are broadly met, in particular a constant growth rate and constant margins. This results in a mixed method for valuation, with an NPV calculation used in the short- and medium-term horizons, and a Sales or EBIT(DA) exit multiple to estimate the Terminal value.

The issue becomes how to estimate the multiple, and here we are not talking about the multiple today, but at the end of the forecasting horizon, so often in 7 to 10 years from now. A common error is to use a multiple that applies today, for example a Sales multiple derived from a peer company whose entity value is known. This is wrong because the industry will be further down the road in 7-10 years from now, so that the long-term growth and profitability of the business will not be the same as what they are today and in the near future.

The only meaningful method here is to get back to expressions (1) and (2) above, and derive values for the multiples based on your long-term assumption for the business. We repeat the formulae for the EBIT and Sales multiple for this purpose here:

$$\text{Terminal Value} = \frac{(1-g/\text{ROIC}) \times (1 - \text{TaxRate})}{\text{WACC} - g} \cdot \text{EBIT}$$

$$\text{Terminal Value} = \frac{(1-g/\text{ROIC}) \times \text{EBITMargin} \times (1 - \text{TaxRate})}{\text{WACC} - g} \cdot \text{Sales}$$

We now review typical values for EBIT and Sales multiples.

5.1 Typical values for Multiples

Figure 5.9 and 5.10 show the values taken by the EBIT and Sales multiples respectively, as a function of the growth to perpetuity and the ROIC. We have assumed WACC =10% (inflation =2.5%), and Tax=30%.

Note that when the ROIC is equal to the WACC, the multiple does not vary with growth: growth does not create additional value and the Terminal Value is equal to the invested capital at the end of the forecast horizon. When ROIC is smaller than WACC, then the EBIT Multiple varies inversely with growth, meaning that additional growth is destroying value. Another way to put it: if the return on capital is less than the cost of capital, you don't actually want to invest more (grow).

Growth \ ROIC	8%	10%	12%	14%	16%
2%	6.6	7.0	7.3	7.5	7.7
3%	6.3	7.0	7.5	7.9	8.1
4%	5.8	7.0	7.8	8.3	8.8
5%	5.3	7.0	8.2	9.0	9.6
6%	4.4	7.0	8.8	10.0	10.9

Figure 5.9: EBIT multiples for the Terminal Value calculation [Source: INVESTAURA].

Growth \ EBIT	5%	10%	15%	20%	25%
2%	0.4	0.7	1.1	1.5	1.8
3%	0.4	0.8	1.1	1.5	1.9
4%	0.4	0.8	1.2	1.6	1.9
5%	0.4	0.8	1.2	1.6	2.0
6%	0.4	0.9	1.3	1.8	2.2

Figure 5.10: Sales multiples for the Terminal Value calculation (ROIC assumed = 12%) [Source: INVESTAURA].

5.2 Estimating the perpetuity growth

When setting the growth rate to calculate the terminal value multiple, remember that this rate should be consistent with the inflation rate assumption implicitly made in the WACC. For instance, if your (nominal) WACC assumes an inflation rate of 2%, then the growth rate should be commensurate. A revenue growth to perpetuity of 2% in nominal terms actually means 0% growth assumption in real terms if the long-term inflation rate is assumed to be 2%. A nominal growth rate lower than inflation actually means a decreasing sales volume in real terms.

Beware that the growth assumption should not be too much higher than inflation as it is a perpetuity rate. Typically, growth will be set at inflation plus 1%-2%, so that in low inflation country, a perpetuity rate of 2.5%-4.5% will be common in practice. This should be broadly similar to the nominal GDP growth rate. Higher growth rate can only be sustained in strongly growing industries, and will have to be justified to decision makers in any case.

5.3 Estimating the perpetuity ROIC

In many cases, the perpetuity ROIC should be equal to the WACC. The business is growing in sales, assets (and employees!) but is neither adding nor destroying value to providers of finance. Shareholders expectations are perfectly met and the share price should broadly remain constant over time. Although profit in the form of NOPAT is increasing, this is entirely compensated by the additional capital charge incurred on the additional retained profit ploughed back in the business to fund growth. It might be better to constrain growth and return net profit in full to shareholders in the form of dividends with a payout ratio of 100%. Unsurprisingly, most managers will prefer to head a large business than a small one, so constraining growth might be wishful thinking.

Obviously, if the management team can operate the business at a higher ROIC than WACC at a later stage, this would generate substantial amount of value; alternatively, considerable amount of value can be destroyed if the business starts operating at a ROIC lower than the WACC, in particular if the competition intensity further increases in the industry.

Most firms will be operating at a ROIC slightly higher than the WACC in the long term, as a ROIC lower than WACC is not economic and would lead some players to exit the business or merge with others to re-establish a ROIC larger than WACC. ROIC is the product the NOPAT margin and capital turnover, as seen in the following formula:

$$ROIC = \frac{NOPAT}{Average\ Net\ Assets} = \frac{NOPAT}{Sales} \times \frac{Sales}{Average\ Net\ Assets}$$

The capital turnover and indicates how many Euros of revenues can be generated from one of net assets in the balance sheet. Capital turnover varies according to the position taken by the business in the value chain. Chip manufacturers and network operators are very capital intensive and should have a low capital turnover. Value between 0.5 and 1 will be common. On the other hand, manufacturers of hardware or software products (B2B or B2C) as well as service providers will have much higher capital turnover, typically between 1 and 10.

The NOPAT margin is the same as after tax EBIT margin, and also strongly depends on the position in the value chain. Capital-intensive business should have EBIT margin between 15% and 25%, less capital intensive business would typically display lower EBIT margin comprised between 5% and 15%. Obviously the EBIT margin that can generated in the long term is function of the level of competition in the segment of the value chain addressed as well as the ability to create high barriers to entry to keep competition at bay – some companies are well-known for being able to derive what could appear as monopoly profits.

To take a numerical example: a network operator with a long-term capital turnover of 1 and a long-term EBIT margin of 20% as well as a tax rate of 30% would have a ROIC of 1 x 20% x (1-30%) = 14%. If long-term WACC for this operator is assumed to be 10%, then ROIC would be 4% points about WACC.

5.4 Two stage terminal value

In some cases, the business has not reached maturity at the end of the explicit forecast horizon, so that a two-stage formula should be used to calculate the Terminal Value at the end of year n, as given by the following relationship:

$$
\begin{aligned}
TV_{n+1}^{\infty} = {} & \frac{NOPAT_{n+1} \times \left(1 - \dfrac{g_A}{ROIC_A}\right)}{WACC - g_A} \times \left[1 - \left(\frac{1+g_A}{1+WACC}\right)^{m-1}\right] \\
& + \frac{NOPAT_{n+1} \times (1+g_A)^{m-1} \times \left(1 - \dfrac{g_B}{ROIC_B}\right)}{WACC - g_B} \times \frac{1}{(1+WACC)^{m-1}}
\end{aligned}
$$

m is the number of years in the first part of the continuing value period. g_A and g_B are the growth rates in the first and second part of the period respectively.

6. Estimating the Weighted Average Cost of Capital (WACC)

The cost of capital is the rate of return that providers of finance expect to generate on the capital that they have provided. A company has two broad options for external financing: to contract debts or issue equity capital. The costs are expressed in the form of interest payments and distribution of dividends respectively.

The cost of capital is calculated as the average between the cost of debt and the cost of equity. The WACC is used to discount the Free Cashflow to derive the NPV, and as the FCF is an after-tax term, the WACC should also be taking an after-tax perspective. Interest payments are deductible from profit before tax, which implies that the cost of debt (the interest) enjoys a tax credit (tax shields). Therefore, the net cost of debt to the business is actually lower than what the company pays to bondholders as interest.

Estimating the WACC is a difficult exercise. In many companies, a single value will be applied across the board to all projects whatever their risks, but the correct approach would be to use a project WACC, i.e. apply a mark-up or a discount to the company WACC to reflect the additional or lower risk compared to the overall business. Monte Carlo simulation can be used to estimate the value of the mark-up or the discount. In addition, project risk might vary over time, so that the WACC might be higher in the first phase, but return to a lower value in a second phase. As the WACC is applied in a compound manner in the NPV calculation, business valuation will be most sensitive to the WACC value. Sensitivity analysis of various WACC values on the NPV is recommended when calculating an NPV. If sensitivity analysis (instead of a time-dependent WACC) is too crude an approach, do call on the help of a financial expert.

6.1 Calculating the WACC

The WACC is expressed as follows:

$$WACC = \frac{D}{D+E} \times C_d \times (1-T) + \frac{E}{D+E} \times C_e$$

C_d and C_e are respectively the cost of debt and the cost of equity, T is the tax rate, D and E are the value of debt and the value of equity. The cost of debt and equity represent current and future expectation so historical values are not necessarily appropriate.

Values for debt and equity should as much as possible be taken at market value and not book value: providers of finance expect a return on the current market value of their investment, not the past historical costs. The market value of debt is usually sufficiently close to book value so that book value provides a reasonable approximation unless interest rates have changed a lot in the mean time, or debt has been re-graded. The market value of equity is typically higher than the share capital invested in the business by shareholders and the related retained earnings in the Balance Sheet. The difference between the market value and book value of equity is also called the Market Value Added (MVA).

The WACC formula shows that we have two sets of calculations to perform: firstly, value debt and equity; secondly, value the cost of debt and the cost of equity. We have learned above that we need to know the WACC to derive the value of equity, and we are now saying that we need the value of equity to calculate the WACC, so we have a clear circularity here.

6.2 Solving the circularity

There are two schools of thought to solve the circularity: break it or iterate.

Break it

In the simpler approach, a target gearing i.e. the relative proportion of debt and equity is taken as long-term financial structure for the business. This target gearing will depend on the industry in which the business is operating. When a business has a very large asset base and generates high cashflows, it will be in a good position to operate at a high leverage, so can borrow a large amount of debt compared to its equity value. For very capital-intensive business with stable cashflows such as utility companies, a ratio of 50% debt to 50% equity will not be unusual.

Managers who follow this approach believe that the current capital structure of the business should not be used to calculate the WACC as the current financial structure might be imbalanced for various reasons, and the WACC is best seen in a forward-looking and long-term perspective. A high level of debt might be used to temporarily finance an important acquisition as it takes more time to raise capital, and some of the debt will be replaced by equity capital at a later stage. Raising capital is also a question of timing and whether management believes that the current share price is undervalued. Vice-versa, in a speculative bubble, the company equity might be overvalued compared to its debt so that the current gearing based on market value might be out of range with the company's target gearing.

Iterate

Alternatively, in a more complex approach, you can accept the circularity and calculate the WACC by iteration. Start with an expected WACC value, derive the value of entity using the NPV approach, deduct the value of debt taken at book value in the balance sheet, and then recalculate the WACC. Two or three iterations should be sufficient to achieve convergence.

Obviously, when a company is quoted on the stock market, then the best estimate of the equity value is the market share value (a market consensus), so that the calculation of the weights in the WACC formula is simplified. As mentioned above, this approach might lead to wrong estimate of the WACC value as it generates a WACC based on current leverage and not on target leverage. In this approach though, the WACC estimation becomes simpler and reduces to estimating the cost of debt and equity.

6.3 A note on inflation

In most cases, nominal Free Cashflows are discounted so a nominal WACC should be used. If future inflation is expected to be different from the current inflation level, then the nominal cost of debt and equity in the WACC should reflect this accordingly. In most developed countries with low levels of inflation, it is usually easier to reason in nominal terms, not only because most people think in nominal terms, but also because all historical data as well as interest rates are in nominal terms and provide a good starting point for forecasting. In countries with high level of inflation, it is easier to think about costs and price and their evolution in real terms so we recommend generating a Free Cashflow forecast in real terms, and apply an inflation index as required in a second stage.

We now turn to the estimation of the cost of debt and equity.

7. Estimating the Cost of Debt

7.1 Introduction

The two main forces behind the cost of debt are the risk of default and the time to maturity. Risk and time to maturity are not fully independent, as the risk of debt is decreasing when the debt is nearing maturity. The higher the risk, the higher the cost of debt is. The longer the maturity, the higher the cost of debt is as the risk of default increases. When debt is guaranteed by a credible government, it can be regarded as risk-free. In this case, the cost of debt is a function of the time to maturity only and becomes dominated by the term structure of inflation. If inflation is expected to be lower in the future than today, then the cost of fixed-rate long-term debt can be lower than the cost of short-term debt.

The cost of debt is determined in the market by the laws of supply and demand. When new debt is issued by companies or governments, it has to attract sufficient interest so must be in line with current market coupon rates. Once debt has been issued, its value and yield will vary over time to adjust to the coupon rates currently offered for new debt of the same maturity and risk. If the coupon rate for new debt of the same structure (risk, maturity) is lower, then the value of the debt previously issued will rise so that the yield that it serves is the same as the coupon rate on the newly issued debt.

The cost of debt is defined as the current yield on equivalent risk class debt with the same maturity period. So to calculate the cost of debt, we need a theory of debt risk. When the risk is small, the debt can be approximately seen as risk-free. In this case, the value and cost of debt are linked by a deterministic relationship so that if one is known, the other can be derived. For instance, if the value of debt can be directly observed on the stock market, then its cost can be inferred.

7.2 Risk-free, fixed-rate debt

We now turn to the case of fixed-rate debt. If the debt is traded as a bond, then the value of the debt D is known. The current cost of debt can be approximated as the yield to maturity, derived from current market value, coupon and face value. Note that the coupon rate is the historical cost of debt when the debt was issued, and is irrelevant for determining the current cost of debt, as the cost of debt varies with time.

The formula to calculate the yield to maturity y is :

$$D = \sum_{i=1}^{m} \frac{Coupon_i}{(1+y)^i} + \frac{Face\,Value}{(1+y)^m} \qquad (7)$$

y is the current yield to maturity i.e. the cost of debt, m the number of years to maturity. *Coupon* is the promised coupon paid at the end of time i, *Face Value* is the value of the bond promised to be reimbursed at maturity. At time $t=0$ when the debt is issued, D is equal to *FaceValue* and y is the same as the coupon rate. When y is small, it can be approximated without complex calculus by the following relationship:

$$y = \frac{1 - D/FaceValue}{m} + CouponRate \qquad (8)$$

When debt is traded, the yield is usually published next to the value of the bond so that you might not have to calculate it yourself.

Note that y is the *promised* yield to maturity. When debt is not risk-free, then its cost would actually be higher than the promised yield due to the risk of default.

7.3 Risky, fixed-rate debt

The formulae (7) and (8) above are only straightforward to apply if the risk is very low so default is unlikely, coupons are being paid as expected and the face value is reimbursed at redemption. Otherwise, the coupons, face value and yield must be replaced by their expected value. When there is some risk of default, the coupon rate will usually be high and the value of debt low, so that the promised yield to maturity will be higher than when the debt is risk-free. The expected yield however, will be lower than the promised yield. We can estimate the expected yield using formula (7) if we know the current market price of the bond and make assumptions about its expected default rate and value in default. The likelihood of default decreases as the bond nears maturity.

The companies Standard & Poor's and Moody's also provide ratings on bonds. They assign a bond rating when a bond is first issued and track it over time. They use letters e.g. A, B, and C and their combination to describe the risk of default. AAA is the higher grade, C the lowest, with a high probability of default by maturity. In D the company is in default.

For non-traded debt, if the bond risk class is not provided by a rating agency like Standard & Poor's, then you should look for a peer-traded bond that has the same risk and same period to maturity. The promised yield to maturity of the debt considered and its peer should be the same. To help you find a proxy, calculate liquidity and stability financial ratios of the company and look for a peer that has financial ratios in a similar range. Alternatively, there are software packages on the market that provide estimates of the bond ratings and cost of debt using financial ratios.

The calculation of cost of debt and value of debt becomes particularly complex when debt is not traded and the risk is high. If a peer of similar risk class and maturity to redemption can be found, then yields should be similar. Otherwise, know-how on options valuation can help further. When the risk of default is high, then the value of debt becomes strongly related to the value of the entity that it is financing. In this case, the value of the entity decreases towards or below the face value of the debt. Indeed, when companies are given limited liability by their corporate status, the value of equity is essentially the same as that of an American call option written on the entity with an exercise price equal to the face value of the debt and a maturity period equal to the maturity period of the debt. At expiration, if the value of the entity is lower than the face value of the debt, then shareholders will choose to default and not reimburse the face value. The value of debt is equal to the value of entity minus the value of the call option. The promised and expected yields can be derived from expression (7). Figure 5.11 provides a summary of the various cases discussed above.

	Fixed rate, low or no risk	Fixed rate, high risk
Traded	- Derive yield from market value of debt, coupon and face value: expression (8)	- Determine risk class - Estimate the expected value of Coupon and Face Value from the probability of default - Apply formula (7) to derive the expected Yield of debt - Alternatively use software package and financial ratios to derive the yield
Not traded	- Find traded peer with same maturity (and no or low risk) - Calculate the yield of peer - The yield of debt is the same as the yield of the peer - The value of debt is the discounted value of coupon and face value	- Determine risk class - Find a traded proxy with of the same risk of default and same maturity. Yields will be the same - Use Monte Carlo simulation to derive the value of the debt. If equity is traded and the volatility of the rate of return on the entity can be estimated, the equity is an American call with exercise price equal to face value of the debt and expiring at maturity of debt - The value of the debt equals the value of the entity minus the value of the call.

Figure 5.11: Steps required for calculating the cost and value of debt in various circumstances [Source: INVESTAURA].

7.4 Variable-rate debt

If the debt has variable rate, then the cost of debt to maturity is equal to the geometric average of one-year forward rates over the investment horizon being considered for a certain risk class. If the risk is small, and the one-year forward rates of risk-free debt are available for this year, next year, and all other years until the maturity year, then the geometric average can easily be derived and the result is a good approximation for the cost of debt.

7.5 Other forms of debt

Debt can be callable. This means that the borrower has a call option to reimburse the face value of the debt before redemption. Callable debt has to offer higher coupon to attract debt holders, so its cost is higher. The advantage for companies is to be able to refinance at a lower cost if interest rates have decreased in the meantime.

With convertible debt, the borrower can convert debt into equity at his discretion if certain conditions are met, typically if the share price has fallen below a certain level. More commonly, convertible bonds give lenders the right to convert the bond into shares over a certain time period at an exchange ratio known in advance. This can be attractive to lenders if the share price increases strongly. The advantage for companies is to finance risky debt at a lower coupon rate and compensate with an opportunity to participate in the increase in the value of the equity should the company succeed and its share price increase.

There are many other forms of debt than those briefly addressed above. Financial institutions do not lack creativity to meet the ever-evolving expectations of their customers. When debt is issued, its terms are set in a contract whose objectives are to protect the lenders against the borrower. Whereas contracts for public debt are fairly standardised, private debt contracts can contain a lot more unusual features, many of them are options either held by the borrower or the lender. To value callable and convertible debt for instance, it is necessary to know how to value options on the underlying equity.

8. Estimating the Cost of Equity

8.1 Introduction

The cost of equity is the rate of return expected by shareholders for holding a risky share in the business so it is the price of the risk that they take. The rate of return is defined as the total rate of return:

$$\text{Rate of Return over the period} = \frac{\text{Dividend} + \text{Increase in share price}}{\text{Opening share price}}$$

Companies' risk can be broken down into specific risk (also called non-systematic) and unspecific risk (also called systematic). As investors can diversify away the specific risk but can't get rid of the unspecific risk, it is only the non-diversifiable risk that they should expect to be compensated for. This is the cost of equity.

8.2 Estimating the cost of equity from historical data

A common approach for estimating the cost of equity of a quoted company is to take a historical view, calculate the rate of return of the company share and average over time. There is controversy in the academia and among practitioners whether it is better to use an arithmetic or a geometrical average. A geometric average is more appropriate to model the behaviour of buy-and-hold investors, whereas arithmetic averages better portray a one-year invest horizon. The geometric average also has the advantage that, unlike the arithmetic average, it is unbiased by the measurement units (days, weeks, months). Note that the arithmetic average is typically 2% points higher than the geometric average. As there is no consensus between practitioners, a pragmatic approach is to take the average between the arithmetic and geometric averages.

Although historical returns provide a convenient approach, they have two major drawbacks:

- the future cost of equity is not necessarily the same as the past cost as the risk of a company's businesses might be changing over time and the price of risk expected by shareholders is also believed to change over (long periods of) time

- the cost of risk of an individual project is not the same as the cost of risk for the company as a whole, which represents an average across all projects and businesses the company is engaged in.

For a non-quoted company or an individual project, a possible work-around is to find a quoted company with a similar risk structure and use it as proxy. Both companies should have a similar un-levered cost of equity. Finding a proxy is not always possible though. In the extreme case, it is necessary to derive the cost of equity from a Monte Carlo simulation applied after having identified the key uncertainties in the input parameters and their volatility. More about this in Part Four, Chapter Thirteen, on Real Options.

8.3 Estimating the cost of equity from a simple model

The challenge here is to find a model for the forward-looking cost of equity. One idea is to express the cost of equity as a function of macroeconomic parameters that are changing over time and can be forecast, in particular the risk-free interest rate and the market risk premium, to derive a measure of the intrinsic risk of the business. Performing a historical regression analysis against changing parameters allows us to derive estimates for parameters that characterise the business and are broadly constant over time.

The most common model used in practice is the Capital Asset Pricing Model (CAPM). It is important to be clear that this is a model only. There are other models available for instance the Arbitrage Pricing Model (APM), which regresses the return on equity not on a single factor, the market risk premium, but on a larger number of macroeconomic indicators. These models are more complex to apply and go beyond the scope of this book.

The CAPM states that the expected rate of return of a given asset can be expressed as the sum of a market risk-free rate and an asset-risk factor, itself a function of the market-risk premium. $E(\ )$ designates the expected value of a variable.

$$E(r_{asset}) = RiskFreeRate + Asset\,RiskPremium$$
$$= E(r_f) + \beta_{asset} \times \left(E(r_{market}) - E(r_f)\right)$$

$E(r_{market})\text{-}E(r_f)$ is the expected value of the market premium. Assuming that β_{asset} changes slowly over time, the value of the asset beta can be obtained by regressing the historical rate of return of the asset on the risk-free market rate and the market-risk premium. By definition, for the market portfolio, the expected rate of return $E(r_{asset})$ is equal to $E(r_{market})$ so that the market beta is equal to one.

The beauty of the CAPM model is that for an asset of a certain risk, we only have to estimate one parameter, beta, and then forecast the other market parameters, which are hopefully easier to forecast, to derive a forward-looking cost of equity for the asset. Note that the market parameters vary from one country to another though.

When beta is higher than one, then the asset is said to be more volatile that the market, and conversely, when beta is lower than one, it is less volatile. Volatile industries are: telecom equipment, air transportation, automotive manufacturers, investment banking. Less volatile ones are: food business, utility companies, telecom service providers, private banking.

8.4 Estimating the risk-free rate

The risk-free rate is the forward-looking rate of return on a risk-free asset. Take a treasury bill as estimate, guaranteed by the state, with a maturity period in line with the project duration. If you are in a business with a shorter product cycle, you might want to take a shorter rate. A 10-year rate is a good compromise for most businesses. Historically, the real-term risk-free interest rate has been between 1% and 2%. The real-term risk-free rate of interest varies from country to country but also varies over time in any given country. Adding an inflation forecast of about 2% in the future should lead to a nominal risk-free rate forecast of 3% to 4% in developed countries. This is the time-value of money, i.e. the market price for deferring consumption today to consumption tomorrow.

8.5 Estimating the market risk premium

As for the (forward-looking) market risk premium, the best estimate that we can generate is based on a real-term historical analysis of the risk premium for the market portfolio, possibly adjusted if we think that shareholders will price the market risk differently in the future. It would be somewhat conceptually incorrect to add a current risk-free rate to a historical risk premium, so we have to make sure that both are forward-looking rates. Once a real-term market premium forecast has been estimated, then our inflation forecast will be added on the top to obtain a nominal-term risk premium.

For the USA, the real-term risk premium was 5% over the last 70-year period, but only 3.6% over last 30 years. Lower rates lead to higher valuations. This could indicate that investors are now ready to live with a lower risk premium that they have been in the past. Both the 1987 and 2000 stock market crashes would rather incline us to be prudent in our valuation though, and use 5% as a real-term market risk premium forecast. In total the expected rate of return on the market portfolio would be about 2%+5% = 7% in real terms and 9% in nominal terms including an inflation forecast of 2% per annum. In the UK, the real-term risk premium on equity has averaged 4% in the 20th century, and market real-term return on equity has averaged 6%. These values are fairly close to those experienced in the USA (7%).

8.6 The dividend growth model

Another approach to estimate the cost of equity is to assume that dividend yield will grow to perpetuity at a constant growth rate. In this case the expected value of the asset rate of return is:

$$E(r_{asset}) = \left(1 + \frac{Div}{S}\right) \times (1+g) - 1$$

which reads that the estimated rate of return on the asset is equal to the dividend yield of the asset plus the estimated dividend growth rate.

Applied to the market portfolio: g is the analysts' consensus estimate for the growth rate of dividends and in the long term equal to a real GDP growth rate of about 2.5% for the market portfolio; Div / S is the dividend yield of the market portfolio, historically about 2.2%. This gives a total real-term return on equity of 4.7%. The risk-free rate forecast is subtracted from the expected return on the market to derive the forecast of the market risk premium.

The advantage of this method is that it is forward-looking and allows premiums to be estimated for markets without long historical series of return, which are often not available. This method implies a future risk premium of only 2.7%, i.e. 1%-2% lower than estimated historically in the USA and the UK. There is also theoretical evidence in the academics for supporting a lower equity risk premium than has been in the past, maybe due to better functioning markets, more information and overall higher market efficiency. To summarise, real-term market risk premium should be in the range of 2.7%-5%.

8.7 Estimating company betas

Now that we have seen how the risk-free rate of interest and the market risk premium can be estimated, the last missing piece of the puzzle is the estimation of betas for companies. Company betas as provided by numerical regression on market portfolio indices are less reliable than an industry betas derived as averages of single company betas. Typically, the variance of beta for a single company is large so the estimate of a company beta is imprecise, whereas the variance for a portfolio of companies in the same industry is a lot smaller. So ideally, when you are provided with a single company beta, check whether it is consistent with the industry beta, which provides a better, less biased, estimate.

Another problem with betas is that their estimation varies depending on the horizon taken for the historical regression. This is partially related to change of business risk, partially to the fact that a smaller sample will yield a more biased beta. The two effects are difficult to split in practice, so that considerable care is required here.

Figures 5.12 and 5.13 show that the beta of telecom service providers are lower than the betas of equipment manufacturers – a reflection that the former businesses are less volatile that the latter.

Company	Geared Beta	Market Cap (€/$bn)	Net debt (€/$bn)	Ungeared beta
Siemens	0.92	55.6	-2.4	0.95
Nokia	1.16	54.5	-12.2	1.36
Ericsson	1.42	33.8	-4.0	1.54
Alcatel	1.30	12.0	-0.8	1.36
Lucent	1.60	10.6	1.1	1.50
Motorola	0.96	36.2	-6.0	1.08
Cisco	1.26	111.2	-8.3	1.32
Avaya	1.68	5.0	-1.0	1.93
Average	1.29	n.a.	n.a.	1.38

Figure 5.12: Beta of key telecom suppliers, April 2005 [Source: Cortal Consors, company annual reports. Betas are measured against the DJ Euro Stoxx 50 except US companies against the S&P 500].

Company	Geared Beta	Market Cap (€bn)	Net debt (€bn)	Ungeared beta
France Telecom	1.30	57.4	44.0	0.87
KPN	0.73	15.7	8.3	0.54
O2	1.09	15.2	0.5	1.07
Vodafone	0.72	133.4	12.0	0.68
Cable & Wireless	1.01	4.4	-2.0	1.43
Deutsche Telekom	0.88	62.6	34.5	0.65
TIM	0.43	43.6	0.3	0.43
Telefonica	1.15	66.8	19.6	0.97
Telefonica Movil	1.50	40.4	5.1	1.39
Average	0.98	n.a.	n.a.	0.89

Figure 5.13: Beta of key telecom service providers, April 2005 [Source: Cortal Consors, company annual reports. Betas are measured against the DJ Euro Stoxx 50 except UK companies against the FTSE 100].

8.8 The impact of leverage

Note that equity betas depend on the company's debt level, with betas increasing with debt. This explains the difference between geared (levered) and un-geared (un-levered) betas in the tables above. When using beta from peer companies, make sure to use un-levered betas before averaging and then re-lever using the target capital structure of the company you are looking into. The relationship between levered and un-levered betas is as follows:

$$\beta_{levered} = \beta_{unlevered} \times \left(1 + (1-T) \times \frac{D}{E}\right)$$

Levered beta is also called asset beta, and un-levered beta equity beta. T is the marginal corporate tax rate. Note that this formula is an approximation as it assumes debt to be risk-free. Intuitively, the effect of increased gearing is to increase the cost of equity capital as it increases the risk on the common stock.

When debt is not risk-free, a more accurate version of the previous formula is provided by an analysis from Modigliani and Miller:

$$\beta_{levered} = \beta_{unlevered} \times \left(1 + (1-T) \times \frac{D}{E}\right) - \beta_{debt} \times (1-T) \times \frac{D}{E}$$

where the beta of debt is measured against the market portfolio and can be obtained by regressing the cost of debt y against the market:

$$\beta_{debt} = \frac{y - E(r_f)}{MarketRiskPremium}$$

As debt interests are tax deductible, the more debt increases, the higher the tax break on debt. Assuming that the cost of debt is not affected by an increase in debt (this is certainly valid at low level of debt), it can be shown that the benefits of increasing gearing more than offset the increase in the cost of equity, so that the WACC declines as leverage increases. It can be shown that this result is still valid even when an increase in the cost of risky debt is taken into account. Nonetheless, there are limits to high gearing, in particular lenders to highly geared companies often impose restrictive covenants which limit managerial actions. With high gearing, the probability of making a loss in any one year also increases, resulting in a delay in obtaining tax relief on debt interest. In practice, at high gearing level, the cost of capital increases, so that the WACC reaches an optimum value at a middle level of gearing that varies from industry to industry.

Sources for beta are the NYSE and Standard and Poor's in the USA, the London Business School Risk Measurement Service (RMS) in the UK, as well as Bloomberg and investment banks like Merrill Lynch. Financial portals in the Internet, for instance from Cortal Consors, as well as Yahoo Finance, also provide beta values for individual companies.

8.9 Estimating beta for a single project

For a new project where no past experience is available, the CAPM cannot be used to estimate the future rate of return on the asset. The only possible method here is to calculate the NPV and use a Monte Carlo analysis. In this approach, the key uncertain input parameters to the NPV calculation are modified a large number of times (typically 5,000) and the rate of return of the project estimated from one simulation to the next. The distribution of the rate of return is also recorded in the model. The average value is then calculated which will give an approximation of the expected rate of return. Note that the results are very sensitive to the variance of the input parameters, the change in the variance over time, as well as the autocorrelation of the input variables over time and their cross-correlation. We will provide a numerical example in Chapter Thirteen.

9. Don't Use the Internal Rate of Return (IRR)

Before we close this chapter on valuation, we would like to urge you not to use the IRR as a financial performance measure in any of your investment decisions, project ranking or budget allocation. It is a pity that generations of students – including the author of this book – have ever been taught about the IRR, as this indicator is in the best case misleading, in the worst case dangerous, and in all cases confusing. Although widely used in literature in the 1980s, the IRR seems to have come out of fashion now in academic books, but not always in corporations. Just don't use it as there is no easy interpretation, and most financial managers misunderstand the term.

The IRR is the cost of capital that leads to NPV = 0 over the time horizon of the valuation, assuming no terminal value for the business. It shows how high the cost of capital would have to be so that no value is created over the time period used. You can also say that this is the cost of capital that makes the NPV break even over the time horizon considered. In most projects, the terminal value will be significant and not nil; in other projects with substantial decommissioning costs (for instance the nuclear industry), the project terminal value might be negative. But assuming a terminal value equal to zero doesn't seem to make much sense.

Another way to look at the IRR is to interpret it as equivalent to the yield to maturity on a corporate bond with variable interest rates i.e. variable coupon and nil redemption value at maturity of the bond. The variable coupons are equivalent to the positive cashflow generated by the business. In the initial phase though the cashflows will often be negative i.e. the interest rate would be negative, and you would be expected to return money to the corporation, a sort of negative coupon. This would make our bond a very strange and unusual bond indeed.

The IRR is often thought to be a compound average ROIC but this is not correct. So you can conclude that the IRR is a mathematically derived figure without any simple economic interpretation beyond the complex ones mentioned above.

Usually, when the IRR is greater than WACC, then the NPV is positive, so the project should be undertaken, while when the NPV is negative, the IRR is lower than WACC. The equivalence between NPV > 0 and IRR > WACC does not always hold however. For some cashflow patterns and projects the IRR does not exist, and for some others, multiple IRRs exist. This happens when there is more than one change in the sign of the cashflow. It can even happen that the NPV is negative, however the IRR is positive and larger than the cost of capital!

Also, when multiple projects should be ranked, a higher IRR for a project does not imply a higher NPV, so that ranking of projects IRR and NPV are not the same. This happens even when project cashflows display the classical U shape. Think about the following: if you have to choose between project 1 with 100% IRR and NPV=€100m or project 2 with 15% IRR but NPV = €1bn, it is more important to you to become €900m richer or have the intellectual satisfaction of generating a 100% IRR, assuming that you would be able to finance any of the two projects? Choose the project you like best.

In addition, there are alternative financial parameters to the IRR that are easier to understand and are much more useful for decision making, in particular the peak cash requirement and cashflow pay-back make the IRR redundant. These results complement the value creation measure provided by the NPV, are easy to understand and relate to the important practical issue of how much funding is required for the project. Funding might be a real constraint, and a project be chosen instead of another because it requires less funding, although its value creation might be lower.

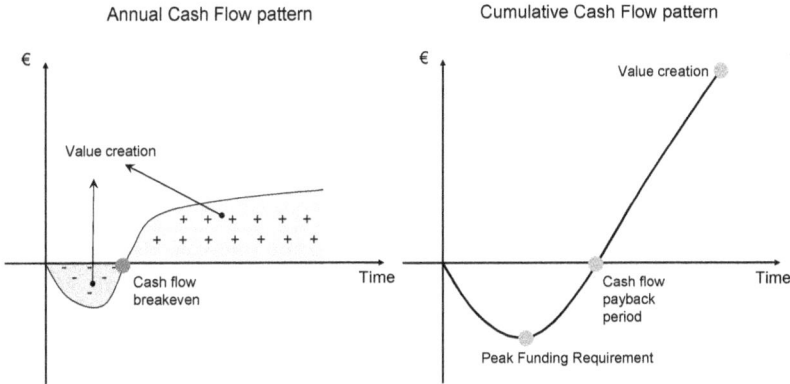

Figure 5.14: The IRR summarises an overall cashflow pattern [Source: INVESTAURA].

Broadly speaking, one might say that the IRR is a parameter summarising an entire cashflow pattern, and captures such key results as the peak cashflow requirement, the long-term value creation and the cashflow payback period in a single measure.

We now turn to a numerical example to illustrate the difficulties associated with the IRR.

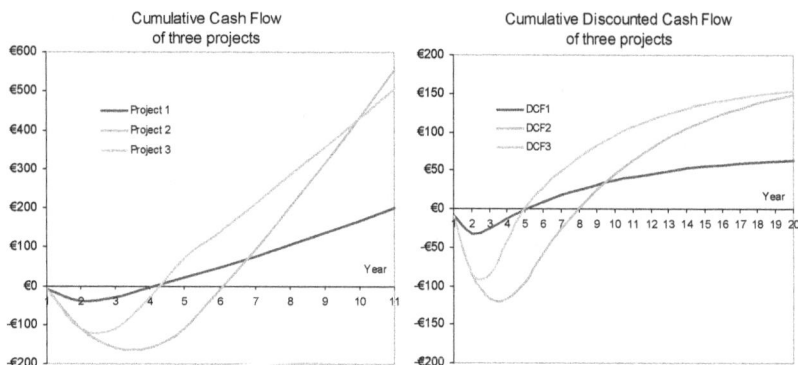

Figure 5.15: Cumulative and Discounted Cashflows for three projects [Source: INVESTAURA].

	NPV	IRR
Project 1	€64m	48%
Project 2	€148m	35%
Project 3	€154m	48%

Figure 5.16: NPV and IRR over 20 years for the three projects shown in Figure 5.15 [Source: INVESTAURA].

When faced with an investment decision and selection between mutually exclusive projects, you can use the following decision rules:

- If two projects have the same NPV, choose the one with the higher IRR. It will typically have lower peak cash requirement and/or shorter cashflow payback (Project 3 should be preferred to Project 2).

- However, very often, a project has a higher NPV but a lower IRR (Project 1 and 2), which usually means a longer pay-back period and larger peak funding requirement for the project with the lower IRR.

- Also two projects can have the same IRR but one has a higher NPV (Project 1 and 3), which can happen with a larger peak funding requirement, the same payback period and a higher positive cashflow for the project with the higher NPV.

As these examples show, rather than blindly relying on a single measure such as the IRR, it is better to analyse the cumulative cashflow pattern of the business and in particular the peak cash requirement and break-even period. The right way to rank projects is to use the NPV that they generate and their required peak funding, not the IRR.

## Chapter Six

Checklist of Common Pitfalls

"All men make mistakes, but only wise men learn from their mistakes"
Winston Churchill, British Prime Minister

In the previous two chapters, we have learned how to prepare a multiple-year financial plan and value a business. Before looking into how revenue and cost forecasts can be generated in practice, we briefly review here the typical mistakes that are made in financial planning and valuation. These mistakes can be easily avoided if you review this checklist every now and then.

1. General

- You are not performing crosschecks on the mutual consistency of inputs or outputs. Usually, inputs will come from various sources and are unlikely to be consistent with one another. Even if they come from the same source, you are often specifying more inputs than necessary, and forecast inputs by assuming a number of simple trends, for instance cost decreases. In this case, you need to check that the evolution of inputs over time is consistent. This is usually done by calculating a set of ratios and check that they behave as expected. You should also check that your outputs are consistent with your expectations. If both tariffs and costs decrease over time, do you expect profit to remain stable, increase or decrease?

- You are using benchmarks without adapting them. Maybe the focus company and its peers are actually quite different, for example using different sales channels or business models, sell to different end-users, or have different capital intensity. Benchmarks are good, but should be used with circumspection.

- You spent a lot of time discussing issues and factors that don't have a lot of impact on the business plan at the end of the day, while forgetting to clarify the impact on very fundamental issues, for instance using scenarios. This is one of the most common problems: getting lost in the (minor) details, only seeing the trees but not the forest. The more details you include, the more likely you are to make calculation mistakes as well.

2. Revenues

- In the launch year you have overestimated revenues because you are not commercially launching in January, but later in the year.

- To calculate revenues, you have multiplied the average revenue per user (ARPU) with the end-of-year subscribers rather than taking the average between the beginning- and the end-of-year subscriber numbers. This overestimates revenues.

- Your revenues are implicitly (but not explicitly) based on the assumption that you will have more than 50% market share in the long term, or even worse that you are active in a market with no competition. If you plan to be a gorilla and not a monkey, then you need to have unique advantages over the competition, and sustain them over time. If not, then remember that any good business idea will attract competition. If you are not clear about your unique selling proposition, or plan to follow a 'me too' approach, then don't expect a high market share.

- Your revenues per user are decreasing too slowly over time. In a service business, price can go down fast as new competitors enter the market and 10% reduction p.a. is not uncommon. In the consumer electronics business, products quickly become obsolete and are replaced with new products; also competition is intense so that much of the benefit of decreasing component costs is passed on to end-users, and price decreases of 30% p.a. can be common.

- Your market share and overall revenue expectations are not consistent with your marketing and advertising plan. How will you acquire customers? Which channels will you use? How much will it cost to build these channels from scratch or pay third party channels for shelf space and customer acquisition? Is your advertising budget consistent with subscriber ramp-up?

- You are underestimating the time required to build up your customer base, especially your first-year plan is too ambitious. Cut revenues by half and double your costs in the early years, and you will probably be closer to reality.

3. Costs

- In a low-inflation country, you have forgotten the impact of inflation on a number of OPEX positions such as salary increases. In developing markets salaries usually increase faster than inflation due to productivity increase and high GDP growth.

- You are not aggressive enough on technology price decrease. High-tech prices usually decrease very rapidly, from -10% to -40% per annum.

- If you subsidise hardware, for instance a mobile handset or a household customer premises equipment (CPE), you have based your subsidy costs on net customer addition rather than gross additions. The difference between net and gross is that you have lost customers during the year as they have discontinued service. This is also called churn or customer attrition. So even if your customer base is constant, you need to win new customers to replace those that you have lost. In addition, loyal customers might get a hardware replacement every few years and this might have to be subsidised as well.

- You have underestimated the cost of sales. If you sell through retailers, the average selling price (ASP) is only about 50%-70% of what the end-user price will be. The difference is used by the sales channel to cover its costs, mainly personnel, space, inventories and advertising.

- You have taken sunk cost into account. Sunk cost is past money spent and not recoverable. It is irrelevant to your business plan and should not impact your decision to invest or not. Including sunk cost in a business plan might lead to wrong decisions. When deciding on a new business opportunity, the only relevant issue is whether future benefits are higher than future costs. The only impact of past costs is whether you have under or overestimated costs before, so the forecasting of future costs should be reviewed in that light. If you have spent billions of Euros on a UMTS license, this should definitely not influence whether you launch UMTS service early, late or at all.

4. Free Cashflow

- You have not accounted for changes in working capital in the business case. The consequences are that you are underestimating capital requirement in the growth phase and overestimating it when growth is diminishing. Therefore you consciously overestimate cashflows in the growth phase and underestimate them in the maturity phase. Working capital is often what makes fast growing businesses get into trouble.

- To calculate Free Cashflow, NOPAT, NPV or EVA, you are not taking tax into account. Tax has to be incurred and has a real impact on value. Just imagine that you did not have to pay personal income tax. Wouldn't you be richer?

- In a valuation, you are calculating the terminal value of the business wrongly because FCF_{n+1} is wrongly extrapolated from FCF_n. See Section 3.4 of Chapter Five.

- To discount the Free Cashflow, you have taken a company WACC rather than a project WACC. When the project risk is higher than the company's average risk, then the WACC should be higher. On the other hand, if project risk is decreasing with time, for instance if the project is undertaken in stages, and stage two only goes ahead if stage one has been successful, then the WACC in stage two should be lower than in stage one.

- You have forgotten to discount the Terminal Value by the cost of capital to express it in today's money, not money in many years from now.

## Part Three

Forecasting
Revenues and Costs

## Chapter Seven

Forecasting is an Art

"Prediction is very difficult, especially if it is about the future"
Nils Bohr, Nobel laureate in Physics

With this chapter, we turn to the difficult issue of forecasting. Understanding customer needs, translating these into products and generating accurate forecasts of market demand are real challenges that keep legions of market researchers, marketing experts and consultants busy. This is especially true in very innovative businesses where there is limited or no historical data available and no experience to relate to. On the supply side, uncertainties can also be large, especially the availability of new technologies, their costs evolution and their respective benefits. However, the challenges on the supply side are not as great as on the demand side, and reasonably accurate forecasts can be derived following careful analysis.

In this introductory chapter, we start by reviewing the issue of forecasting from a holistic perspective and discuss the alternative methods that are used by practitioners. In the next chapters we will show how numerical forecasts for supply and demand can be generated for your business plan.

Overview of Chapter Seven

1. We Are Still in the Stone Age 150
2. Two Types of Uncertainty...151
3. Using Rules of Thumb..152
4. Modelling...153
5. End-User Surveys 160
6. Pilot Project 162
7. Commercial Launch 163

1. We Are Still in the Stone Age

Let's face it: our understanding of end-user requirements and market demand has remained rather primitive until today. We have split the atom, sent men to the moon and returned them safely to earth, designed instant communication systems that can connect any two people on earth, but we still don't understand well what end-users want. The proof is that today 80% of new products are withdrawn from the market within one year of introduction due to their lack of success. Why is this?

The explanation is actually simple: we cannot look into end-users' brain and are not particularly good at modelling human preferences. How people think, take decisions and behave is difficult to understand and forecast. Even if we could look into people's heads, we might not be any wiser, as complex factors including emotions and memories influence decision-making without end-users being able to articulate them in thoughts or language. People themselves often do not clearly know what they want and find it difficult to articulate their needs. So asking end-users will usually only give you very rough answers.

Take SMS messaging for instance: developed as a side feature in GSM networks, SMS was initially provided free of charge in the early 1990s. Who would be ready to pay for such a primitive service requiring users to type words on a minuscule keyboard designed for numbers and not alphabetical characters? Person-to-person SMS was never really designed nor marketed by mobile operators in the first place. SMS messaging was incidentally discovered by young consumers who turned it into big business and a money- making service for mobile operators.

But let us return to only a couple of years before the SMS boom and consider mobile telephony: who would ever have thought in 1990 that one day 80% of the population in developed countries would own a mobile phone and use it to communicate any time from anywhere? No one really – apart from a couple of Nordic men maybe. Mobile networks very initially designed for much lower capacity and targeted at a small, often elite, percentage of the population. In the late 1980s, I remember meeting a Finish guy during a summer internship. One of his favourite occupations was to tell me that in Finland, people were moving around with portable wireless telephones that they could use to call other people. I thought that he was pulling my leg and simply showing off.

A big unknown remaining in the telecom industry today is: "what are the mobile applications and solutions that end-users will be ready to pay for tomorrow?". People have been asking this one and the same question for almost ten years now, and we hear repeatedly that "there is no killer application" and "there will be hundreds of services that end-users can choose from". Thank you, this might bring us some comfort, but is not very helpful. Is there any useful application at all? From looking at the WAP disaster, we can at least say: service will have to bring real value to people, and be simple to use.

2. Two Types of Uncertainty

One solution to this daunting question is to realise that uncertainty, like risk, can be split between reducible and irreducible uncertainty. Reducible uncertainty comprises factors that can be resolved to a large extent if you are ready to invest a comparatively small amount of time and money. On the other hand, you can do nothing about irreducible uncertainty, because most forces are outside your control, very diverse outcomes might materialise and there is no way at this stage that you can narrow down the range of possible futures. For irreducible uncertainty, we can only accept that life is very complex, influenced by a multitude of players and events beyond our control, and there is little one can do about it. The only strategy here is either to wait until the uncertainty has resolved, at which point it might be too late. Or enter the market now, hoping that forces will turn out in your favour. Scenario planning is also a powerful technique to devise robust strategies and identify no-regret moves.

Fortunately, a lot of uncertainty in life is of reducible nature. In this case, uncertainty really is a lack of information or knowledge, but we can improve our understanding and resolve the uncertainty to some extent, if not in full. Here, by spending money on R&D, market research, market testing, pilot projects, you should be able to obtain valuable information to help you forecast the future. Various methodologies can be used to derive the potential size of a new market and we will review them in turn from the simplest, lowest cost, to the more complex and more expensive:

- intuition forecasting
- modelling, including benchmarking and regression analysis
- end-user interviews, without or with prototype
- pilot project
- commercial launch.

The first three methods will be examined into detail below as they can be applied in the business plan development phase before the decision to invest takes place. Typically, applying any method from the list above will cost you 10 times more than the method immediately preceding, so if intuition takes you one hour, modelling will take you one to a few days, interviews a few weeks, and a pilot project a few months. Finally, service launch typically involves a lot more human and financial resources as well as commitment over one year and more.

3. Using Rules of Thumb

This is also called *intuition forecasting* or *judgmental forecasting* and is the simplest and cheapest method that is available to you. Common sense can achieve valuable results, and many mistakes can be avoided if good logical thinking has been applied systematically and you are listening to your gut feeling. This approach is unlikely to let you achieve groundbreaking results. On the other hand, your grey cells can help you derive the maximum size of a market.

Let us assume that you were in the year 1999 and trying to estimate the maximum long-term penetration of mobile telephony in Germany. In December 1999, there were 10 million subscribers in the country and mobile penetration was a mere 12%. By that time though, it was clear that the mobile phone was turning into a very personal item. The concept of 'one mobile phone' per family, dominating in the mid 1990s and thought to lead to long-term penetration targets around 30%-40%, was not a valid view of the world any longer. The unit of measurement was not the household anymore, but the individual. Your reasoning might have been as follows: looking at the current age pyramid, people below 6 and above 75 years of age make about 15% of the total population. Assuming that this part of the population would mostly (80%) be excluded from the market and that of the remaining population (7-75 years old), about 15% of people are technology averse enough to refuse to use a mobile phone, gives you a total of 67% of the consumer population as potential mobile subscribers at some stage in the future.

To these can be added business subscribers who get their subscription and bill paid by their employer, with the mobile phone being used as a tool for work. The working force makes up 40% of the total country population. Looking into the various occupation groups, you can quickly exclude 50% of the working force as unlikely to get a mobile phone financed by their employer for their daily job: just take the 10% unemployed, the 25% factory workers, the 10% teachers and civil servants, who are unlikely to have employer-sponsored mobile phones – and you already get 45%. The remaining addressable working force makes up 20% of the total population.

The total now adds up to 67%+20% = 87%. On top of this there are people who might have more than one private subscription. This is unlikely to be widespread because it is rather inconvenient to carry more than one phone with you around or have more than one phone number, so let's add another 10% to our 67% identified above. This gives you a total of 87% + 6.7% ~ 94%. By the way, in this calculation, one can also derive that at saturation, business subscribers would make a maximum of 20% of all customers, which is quite close to what we have today. Now, if you accept the logic of this argumentation, you would have excluded any forecast that sees mobile penetration reach substantially more than 100% in the long term. In 1999, there were many who forecast 150% penetration as long-term saturation.

But maybe I misunderstood the forecast at the time and the additional 50% were meant to be machines, and dogs? You can certainly argue that we forgot to include cars and other vending machines that might at some stage 'become connected'. But then why assume only another 50% on top of the number of human subscription, and not 500%, considering that on earth, there are 6 billion people, but 30 billion machines i.e. 5 times as many? In addition, it is rather unlikely that the average revenue per user (ARPU) that an operator would generate from this additional segment would be as high as the voice ARPU valid at the time, in particular because you will be more likely to call them rather than they call you. But maybe I am wrong and your coffee machine will soon call you and say "Hey, coffee is ready, come and have some".

So without doing any complex calculation we have seen that you can use your brainpower, common sense and logical deduction to derive rules of thumb that can provide estimates of what could happen in the future.

4. Modelling

Modelling is logical deduction taken to the next step. When you have to make so many assumptions and intermediate calculations that the outputs cannot simply be derived in your head from a couple of inputs, then you need a model or a computer program. When calculating in one's head gets difficult, then Microsoft Excel® spreadsheet software is a convenient aid.

Modelling is about deriving one or more outputs, also called explained variables, from one or multiple inputs, also called explanatory variables.

Explanatory variables should be observable or at least easier to forecast than explained variables. If historical data for comparable products and services, or data from other countries and industries are available, modelling will usually start with data analysis. Benchmarking and regression analysis are two common techniques employed. The objective of benchmarking is to compare various sets of data with one another for instance mobile penetration across countries. Regression analysis is about deriving meaningful relationships between various sets of data, and identifying potential explanatory variables.

Most forecasts will be expressed as a function of time. These forecasts can be split in two main families, for which we will provide example in the following chapters:

- in autoregressive forecasting, the value of the explained variable at time n is a function of the explained variable at time n-1, and possibly other variables
- in cross-sectional forecasts, the explained variable is function of other explanatory variables only.

For instance, you can regress mobile penetration against time, GDP per capita, the number of operators in the country, or against all three in one step: this is called multiple regression analysis. Note that in the Microsoft Excel® spreadsheet software, the LINEST function is particularly useful to undertake regressions.

4.1 Benchmarking and regression analysis

Benchmarking is a useful technique as long as the variables that are being compared are indeed comparable. When benchmarking mobile penetration in Western Europe, one might reasonably argue that Europeans can be treated as a homogenous group of people as far as their mobile communication needs are concerned. On this basis, one might draw the conclusion that the penetration level achieved in more mature markets such as Finland and England are likely to be achieved by some other European countries with a certain time lag. The same logic might apply to Asia, although it is a much less homogeneous region from a cultural point of view. Figure 7.1 provides some indication that service take-up can vary tremendously across countries in the same region, and mobile penetration can be related to the wealth of the country as measured by the GDP per capital.

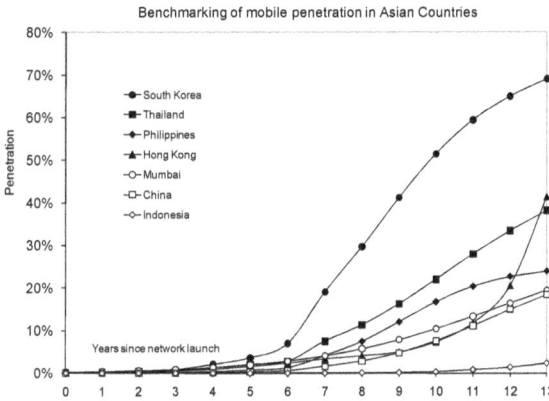

Figure 7.1: Benchmarking [Source: Operator annual reports, INVESTAURA]

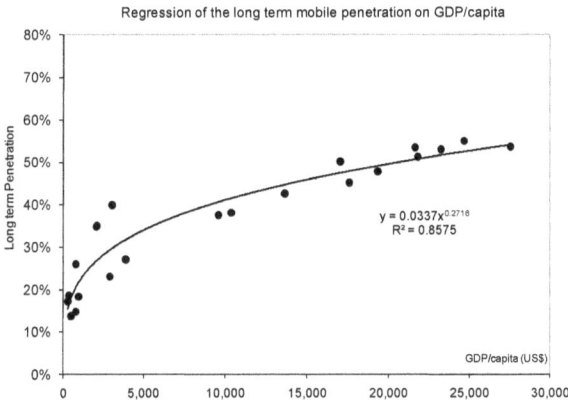

Figure 7.2: Regression analysis [Source: Operator annual reports, INVESTAURA].

As a second example, let us consider the success of i-mode in Japan and think about whether this is a good indication for Europe. The experience that we have collected in Europe from 2002 to 2004 with i-mode seems to indicate that it is not the case. In Japan, within 20 months of its launch in early 1999, i-mode had achieved 50% penetration of mobile subscribers. In Europe, it has achieved about 10% in the same time period. Various explanations have been provided: the Japanese spend vast amount of time commuting in cities between their home and their work place, and fortunately they are provided with a good indoor coverage in trains; also Japan is known to have a lower penetration of PCs at home and Web content in Japanese was more limited at that time. So i-mode applications came at the right time to fill in a latent demand.

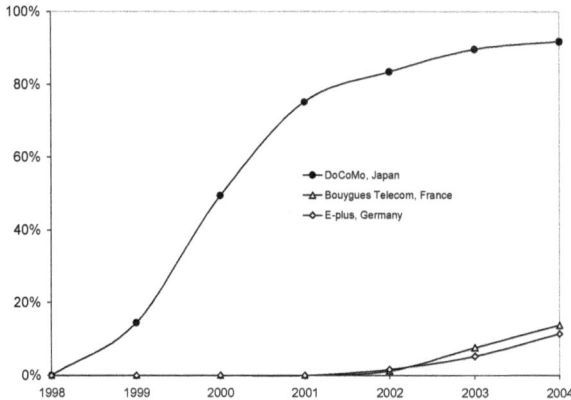

Figure 7.3: Penetration of i-mode in Japan, France, and Germany [Source: E-plus, Bouygues Telecom, NTT DoCoMo].

We can learn from this that benchmarking can provide valuable insight, but should be used with caution. This brings us to the main difficulty in regression analysis and modelling: specifying the model correctly, i.e. defining a set of mathematical relationship between explained and explanatory variables that correctly and meaningfully replicate observation and have predictive power:

- By *correctly* we mean that R^2, the square of the regression residuals, should be high and as much as possible between 0.7 and 1. R^2 is a measure of the goodness of the fit, and the extent to which the explanatory variables explain the derived variable.

- By *meaningfully* we mean whether the coefficients derived from the regression are statistically significant, an indication that we have included the right explanatory variables in the first place. This can be derived from the t-statistic and checking whether the positive or negative sign of coefficient are consistent with our expectations.

- By *predictive power*, we mean that the model should not only explain the past and provide a good fit to historical data, but also generate accurate predictions.

A good model is one that captures the cause-effect relationship in a correct manner. The Appendix provides further information on regression analysis.

4.2 Modelling demand with no historical data

When no historical data is available to support the benchmarking and regression analysis above, then modelling becomes an especially subjective exercise that requires on a lot of judgment. For example, to forecast revenues, a simple approach is to assume a relationship between demand and price, and define price as an exogenous variable set by the market and the level of competition. In the market introduction phase, price for products and services are usually set at a fairly high level by companies, due to high costs on one side, but also because they are unsure about the end-user willingness to pay and need to collect first market response. As the price is lowered at a later stage, the addressable market and customer demand correspondingly increases.

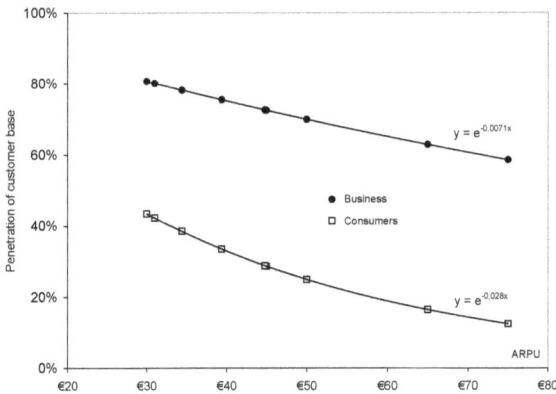

Figure 7.4: Willingness to pay for mobile services. The slope of the curve is the elasticity of price to demand [Source: INVESTAURA].

The demand to price curve can be approximated from willingness to pay data collected in interviews with potential customers. The models set up following this approach are called *predictive* models, because their predict results from one or more predicting variables.

An alternative modelling approach consists of making assumptions for a larger number of input variables and their evolution over time, and then performs a number of crosschecks on the calculation results. These models are called corroborative models. This is often simpler than trying to derive complex relationships between one or more demand variables and other explanatory variables. For instance, from ARPU and traffic forecasts that have been prepared independently of one another, you can derive the service tariff as the ratio of ARPU over traffic, and check whether the levels and pattern obtained make sense. This is exactly the approach that we have taken in the UMTS business plan in Chapter Two.

4.3 Example: consumer spending on mobile data

Let us finish this section with an example showing that modelling does not always have to be complex after all. You may or may not agree with the assumptions made, but assumptions and a model are better than nothing at all. The objective is to estimate the maximum data ARPU that mobile subscribers might be willing to spend on mobile data application in the year 2010. By then, services deployed on technologies such as UMTS and WLAN should have reached a certain level of maturity.

Why are people ready to spend money on a product or service? Because the product provides them with value. Value can come from convenience, efficiency in doing one's work and simplifying someone's life, but also entertainment and emotions. Let us make the simplifying assumption that some consumer subscribers will use mobile data for entertainment only and business subscribers to increase their productivity.

Consumer spending on mobile data

Consumers will pay for their mobile data service from their entertainment budget, amounting to 8% of total budget available in an average German household in 2003. However total budget is increasing at a rate of 3% p.a. in nominal terms accounting for 2% inflation and 1% real term increase. In addition the entertainment share of total budget is further increasing in accordance with historical trend by 7% every year.

Estimation of mobile data ARPU	2003	2004	2005	2006	2007	2008	2009	2010
Monthly disposable income per person	€1500	€1545	€1591	€1639	€1688	€1739	€1791	€1845
Income nominal growth	3%							
Entertainment budget % of disposable income	8%	8.6%	9.2%	9.8%	10.5%	11.2%	12.0%	12.8%
Entertainment budget annual increase	7%							
Monthly entertainment budget	€120	€132	€146	€161	€177	€195	€215	€237
Entertainment budget on top of 2003 level	€0	€12	€26	€41	€57	€75	€95	€117
Share for mobile data	20%							
Mobile data budget	€0	€2	€5	€8	€11	€15	€19	€23
Additional upside	10%							
Total consumer mobile data budget	€0	€3	€6	€9	€13	€17	€21	€26
Mobile data budget % of disposable income	0.0%	0.2%	0.4%	0.5%	0.7%	1.0%	1.2%	1.4%

Figure 7.5: A simple model for consumer mobile data [Source: INVESTAURA].

In nominal terms, the entertainment budget is increasing by 3% + 7% ~ 10% every year. Let us assume that mobile data would capture 20% of that growth – mobile data is competing with many other sources of entertainment such as holiday spending, consumer electronic hardware, and home entertainment. Let us also assume that mobile data would substitute other consumption positions for instance some of household expenditure for postcards and stamps creating an upside of +10%. The model leads to an estimate of €26 per consumer per month spent on mobile data in 2010, or 1.4% of disposable personal income. Knowing that household spending on telecom currently amounts to 3% of household income in Germany, then adding another 1.4% point by 2010 seems high, but not unrealistic.

Business spending on mobile data

Take an enterprise mobile worker whose productivity can be increased by the use of mobile data for example mobile email and corporate Intranet access. Let us assume that this leads to cost savings corresponding to 20 min of work per day i.e. 4% of an average 8-hour working time, for instance by working while commuting in the train. More than half an hour saved per day is possible for specific professional groups such as field-service employees, but unlikely to apply across the board in the long term to a very large customer base of business users. Assume that the time saved is shared equally between the employee, who works 10 minutes less to produce the same results, and his company, which can also reduce its costs by an equivalent of 10 minutes (due to the effective 10 minutes of additional work the employer benefits from). Assuming an average cost to the employer of €3000 in 2003, but €3700 in 2010 per mobile-data-enabled worker leads to a saving of 4% / 2 x €3700 = €74 / month to the employer. Assuming that employers are ready to give away 50% of those benefits to their service provider, this results in an ARPU of €37.

So the average data ARPU per subscriber in a long-term view would be (74% consumers x €26 + 20% business x €37) / 94% = €28 per mobile data user.

An ARPU potential of €28 in 2010 would have led you to reject any data ARPU suggestion of €70-€100, which was not that uncommon in the late 1990s, but has proved to be unrealistic.

To conclude this subject, remember that modelling should be an instrument to support thinking and decision-making. A good model should help you provide an answer to a question, or let you clarify what you have to believe for a certain future to materialise. A valuable fall-out product of modelling is also to derive a much better understanding of the key drivers influencing a business. On the other hand, you should not let yourself get drowned in too deep a level of detail, and modelling should not become an end in itself. Although it can potentially be an enjoyable pastime, your objective is not to model complex questions, but to bring answers to real business problems.

5. End-User Surveys

To complement modelling and also provide inputs to business planning, it is essential to talk to end-users and develop a good understanding of their needs. A prerequisite is to make your product or service as simple, clear and easy to understand as possible. End-users can find it hard to relate to something that they have never seen or experienced before in their lives. The product that you might show them might require a shift in their current perceptions and habits. In most cases they will only have a very vague idea of whether they would use the product or not, and even less if they would buy it.

Therefore, you should not be blinded by the results and apparent accuracy that you get from end-user interviews, but use them as indication for your product development and fine tuning of the business plan.

5.1 Telephone interviews

A classical technique is to conduct interviews on the telephone, which unfortunately does not allow you to show any additional material, in particular pictures of a prototype that would help end-users relate to your questions. Results are then analysed for each market segment. Consumers can be split according to various criteria that must be relevant to your business. Typical criteria include not only age, gender, disposable income and spending patterns, but also behavioural characteristics such as values, lifestyle, needs and social networks.

Price issues should be raised as late as possible in the interview. Results will usually be biased downwards when people let their answers be influenced by any price perception. This happens even if you have told people to assume that prices would be acceptable, because some will reject the assumptions and still assume that price will remain beyond their means, or at least their willingness to pay.

Market research conducted over the telephone will provide a high-level indication of end-user preferences, but nothing more than this. Experience has shown that to generate more reliable results, your questionnaire should follow a number of guidelines:

- questions should let interviewees choose from an even number of alternatives, otherwise many interviewees will tend to give you middle-of-the-road answers

- the product should not be defined too narrowly because you are usually interested in understanding the long-term potential of a product that will most likely change over time
- you should express the functionality and benefits of new products in terms of an experience that respondents can relate too
- you should not prescribe prices too early as this may lead to unduly negative reactions
- prior to the interview, you should conduct a pilot of the questionnaire on a small number of respondents, for example colleagues, to remove any ambiguity and check whether they have problems answering the questions
- when designing a questionnaire, you should begin by asking yourself what the survey results will be used for. Which decision should be taken based on the questionnaire results? What format will be most useful? Do the questions being asked provide the right level of detail for decision making?

You should primarily interview your focus market segment. When services are addressed to the mass market, interviewing 10-20 year old people is very beneficial, because this age class is likely to be part of the early adopter segment for most innovation and can exert a snowball effect towards younger and older generations. In addition young adults are demanding people that won't give you a second chance if they are not immediately convinced, and display the confidence required to think for themselves and let you know what they think openly.

5.2 Face-to-face interviews

Interviews undertaken face-to-face and in an unconstrained environment create more room for rapport between interviewers and interviewees, leading not only to a better understanding of what people like and dislike, but also to their background motivation. Often, a prototype or mock-up product will be available, whether faked or not, for people to experiment with. These interviews will bring you a lot of valuable information about the product design and help you iron out apparently secondary details that can none-the-less make a huge difference in practice. Think about a portable gaming console where the game cartouche is place under the console battery, making cartouche changing a tedious exercise. Or think about providing mobile ticketing to teens for a pop concert: teens will value the convenience of getting an entry place, but might tell you that they hate the idea of not holding a paper ticket with a cool picture of their idol that they can collect and show to their friends. So a mobile ticketing solution might be attractive to end-users, but ideally combined with a real ticket sent to their home address in advance.

There are many other techniques to engage with potential customers and learn from them. Focus groups provide an interesting approach. The idea here is to conduct a loosely structured discussion and encourage the free flow of ideas. This allows as much information and end-user wishes to be collected before presenting interviewees with the product that you plan to bring to market. Other techniques use pictures and especially association to help understand the emotional value that products provide to users.

6. Pilot Project

A pilot project marks the stepping-stone between the analysis phase and the commercial launch. Its objective is to replicate on a smaller scale the circumstances that would apply in a market environment, end-to-end verification that various technologies and processes can be integrated and successfully work together, test various prototypes and pre-commercial services. Last, but not least, collect feedback from end-users on the product or applications being offered. A pilot project usually takes place over a short period of time spanning 1 to 6 months. It should be sufficiently long so that the bias created by novelty and curiosity, which later wears out, can be observed and accounted for.

A pilot project typically involves multiple players and companies bringing complementary expertise and sharing the costs of the project as well as the learning. It traditionally comprises three phases:

- a development phase including requirement analysis, solution implementation and integration
- the trial phase itself, involving end-users in near-real-life circumstances
- finally the post-trial phase where key results are summarised and analysed as well of recommendation generated for a potential full-scale launch.

The only major inconvenience of a pilot project is that it is rather difficult to keep confidential, considering the number of players and people involved, so that competition is informed well in advance about your next likely move and your potential strategy, and you cannot capitalise on a surprise effect.

7. Commercial Launch

Congratulations if you have reached that stage as product or service line manager. From the many products or service ideas that are investigated and trialled by a company, only a small portion manage to make it to the commercial phase. Ahead of the market launch, a clear strategy will have been formulated, a product developed to commercial maturity, a marketing campaign prepared, production ramped up, sales channels as well as customer care staff trained so that everybody is 'go' for day one.

Only the commercial phase will tell you whether your business idea was really a good idea or not. Whatever the amount of analysis and piloting you might have performed to minimise risk, the line of demarcation between success and failure is often quite thin. In the fast-moving consumer goods industry, the timing of market launch is particularly critical. If your product comes too late to market, for instance in January rather than November of the year before, your might have lost 50% of your potential business volume with that product due to the missed Christmas sales period. You might also be half a generation too late compared to your most agile competitors in terms of product features, which will force you lower your prices – this is unlikely to keep your product business plan profitable in any case.

Some countries such as the USA, Japan and Korea are well known for their higher readiness than in other countries to experiment and reach commercial launch. This can be explained by some of the following factors:

- a well developed venture-capital industry ready to finance start-ups with seed and growth capital, and possibly having developed better skills at selecting new promising business ideas
- a technology-aware society that is avid for new products and services
- a learning and forgiving attitude towards failure rather than finger pointing, and a readiness to bounce back.

Now that we have seen how challenging it is to forecast what the market wants and discussed alternative approaches, we return to the more analytical issue of forecasting supply and demand in the next chapters.

## Chapter Eight

Forecasting on the Supply Side

"640kbytes should be enough for anybody"
Bill Gates, Microsoft, 1981

Earlier in this book, we have discussed valuation techniques that should become routine over time with regular and rigorous practice. Unlike valuation, forecasting cashflows for new businesses will always require considerable experience and personal judgment. In this chapter, we look at the supply side and how technology characteristics and costs can be forecast in practice.

Overview of Chapter Eight

1. Forecasting Technology Capacity Evolution...166
2. Forecasting Technology Costs (CAPEX) 170
3. Forecasting Operating Costs (OPEX)...174

1. Forecasting Technology Capacity Evolution

The uncertainty on the supply side mostly relates to the availability, the capability and the costs of existing and future technologies. Uncertainty can be considerably reduced by talking to hardware manufacturers, chipset makers, suppliers of enabling technologies, technical experts working in research centres, as well as analysts specialising in technology innovation.

The good news is that many technology characteristics display constant growth rate over time. This means that capacity is growing exponentially and when plotted on a logarithmic scale, capacity is a linear function of time.

This is especially the case at the component level, as shown by the following examples.

- The number of transistors per chip has been correctly predicted by 'Moore's law' to double every 2 years on average since the 1960s, giving an annual growth rate of +40%.

- The number of Million Instructions Per Second for microprocessors expressed in MIPS. This is closely related to Moore's law and growing at +45% per annum. This is not only the result of shrinking processor size (so increase in transistor density) but also continuous increase in processor clock speed.

- The storage capacity in bits per square inch for various types of memories (DRAM, Hard Disk Drive, Flash Card). For DRAM, it has increased at +40% p.a. for the last 30 years. For HDDs, the growth rate has accelerated from 25% p.a. between 1970 to 1990 to 60% p.a. from 1990 to 1998 and +100% from 1999 to 2003, but has been slowing down to 40% p.a. since then. Do you remember the time when 1 Mega Byte of RAM capacity in a computer was regarded as a real feast? This was the Atari around the year 1988. Today most PCs come with 512MB to 1GB of RAM. The same applies to hard disks: the first Giga Byte hard disk came to market in 1997, but 10 years later most new PCs are equipped with a hard disk of 80 Giga Bytes or more.

- The bandwidth of optical fibre expressed in Mega bit per second (Mbps). This has increased by a factor 10,000 between 1983 and 2003 or +60% p.a. This is partly due to the development of fibre of higher quality grade, partly to the development of better diode and laser technologies.

- The data rate of end-user modems expressed in kbps: modems have evolved from analogue over ISDN to ADSL and further xDSL technologies are being rolled out now. Although data rates have increased in steps rather than year-on-year, the equivalent annual growth has been +55% p.a., or a doubling in data rate every 19 months.

- The energy density per unit of battery weight, usually measured in Watt-hour per kg (Wh/kg). This is evolving rather slowly at +10% p.a. within the same battery technology family, for instance Nickel Metal hybrid (Ni-MH), whereas a technology change from Ni-MH to Lithium-ion (Li-Ion) can double the energy density. Fuel-cell batteries are expected to provide a ten-time improvement compared to current Li-Ion batteries. Considering the low battery capacity growth rate compared to other components, batteries are often a limitation factor in product development today. This can be partly compensated by the development of smart power management techniques, such as the time-slicing technology used in DVB-H handsets where the handset receives data in bursts and powers down when not receiving data.

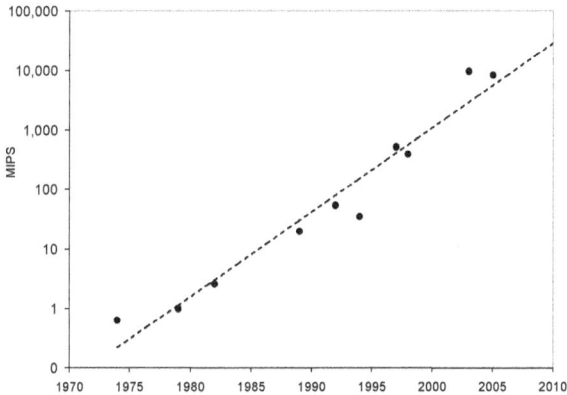

Figure 8.1: MIPS capacity of Intel microprocessor. 8086 to Pentium 4 [Source: INVESTAURA using data from Motorola, Intel, AMD].

Even if a generation change is taking place and generates a step increase in capability, over the long term a fairly linear pattern might emerge when you look at the envelope of capacity increase over multiple generations. Note that in this case, it is not the logarithm of capacity that appears to be linear, but capacity itself, so the rate of change (growth) is not constant, but diminishing over time.

In mobile networks, improvements in air-interface capacity are driven by improved modulation techniques that increase the number of bits per Hertz, the usage of larger spectrum blocks to transmit information as well as multiple-antenna systems such as multiple-inputs multiple-outputs (MIMO) solutions. The limits shown in Figure 8.2 are as defined in accordance with the Shannon's theorem, which states that there is a maximum bit rate than can be achieved over a certain transmission medium defined by its bandwidth and its signal-to-noise ratio.

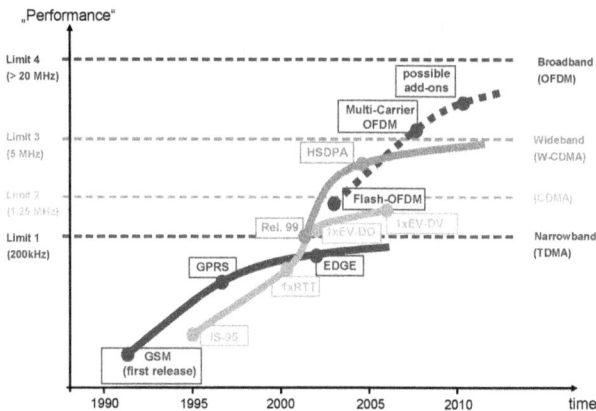

Figure 8.2: Increase in performance of mobile radio systems [Source: Siemens AG].

That the IT and consumer electronics industry could maintain growth rate between 30% and 60% over long periods of time is really remarkable, not only because of the great technical performance enhancements involved, but also because of the seemingly insatiable readiness of the market to absorb those capacity increases and build new products around them. We rarely have time to stop for a second and appreciate what an exponential growth of 40% per annum really means in absolute term: after 10 years, your initial capacity will have been multiplied by 30; after 20 years, the capacity is 800 times higher; after 30 years, the unimaginable figure of 24,000 times the initial capacity is reached. Applying the same process backwards illustrates the extraordinary achievement in reducing the size and density of transistor on a chip: if a transistor of the early 1970s were to be magnified to the size of a 1.80m adult, then our transistor of the year 2010 would have a size smaller than that of an ant. If the airplane industry had made the same progress as the microelectronics industry in the last 30 years, then flying from London to Sydney would take 2 minutes, and the flight ticket would cost less than 4 cent.

The good news for forecasters is that in practice, technology improvement is reasonably predictable, as most technology performance grows linearly or exponentially (i.e. the growth rate is constant). So to generate a short-term forecast, look at the current and past performance, perform regression analysis, and use the results to extrapolate into the future.

You must think that there is a physical limit somewhere and you are right: there are physical limits, whether this is the distance between two atoms on a chip or the maximum number of bits per Hertz than can be transmitted according to Shannon's limit. You can't beat physics after all. But there again, as we near from those limits, new technologies and concepts are introduced, often providing a magnitude improvement over what was possible before, and putting off past barriers. In the 1950s, people were concerned that you would have to recruit a large number of staff to switch telephone communications manually, especially with the rapid increase in the number of telephone users. But then mechanical switching was introduced and used until the 1970s, then electrical analogue and later digital switching followed, and we are now going into optical switching. Using manual switching, the total current population on earth would not be enough to carry the giant task of handling the annual 2,000 billion telephone calls and more than 1,000 billion SMS's.

So it is with technology. It frees our hands and brains for more noble purposes, and makes us humans more and more machine-assisted. In 15 years from now, your office PC will be about 150 times faster than it is today. If this is not impressive, then expect that *all* mobile users own a handset that can be used as PDA, TV set, camcorder, music player, travel navigator, virtual assistant, payment device and many other uses by the year 2025. Some handsets on the market in 2010 already provide a lot of this – but remain pricey, and bulky.

2. Forecasting Technology Costs (CAPEX)

Obviously, market acceptance for such incredible increases in technology capabilities has only happened because the cost per unit of capacity has decreased at an even faster rate. The magic here is that the increase in capacity could be achieved without any significant increase in component price, and in many cases at a lower cost, so that the total component price has decreased while its capacity has increased. This simultaneous increase in capabilities and decrease in costs is really what has opened up a mass market for many new products.

At the product level, and by squeezing more and more transistor on a chip, you need fewer chips to make a product, helping costs decrease further. When a product becomes very mature though, floor effects become apparent, and its price stabilises at a minimum level. Once great savings have been achieved in the chips making up a product, the total product price becomes dominated by plastic, buttons and other mechanical parts that do not decrease at the same speed as chips, so that the overall product price decrease flattens out or even stops. This is manifest in DVD players today (about €50 per unit) as well as desktop PCs, whose minimum price has been fairly stable at €500-€800 for many years, but of course with vast increases in capability.

Let us now look at a few cost decrease examples.

- The cost of transistors in microprocessors. This has been decreasing by a factor of 100 every 10 years, i.e. -37% p.a. from 1 dollar in 1965, to 1 cent in 1975 to 1/10,000 of a cent in 1985 and so on.

- The cost of memories (DRAM, Hard Disk, Flash card). In 1973, a DRAM chip of 1kbit cost $80; in 2002, a 1 Gbit (so 1 million kbit!) cost $50, giving a price decrease of 39% per annum. In 1981, 1GB of HD capacity cost €300,000, in 2003 only €1, an annual price decrease of 77%: this is faster than the increase in Hard Disk capacity, and has made Hard Disk become mass-market products in PCs in the 1990s. Flash-based cards with 1GB capacity have come to market at about €100 per unit in 2004, and cost about €10 in 2007 (-50% p.a.). Mini Hard Disk drives of 8GB capacity emerged in 2005 at about €100 as well, and are about 10 times cheaper than Flash Card on a GB basis, however they are heavier and more sensitive to shock so still rarely used in mobile devices.

- The cost per Mbps and km of transport capacity for submarine cable. This has decreased by 3 orders of magnitude in the 40 years from 1959 to 1999 i.e. -16% p.a. This is a rather low rate of decrease as installation and maintenance cost dominate the total system costs. The cost of fibre optic cables has decreased much faster on a circuit capacity basis.

- The cost per kbps of mobile base station capacity. Historically, this has been about -10% p.a. but will accelerate with generation change from 2G to 3G and 3G to 4G.

- The cost of a fax machine decreased from $2000 in 1984 when Sharp introduced the first low-price machine, to $250 in 1993, giving a price decrease of 20% per annum.

- The cost of UMTS handsets. In Europe, first handsets were available to end-users at a price point of about €800 (without subsidies) in March 2003, and €450 in March 2004, suggesting a price decrease of 40% p.a. This sharp price drop is unlikely to be representative in the long term but reflects a transition from first generation to second generation UMTS handsets, and directly related to the decrease in the number of high-value Integrated Circuits from above 100 in 2002 to 40 in 2004 (i.e. a decrease of 40% per annum as well). Historically, the cost of mobile handsets has decreased annually by about 15%.

The experience curve

Rather than using a time dependency and assume that cost (or price) decrease is constant over time as we have done so far, you might want to use a volume dependency known as the experience curve. This simple model has been popularised by the Boston Consulting Group and states that a constant price decrease happens every time cumulative production volume doubles. Mathematically, the relationship between unit price and cumulative production volume is:

$$p_t = p_0 \times \left(\frac{CV_t}{CV_0} \right)^{CEOS} \quad \text{with } CEOS = \frac{\ln(1 + pd)}{\ln 2}$$

CEOS is the cumulative economies of scale coefficient derived from pd, the price decrease observed when cumulative production volume doubles. p_0 is the unit price associated with the cumulative volume CV_0.

When historical data are available, the price decrease coefficient can be obtained by plotting the log of cumulative volume against the log of prices, and is simply the slope of the best-fit line. When no historical data is available, an educated assumption is required. *pd* varies by technology but - 20% is a good average value. The learning curve provides a powerful model when the price decrease is not constant from one year to the next but diminishes over time, as can be seen in Figure 8.3. For this forecast we have assumed a 19% price decrease every time handset volume doubles.

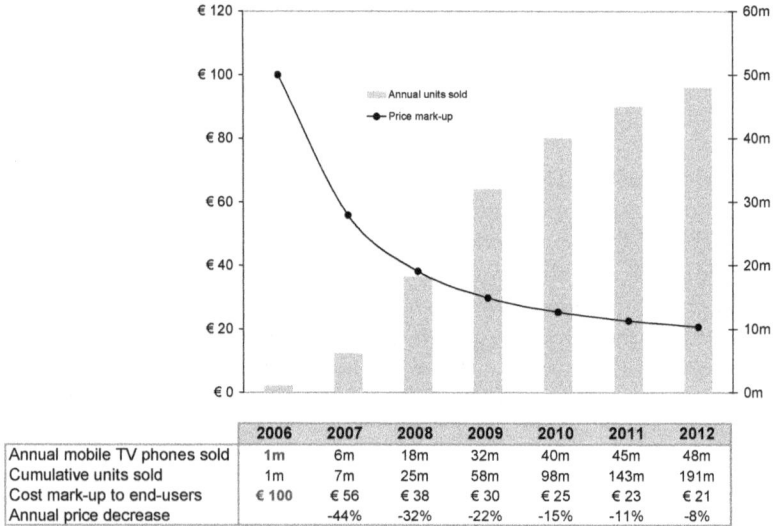

	2006	2007	2008	2009	2010	2011	2012
Annual mobile TV phones sold	1m	6m	18m	32m	40m	45m	48m
Cumulative units sold	1m	7m	25m	58m	98m	143m	191m
Cost mark-up to end-users	€ 100	€ 56	€ 38	€ 30	€ 25	€ 23	€ 21
Annual price decrease		-44%	-32%	-22%	-15%	-11%	-8%

Figure 8.3: Forecast for mobile TV handset sales volume in EU 15 as well as cost decrease [Source: INVESTAURA].

So far we have used the term *costs* rather loosely, so we need to clarify what we mean. A number of costs can be associated to a product, depending on the point where you measure costs in the value chain as the product moves from manufacturing to the end-user. We can at least distinguish between three different costs.

- Bill of material (BoM) costs: this includes the cost of the product components (hardware, but also licence costs for software) as well as the cost of manufacturing and assembling a product from its parts.

- The price at which the product is sold to the sales channel, also equal to the cost incurred by the channel to source the product. This is often called the Average Selling Price ASP. Obviously, this will be higher than the BoM because manufacturers need to cover their fixed costs in particular R&D, Marketing, Sales, Logistics, the office of the chairman, and generate a profit as well. The channel might comprise a wholesaler that resells to retailers and in this case includes more than one entity in the value chain.

- The price sold to end-users i.e. the cost paid by end-users to the channel to acquire the product or service. Here again, this amount will be higher than the cost incurred by the channel itself to acquire the product or solution, because the channel is adding value, in particular holding products on display and advising customers on product features and usage. A good rule of thumb is that the channel is reselling at double the cost it incurred when buying the product.

Price decreases per unit of capacity in the IT and consumer electronics industries vary from 20% to 50% per annum, depending in particular on the amount of innovation from one product generation to the next. PC capabilities increase very rapidly, and this tends to compensate for the rapid fall in price per unit of capacity – whether measured in processor MHz, hard disk capacity, or CD burning speed – leading to fairly stable prices. At equivalent capacity, the price of consumer electronic products decreases at about 35% per annum. Moore's law really is everywhere.

In the telecom industry, cost decreases have historically been lower, ranging from 5% to 15% in the 1990s depending on the product. However, as telecom and IT are converging, we can expect an increasing number of telecom product to become commoditised, in particular routers in the low-capacity segment, or products based on off-the-shelf IT technologies. Although price decrease can partially be compensated by an increasing share of software to implement value-added features, as well as manpower-intensive system integration and services, an average price decrease of 10% to 20% per annum is likely to be witnessed in the future.

With decreasing cost, size and weight, a new range of applications that would not have been possible only 5 to 10 years ago can now become reality, today and tomorrow.

3. Forecasting Operating Costs (OPEX)

High-tech businesses are capital intensive. However, as in any other business, the highest share of costs in the long term is made by operating costs, also called operating expenditure (OPEX).

- Marketing and advertising, including design costs (idea, picture design, video-clip), advertising space (print, billboard, radio, TV, Internet), marketing brochures, mailing, marketing events, sponsoring, promotions.

- Sales costs, covering the costs of sales channels, whether own or external. This includes the costs of sales staff, sales outlets (rental fee, shop decoration), sales commissions, sales staff training costs, costs of packaging and logistics to deliver goods to sales channels or end-users, subsidies of equipment sold to end-users.

- Billing and customer care costs, including print shop and postage costs, call centre costs, warranty costs for malfunctioning equipment, retention costs to encourage customer repurchase.

- Cost for central function staff not included above: salaries, office space, office stationeries, utilities, and other staff benefits such as company cars. Office PCs and desks, on the other hand, are treated as capital investment unless they are leased.

- Telephone costs and recurring IT costs, to maintain staff PCs and back-end servers, the corporate Intranet and Internet as well as Web applications.

- Infrastructure and building running costs such as maintenance, power, fuel, ground lease and other warehouse costs.

An accurate estimation of OPEX requires a good understanding of the business and key processes, in particular how the business markets and sells goods or services to customers, and how it is internally organised to create new products in an efficient and cost-optimised manner.

Often, business processes will not be modelled at a high level of detail in a business plan. The key OPEX drivers will be identified, and the relationship between costs and drivers approximated through more or less complex expressions, changes over time due to learning curve effect, economies of scale or the impact of inflation. In most cases, the OPEX drivers will already have been forecast in the business plan: revenues, number of customers or new customers, volume of goods sold, number of installed units of equipment, net value of assets and so on.

For instance, for a telecom service provider, the key OPEX positions are interconnection and leased line costs, handset or CPE subsidies, advertising costs, staff costs, and maintenance costs:

- interconnection and leased line costs can be related to annual traffic, which can be related to the number of customers
- CPE subsidies are a function of the number of new customers, as well as customer retention
- advertising costs can be estimated bottom-up, or linked to annual revenues
- staff costs require estimating the number of staff, which in turn can be related to revenues or the number of customers using industry benchmarks. When this approach is too crude, the number of staff required should be estimated for each key activity, for instance sales, customer care, production and operations, and central function staff.
- maintenance costs can be estimated as a percentage of the asset value, for example 10% per annum.

Be careful not to model OPEX in a too simplistic manner either. OPEX are the costs that make or break a business plan. As most businesses have an EBIT margin between 0% and 20%, and OPEX amount to up to 95% of all costs, you can deduct that OPEX represent between 75% and 95% of revenues. So an under- or over-estimation of OPEX by only 10% will have a positive or negative impact of about 8 percentage points on the EBIT margin. And you will certainly agree that a -3% EBIT margin is certainly not the same as a +5% EBIT margin nor it is the same as a +13% EBIT margin.

So the estimation and forecasting of OPEX should be done with great circumspection, especially if you use a simplified top-down approach rather than a bottom-up estimation based on a detailed understanding of business processes. In particular, fixed costs are often underestimated if they are linked to the number of customers or revenue in the early phase, as revenue is not a good cost driver for the core staff necessary to launch the business and the initial marketing campaign.

Economies of scale are also very difficult to model in a top-down approach: where should the thresholds be set? How do the variable costs per sub go down as the number of subscribers increase? What is the minimum size the business should achieve to break-even? A crude OPEX modelling does not allow the business plan to provide any answer to those questions.

Note that the modelling of OPEX in a business plan also depends on what the business decides to do itself (make) and what it decides to outsource to others (buy). Strategic and core activities should remain in house, whereas activities in which the business has little expertise or can add little value should best be bought from third parties. Outsourcing gives the potential advantage to benefit from the economies of scale of larger suppliers, resulting in lower cost than performing the activity on your own. With 'pay-as-you-grow' pricing models, activities outsourced to others should have much lower fixed costs than if they are retained in-house. On the other hand, outsourcing bears the risk that due to reduced control on the outsourcing supplier, the quality, quantity, and time performance of the partner is not good enough for you and much energy is lost in managing the partner or comforting unsatisfied customers. Also, if the outsourcing supplier also supplies your competition, your competitive advantage may be lost, or the competitor may influence the supplier to your disadvantage. Even more dangerous, the outsourced activity might turn out to be strategic after all, with a large chunk of profit going lost to the outsourcing partner due to his increased bargaining power with no alternative sourcing.

In the previous section we have seen that capital costs for machines and equipment often decrease over time and with volume as manufacturing processes improve. For operating costs, the opposite is often true: many cost items increase with time, for example salaries, but also utility costs and space rental. So make sure to identify whether OPEX are falling or increasing, and when costs components are under the influence of positive as well as negative cost trends, estimate the respective size of each cost trend and determine whether their combined impact is negative, neutral, or positive.

Last recommendation: try to remain conservative but realistic while estimating costs, and include allowances for wastage, sickness, recruitment, training, lost employees, insurance, legal fees, consulting fees, theft, medical care, pensions, social events and the Christmas party. Experience shows that costs are almost always underestimated.

## Chapter Nine

Forecasting Demand

"There is no reason anyone would want a computer in their home"
Ken Olsen, Chairman and President, DEC, 1977

Demand forecasting is a mixture of art and science. Substantial experience pays off, but a share of luck will always remain. It is also a wide topic, and unsurprisingly, there is a large divide between the theory, often complex and difficult to implement, and the level of simplicity required in business practice. The deeper you dig into the forecasting instruments available, the more sophisticated they become, while often adding only marginal improvement to the forecasting quality.

In this chapter we provide a summary of the demand forecasting know-how that any business planner should have in his toolbox. If you are lucky enough to have access to people with strong forecasting skills in your organisation, for instance from your marketing department, then the best approach will be to refer to those experts when faced with a forecasting issue. Unfortunately, when you do not have access to expert opinion, you will have to rely on yourself, and this is where this chapter will prove helpful.

Overview of Chapter Nine

1. The Diffusion of Innovations in Markets....................................178
2. Main Parameters Characterising an S-curve 186
3. Review of Various S-curve Models..188
4. Forecasts Must Have Predictive Power......................................200
5. More Complex Models 203
6. Monte Carlo Simulation..216
7. Lessons Learned from Demand Forecasting 223

1. The Diffusion of Innovations in Markets

Demand forecasting is closely related to the adoption of innovations within a target population. Looking back on the still recent dot.com bubble crash, one major mistake made by all of us was timing: we have often misjudged the speed of adoption of new, but often immature technologies and applications, and placed huge investment bets on the start-ups that developed them.

In order to avoid repeating the same mistakes in the future, we need to base our investment decision on better prediction models. Prediction tools must improve, and diffusion models can provide the starting point. Everett M. Rogers, who wrote "Diffusion of Innovations" more than 40 years ago, has provided us with a powerful framework. We also have the ability to analyse the data – Microsoft Excel® spreadsheet software is the right tool to help here. We also have large amount of historical data and lessons learned from decades of technology innovation. So let us use all these instruments.

1.1 S-curve and customer segments

Rogers has extensively investigated since the 1950s how innovations diffuse in society, and has introduced the notion of S-curve, an S-shaped curve that shows how usage of an innovation evolves in a population over time.

His famous S-curve can be broken down in five distinct user segments and phases, also described particularly well by Geoffrey Moore in "Crossing the chasm".

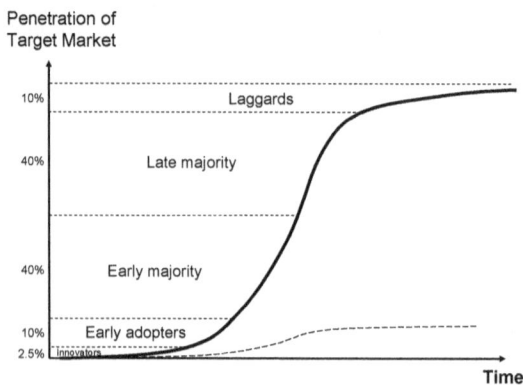

Figure 9.1: The innovation diffusion S-curve and the five customer segments [Source: INVESTAURA].

- *Innovators* are the first to adopt new products and services. They are technology freaks par excellence, and like experimenting and playing around to find out what they can do with their new toys. Innovators typically represent a few percent of the target user base.

- *Early adopters* also invest early on in new technologies, not as technologists, but to address their concrete problems. They typically represent about 10% of the target population.

  In companies, early adopters are opinion influencers. Often they will not be decision makers themselves, but are key to convince others. Early adopters are usually at the centre of extensive communication networks, for instance internal management circles, industry fora, or are very sociable individuals in their private sphere.

  When a critical mass of early adopters has developed, the process of technology diffusion becomes self-sustaining and like a snowball effect, it spills over to the early majority. On the other hand, competing and incompatible standards slow down the rate of adoption and the transition from early adopters to the early majority.

- The *early majority* is happy to wait and see until a main stream of users and technical standards have materialised under the influence of the early adopters. Only then are they ready to invest in innovation to satisfy concrete needs. They typically represent 40% of the target market. In corporate life, these are decision makers who need to be convinced by references before they allocate budget.

  The early adopters and early majority usually have higher socioeconomic status than later adopters. Being financially better off than late adopters, buying pricey technology early is less risky to them. Studies have also shown that the early adoption of innovation tends to strengthen their economic position and widen the gaps between the higher and lower individual in a system. Paradoxically, the individuals who adopt first generally need the benefits of the innovation comparatively less than later adopters.

- The *late majority* has similar characteristics and expectation as the early majority, except that they are risk averse and uncertain about their ability to master innovation. As a consequence, they prefer to wait until products have been further developed and designed for the mass market, and provide an increased level of user-friendliness compared to previous generations. The late majority is made of followers and represents 30%-40% of the target market.

- *Laggards* are technology averse and resistant to change. If they buy technology at all it is because the technology has become so pervasive that they have little choice not to use it. As a market, they are usually of limited interest to technology sellers as they require low price, a lot of support and their profitability is the lowest. Laggards amount to about 10% of a total market.

Note that some innovations stagnate in the early adopter market and fail to reach critical mass to develop to the following stages. The transition from the early adopters to the early majority can be particularly challenging, as described by Moore in "Crossing the Chasm". As marketers the best approach is to look at the five categories of adopters as different target segments to be addressed sequentially, usually with different products, communication messages and sales channels to meet the specific needs of each segment.

The self-sustaining pattern of growth in the early majority phase has been extensively documented in innovation diffusion, and attempts have been made to model the effect. For example the Bass diffusion model has specific factors for early adopters and imitators (early majority) in a market – see Section 3 below.

1.2 Factors influencing the degree of adoption

Rogers has identified the five factors influencing the adoption of any innovation, and ultimately its degree of success, as shown in Figure 9.2. When assessing the potential for an innovation, whether it is a new product or service, benchmarking the benefits provided by the innovation against the five factors will help identify potential barriers to adoption and areas for improvement.

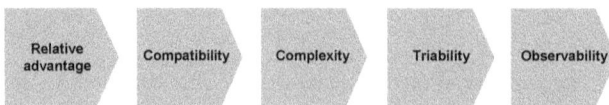

Figure 9.2: Factors influencing the rate of adoption of an innovation [Source: INVESTAURA].

Research findings have shown that the first three factors, the relative *advantage*, *compatibility* and *complexity* consistently influence the level of innovation adoption. Those technologies that score best on those criteria are likely to reach the highest saturation level among potential adopters.

We will now review the individual factors in turn.

Relative advantage

An innovation will be adopted more widely when it is considered superior to the alternative solution that it replaces. The relative advantage might be measured in economic terms (the new technology is cheaper than the old, or as expensive but more powerful) but it could also be a convenience factor (receiving email is faster than writing letters and going to the post) or a status aspect ("I need this product in order to look cool"). Relative advantage is important because a new product is rarely without alternative, whether it is using digital cameras rather than analogue ones, or watching video on demand rather than renting DVDs from a DVD shop. However, relative advantage is not enough to guarantee fast diffusion speed, and the market abounds of superior technologies that never made it to success, from the Dvorak keyboard to the Betamax or Video 2000 video recorder.

Compatibility

Compatibility measures whether the innovation is consistent with the set of norms, values and other cultural aspects or religious beliefs that predominate in the population. This also includes naming issues: a product wearing the wrong name or the wrong colours in a society that associate special meanings to these attributes has a low level of compatibility.

Complexity

Complexity is the level to which an innovation is seen as being complex to use in practice, maybe because its user interface is not intuitive, or it requires too many successive steps to be applied, like swallowing pills every hour ten times a day. This is an area where well-thought-out solutions bundling hardware and software like the iPod and the iTunes application can have a real competitive advantage: each component is easy to use on its own and the components have been optimally designed to interact with each other.

Triability

Triability is the degree to which an innovation may be experimented with on a limited basis. It lowers barriers to entry for customers, especially the late majority. Triability can help convince those who are risk averse and would delay their usage of the technology because they are not sure whether it will satisfy their requirements or be superior to the previous practice. For instance, many telecom service providers provide new services for free in an initial launch phase, for example unlimited mobile TV access, to encourage their subscribers to use the service.

Observability

Finally, innovations that have a lower degree of observability will spread more slowly than others, because observable innovations advertise for themselves. These could be innovations used in the home only rather than outside, or innovations that have been allocated more limited shelf space than other products.

According to Rogers, "the five attributes of innovation have been found to explain about half of the variance in innovations' rate of adoption". The other half is influenced by:

- the intensity of the promotion efforts, in particular with aggressive marketing campaigns
- the right timing and combination of mass-media and interpersonal channels – see the next section
- whether the adoption decision is taken individually, collectively by consensus, or authoritatively by the state or a company's management, as collective decisions are slower to diffuse, and authoritative ones faster.

1.3 Additional learning from diffusion research

Impact of mass media versus interpersonal communication

Before the decision to adopt a new technology is taken, individuals go through a series of stages in the innovation-decision process, starting with the knowledge stage, followed by the persuasion stage where they form a positive or negative opinion about the technology, before reaching the decision stage.

Mass-media communications are most effective at increasing the knowledge level of the market, while interpersonal relationships have higher influence at the persuasion stage. So a large-scale marketing campaign can increase awareness for an innovation considerably, but convince few people to adopt.

This is also often the curse of the company coming first to market: it spends a considerable amount of time and resources to increase knowledge on the market, without managing to convince end-users to adopt, as potential buyers have not reached the decision stage yet, while the company coming second to market reaps a high market share. The impact of mass media versus interpersonal communication channels is taken into account in the Bass model.

Network externality effects for interactive innovation

When the innovation is interactive like telephone, fax, email or video-telephony, network effects tend to slow the adoption of innovation as long as a critical mass has not been achieved, but accelerate innovation take-up once a critical mass has been formed. Early adopters have few people to interact with. On the other hand, the more people that join in, the more valuable the service is to early adopters.

The *critical mass* is defined as the transition point between early adopters and the early majority. This transition point is typically located between 5% and 15% of the target market for innovations that do not display externalities, and between 15% and 20% for innovation with externalities. For instance the fixed telephone had a very slow adoption curve. The first telephone appeared in the USA in 1870, full penetration was only achieved 100 years later. Mobile telephony did not suffer from this initial barrier, as communication with all fixed-network telephones was possible from the beginning.

The concept of critical mass has important consequences for marketers of interactive technologies. They should plan specific measures to get over the critical mass hurdle. One possibility is to provide 'bundles' to families so that at least family members can use the service or product between themselves. A second common approach is to disseminate the innovation in consumer electronics hardware and activate the technology or service only once a large enough share of the installed base, typically 20%, has been equipped. Another more radical approach would be to mass subsidise the innovation.

In practice, the diffusion of innovations that present network externalities can be modelled with an S-curve and a long time to take-off, but a fast adoption speed beyond take-off. The time to reach 20% penetration will be longer than that for other innovations, but the characteristic duration, which is the speed of diffusion beyond critical mass, will typically be shorter.

Benchmarks for the time to critical mass and characteristic duration

In a recent study of the diffusion of 10 households products in Europe, Tellis, Stremersch and Yin (2003) have found that it takes on average 6 years to reach the critical mass, with considerable variance between information and entertainment products (brown goods) such as TV, CD player and PC that required 2 years only, and kitchen and laundry products (white goods) that required 8 years, so four times longer.

The *characteristic duration* provides a complementary measure of the diffusion speed. It is the time required for the innovation to grow from 10% to 90% of the saturation level. Van den Bulte has studied the diffusion of 31 household durables in the USA from 1924 to 1996 and shown that the speed of innovation has increased by 2% per annum: the average characteristic duration has reduced from 13.8 years in 1946 to 6.9 years in 1980. However, the increase in the diffusion speed could mostly be explained by changes in purchasing power, demographic changes and the nature of the products investigated, so that when these factors are accounted for, no systematic change in the speed of innovation could be demonstrated.

Innovations can also be clustered according to the level of saturation of the target population that they reach as well as the speed of diffusion. The level of saturation is correlated to the five characteristics identified by Rogers as discussed in Section 1.2. The speed of diffusion depends on a multitude of factors, in particular:

- the amount of mass-media coverage and advertising
- the nature of the innovation e.g. brown goods diffuse faster than white goods
- the characteristics of the population in the country, and in particular whether 'innovation' or 'imitation' behaviour dominate, as we will see in the Section 3.

The additional cultural factors intervening here are not fully understood and require more research.

Cross-country comparison: similarities and differences

The study by Tellis, Stremersch and Yin has found that the speed of innovation diffusion varies between countries. Research findings show that the time to take-off varies, among other things, substantially by country. The probability of a shorter time to take-off was also higher when the product had already reached a critical mass in a neighbouring country, showing that connected countries influence each other through business, but also individual ties.

In Scandinavian countries (Denmark, Norway, Finland and Sweden) the time to take-off was 4 years on average and almost half as long as in Mediterranean countries (France, Italy, Spain, Portugal and Greece) that averaged 8 years. Other countries in Western Europe (Germany and the UK) required about 6 years. This result is also confirmed by studies of the mobile market.

Interestingly, economic wealth, while being a factor, is neither a strong nor a robust explanation for the difference, and does not have a significant effect on the time to take-off. The differences are thought to relate to cultural factors and further research will be necessary to identify and quantify the cultural drivers.

When marketing a new product in Western Europe, it might therefore be a better idea to start in one of the Nordic countries than one of the larger population countries, as it provides a better chance that the take-off happens earlier. This can help win further internal support for the new product within the organisation, whilst limiting costs for market launch.

2. Main Parameters Characterising an S-curve

We have seen previously that technology adoption follows an S-shape profile over time. To determine the shape of an S-Curve, we need a minimum of three points:

- the number of adopters in the first commercial year, or a later year, for instance the time it takes to reach the critical mass of 10% of the saturation level (the 'early mass market')
- the long term saturation level
- a third point describing how fast the saturation level will be reached, for instance the 50% of saturation point (end of 'early majority'), or the 90% point (end of 'late majority').

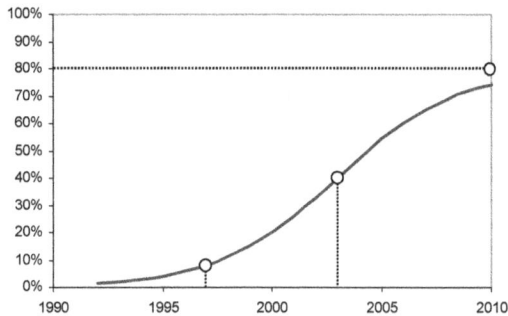

Figure 9.3: Typical S-Curve based on three parameters: Saturation = 80%, 10% of saturation reached in 1997, and 50% of saturation reached in 2003 [Source: INVESTAURA].

The three points on the S-curve correspond to three different horizons for the forecasting activity, each requiring a specific approach:

- The short term, typically the first and second year, is the phase closest to you. You should be able to generate a short-term forecast here with reasonable precision. The number of adopters in the short term has to be consistent with your current set-up and objectives, for instance the number of points of sales, the size of the marketing budget, and any sourcing constraint. If you use analyst forecasts, note that their short-term predictions outperform a naïve extrapolation for a forecast horizon of up to 16 months, and their forecast accuracy is greater when the data is increasing over time rather than decreasing. Analysts, like most people, are reluctant to make a negative forecast, and show a bias towards optimism.

- In the long term, the market penetration reaches saturation. The five factors identified by Rogers can help you forecast the saturation level. You need to take a broad perspective, and think about life style changes, disruptive innovations, competitive forces and the overall industry evolution. Scenario planning can also help estimate the range of possible long-term saturation levels. As Bill Gates once stated, we often overestimate the impact of innovation in the short term but underestimate changes in the long term.

- In the medium term the mass market is addressed and penetrated as fast as possible by suppliers fighting for growth and market share. The key factors influencing the characteristic duration have been discussed above. Various S-curve patterns associated to differing diffusion assumptions can be chosen from, as we will see next.

Once you have a short-term forecast and a long-term saturation level, the challenge becomes how many years are required to reach 10% ('critical mass') and 50% ('early majority') penetration levels, and beyond this how quickly the S-curve will reach the saturation level ('late majority'). Figure 9.4 shows that three points do not define the S-curve uniquely, so a fourth point can be helpful.

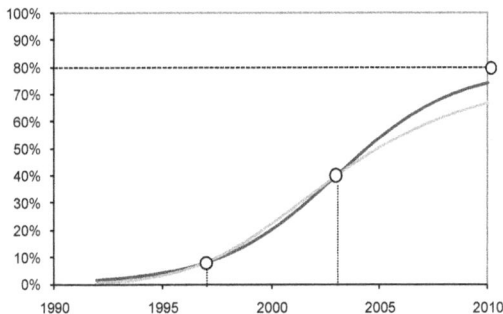

Figure 9.4: Two S-curves: in blue the logistic curve from Figure 9.3, and in green, a modified logistic curve [Source: INVESTAURA].

Selecting the right S-curve and its parameters will be the topic of discussion of the next section.

3. Review of Various S-curve Models

Many human characteristics are normally distributed. The diffusion of most innovations has been empirically shown to approach normality, with the distribution of adopters over time following a Gaussian curve. As there is no simple mathematical expression for a normal curve, other models have been developed that also provide good fits with observation. In this section, we present the five most commonly used diffusion models. All these models assume that the diffusion rate of the innovation is proportional to the remaining number of adopters to reach saturation. The models predominantly differ in the assumptions they make about the coefficient of diffusion. We start with the most widely used model, the logistic curve.

3.1 The logistic model (also called Fisher-Pry model)

The logistic model assumes that the rate of change in demand is proportional to the current level of demand. Intuitively, the assumption is that diffusion occurs through 'contacts' between members of a population rather than through external influences like mass media and advertising, and the pressure to conform plays an important factor in the decision to acquire a product. For this reason, the logistic model is also called the 'internal influence' model.

The logistic model is one of the most employed models due to empirical evidence and its relative simplicity. It is often met in nature, biology, physics, medical science, and this is what makes the logistic curve more used than any other forms of S-curve. For instance, the weight of a growing pumpkin is very well approximated by a logistic curve.

Mathematically, the number of adopters is given by the following formula:

$$Y(t) = \frac{S}{1+e^{a-\beta \times t}} = \frac{S}{1+e^{-\frac{t-t_{50}}{t_{50}-t_{10}}\times \ln\left(\frac{90\%}{10\%}\right)}} = \frac{S}{1+e^{-\frac{t-t_{50}}{t_{50}-t_{k}}\times \ln\left(\frac{1-y_{k}}{y_{k}}\right)}}$$

t_k is the point in time associated to demand $Y(t_k)$, for instance demand in the first year.

The steepness of the logistic curve can be measured by the time that it takes to go from t_{10} to t_{90}. This is also called the characteristic duration Δt. The latter is related to β, the *coefficient of imitation* through the following relationship:

$$\Delta t = \frac{\ln(81)}{\beta}$$

Y can also be expressed as a function of the characteristic duration and the time when 10% or 50% saturation has been reach:

$$Y = \frac{s}{1 + 9 \times e^{-\frac{\ln(81)}{\Delta t} \times (t - t_{10})}} = \frac{s}{1 + e^{-\frac{\ln(81)}{\Delta t} \times (t - t_{50})}}$$

Let us define y as the ratio of Y normalised by the saturation level s. Differentiating the previous expression gives the following relationship for the rate of change in demand, which confirms the assumptions made by the logistic model:

$$\frac{dy}{dt} = \beta \times y \times (1 - y)$$

In many business plans, it might not be appropriate to assume that the acquisition of a product or service is the result of 'contacts' with existing users who have adopted before, but rather the result of attention created by advertising, which is an external influence. In this case the rate of change cannot be assumed to be simply proportional to the existing level of demand. The logistic has also come under attack because of its symmetric shape, which often contradicts experience.

The logistic curve displays exponential growth in the first phase up to the 10% point, although growth might not be perceived as exponential due to the low level it is starting from. In the second phase, between the 10% and 90% points, the pattern of growth is very steep and approximately linear. Finally, the curve comes asymptotically to the saturation level in an exponential decay manner.

Note that the logistic curve can be modified to take the impact of economic growth into account, either as a faster take-up speed to saturation or as a saturation level increasing over time. The impact of a falling price level can also be taken into account in the same way. The advantage of those methods is that the model, although more complex and including more parameters, remains a function of time only.

The expression giving y can easily be transformed into a linear form as follows:

$$\ln\left(\frac{1}{y}-1\right) = a - \beta \times t$$

When historical data are available, linear regression analysis can be applied to estimate the parameters a and the coefficient of imitation β.

3.2 The exponential model

The exponential model applies to products that are already well known to end-users, for instance because extensive advertising has already taken place. The exponential model is also called the 'external influence' model as it is based on the assumption that there is little or no influence between the members of the target population, and all influences come from outside via mass media or an authoritative decision, for instance from a company's management.

The model is also appropriate in the early phase of a new product introduction to depict the adoption of *innovators* and *early adopters*, who do not acquire a product because it is already widely spread in their environment (which is never the case initially). In this case no imitation is taking place between members in the system.

Unlike the logistic model, the exponential model assumes that the growth in normalised demand is proportional to the market remaining to be penetrated, but not to the market already penetrated:

$$\frac{dy}{dt} = \alpha \times (1 - y)$$

Solving this differential equation leads to:

$$Y = s \times (1 - e^{a - \alpha \times t}) = s \times \left(1 - 0.5 \times e^{-\frac{t - t_{50}}{t_{50} - t_{10}} \times \ln\left(\frac{90\%}{50\%}\right)}\right)$$

This can be expressed using the characteristic time instead:

$$Y = s \times (1 - 0.9 \times e^{-\frac{\ln(9)}{\Delta t} \times (t-t_{10})}) = s \times (1 - 0.5 \times e^{-\frac{\ln(9)}{\Delta t} \times (t-t_{50})})$$

The exponential model can also be linearised and the parameters a and α, the *coefficient of innovation*, be estimated via linear regression. Simply regress $\ln(1-y)$ against time, as shown in the following relationship:

$$\ln(1-y) = a - \alpha \times t$$

The take-up of broadband services in South Korea is relatively well approximated by an exponential model.

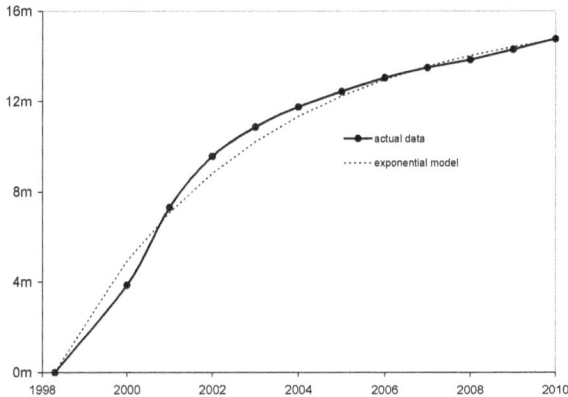

Figure 9.5: Broadband take-up in South Korea [Source: INVESTAURA]

3.3 The Bass model

Whereas the logistic model has its background in the natural sciences, the Bass model has been developed by marketing scholars to predict the rate of adoption of consumer durables like washing machines and TV sets. It has later proved valuable for a large range of other goods and services. The model is not only consistent with the innovation diffusion theory developed in the academia but its validity has also been largely confirmed by empirical evidence. The model assumes that the early adopters buy a product predominantly under the influence of mass-media coverage as interpersonal effects are missing early on, whereas interpersonal channels creates persuasion effects on later adopters as knowledge of the product is already available among other users.

The Bass model can therefore be seen as a combination of the exponential model (for early adopters) and the logistic model (for imitators). It is obtained by integrating the following differential equation:

$$\frac{dy}{dt} = (\alpha + \beta \times y) \times (1 - y)$$

The parameter α captures the external influence and measures the propensity to innovate; the parameter β is the coefficient of imitation and represents the internal influences. When α is similar or larger than β, then the S-curve obtained is similar to an exponential to saturation. When the parameter β is large compared to α, the resulting S-curve is very close to a logistic. This is the most common case empirically as interpersonal communications are known to have a larger impact than mass-media channel. Research of an extensive number of innovations has shown that on average, β is equal to 0.38 and α to 0.03. These values are consistent with $t_{10}=2.3$ years and $t_{90}=11.8$ years, giving a characteristic duration of $\Delta t=9.5$ years. Also, countries that tend to import their innovation from other countries, for instance Europe vis-à-vis the USA, have a higher coefficient of innovation.

The value for Y is given by the following relationship:

$$Y = s \times \frac{1 - e^{-(\alpha + \beta) \times t}}{1 + \dfrac{\beta}{\alpha} e^{-(\alpha + \beta) \times t}}$$

Like previous models, the Bass model is also determined by three parameters. Unfortunately in this case the parameters cannot be expressed mathematically as function of Y at two points in time. In addition, the expression for Y cannot be transformed in a linear function of the parameters, so a simple linear regression technique cannot be used either when historical data are available. A more complex iteration technique must be employed in this case, as follows:

- make assumption for the starting values of α and β
- calculate Y(t) using previous expression
- calculate the residuals of the regression
- change the parameters α and β so that the sum of the residuals squared converges to zero.

This iterative estimation of α and β can be performed in a Microsoft Excel® spreadsheet, using the Solver. Also check that the results make sense, in particular make sure that α and β remain positive.

In the table below, we have expressed the values of α and β as function of the time required to reach 10% and 90% of the population saturation. If you are assuming other values for t_{10} and t_{90} you can interpolate between the values calculated. The values marked in grey are typical in the telecom industry for new products and services.

t_{90} / t_{10}	4	8	10	20
1	(0.05 ; 1.3)	(0.08 ; 0.41)	(0.09 ; 0.26)	(0.10 ; 0.02)
2	(0.003 ; 2.2)	(0.03 ; 0.66)	(0.03 ; 0.46)	(0.05 ; 0.13)
3	(10^{-6} ; 4.3)	(0.007 ; 0.85)	(0.01 ; 0.59)	(0.03 ; 0.19)
4	n.a.	(0.002 ; 1.09)	(0.005 ; 0.72)	(0.016 ; 0.23)
5	n.a.	(10-4 ; 1.47)	(0.001 ; 0.87)	(0.01 ; 0.26)

Figure 9.6: Values for α and β as a function of the number of years t_{10} and t_{90} [Source: INVESTAURA].

Values for β in the range of 0.3 to 0.6 are common for IT innovations. Values below 0.3 correspond to slow diffusion processes. This can happen when externality effects slow the diffusion process, as has been the case historically with the diffusion of the fax machine and email. Values for β above 0.6 correspond to very rapid diffusion. For a technology used in a corporate environment, this would depict the situation where competition is intense and forces companies to imitate rapidly if they want to keep up.

It would be nice to express the Bass model as a function of the characteristic duration Δt and the midpoint t_{50} rather than α and β. Unfortunately there is no analytical formula to perform this conversion. None-the-less, the characteristic duration Δt, the midpoint t_{50} and t_{10} can be shown to be equal to:

$$\Delta t = \frac{1}{\alpha + \beta} \times \ln\left(\frac{1 + 0.9\frac{\beta}{\alpha}}{1 + 0.1\frac{\beta}{\alpha}} \times 9\right) \qquad t_{50} = \frac{1}{\alpha + \beta} \times \ln\left(2 + \frac{\beta}{\alpha}\right) \qquad t_{10} = \frac{1}{\alpha + \beta} \times \ln\left(\frac{10 + \frac{\beta}{\alpha}}{9}\right)$$

The following tables give values for Δt and t_{50} for a range of α and β values. The value marked in grey are the average values mentioned above.

β \ α	0.001	0.01	0.03	0.2
0.1	42.7	34.6	25.4	8.4
0.38	11.5	10.7	9.50	5.2
0.8	5.5	5.3	5.0	3.4
2	2.2	2.2	2.1	1.7

β \ α	0.001	0.01	0.03	0.2
0.1	45.8	22.6	12.9	3.1
0.38	15.6	9.5	6.8	2.3
0.8	8.3	5.4	4.0	1.8
2	3.8	2.6	2.1	1.1

Figure 9.7: Characteristic duration Δt and midpoint t_{50} for various values of α and β [Source: INVESTAURA].

The Bass model is probably the most popular model used in the marketing and business academia – at least by 'power users'. It can also be modified for instance to account for technology price decreases, which increases the relative advantage of the technology and accelerates technology adoption.

3.4 The Gompertz model

The Gompertz model was originally used in biology to model that the death rate in a population increases exponentially as the age of individuals in the population grows. In the diffusion of innovation, the model is most appropriate when a new technology offers no substantial advantage over an old one in terms of price and features, so that purchases of the new technology are driven primarily by equipment deterioration rather than technological innovation. It can also be used to model innovations that diffuse at varying speed across different groups of adopters. In practice, the Gompertz model generates forecasts that are fairly close to those obtained from the extended logistic model discussed in the following section.

The Gompertz model states the following relationship between the number of adopters Y and time t:

$$Y = s \times e^{-e^{a-\beta \times t}} = s \times e^{(\ln 50\%) \times e^{-\frac{t-t_{50}}{t_{50}-t_{10}} \times \ln\left(\frac{\ln 10\%}{\ln 50\%}\right)}}$$

After normalisation and differentiation, the Gompertz model can be turned into the following differential equation:

$$\frac{dy}{dt} = -\beta \times y \times \ln(y)$$

Here as well, the parameters α and β can be estimated using linear regression analysis and the following expression:

$$\ln\left(\ln\left(\frac{1}{y}\right)\right) = a - \beta \times t$$

The logistic, the exponential and the Gompertz models each use three parameters and they are the simpler models to use in practice.

3.5 The modified / extended logistic model (also called the Weblus model)

The modified logistic curve is particularly appropriate under the assumption that the target customer base is not homogeneous and a very fast adoption by the more well off part of the population takes place at the beginning, followed by a slower adoption by the rest of the population. The modified logistic curve is also thought to be more appropriate when the existing level of adoption does not necessarily make the additional take-up easier to achieve, as is the case with innovators, or when interpersonal contacts might be less pronounced. It can also be a better model when a replacement process is taking place without the new product necessarily bringing a breakthrough innovation compared to the previous generation.

The modified logistic curve follows the formula:

$$Y = \frac{S}{1 + e^{a - \beta \times \ln(t - t_0)}}$$

$$= \frac{S}{1 + e^{-\frac{\ln(t - t_0) - \ln(t_{50} - t_0)}{\ln(t_{50} - t_0) - \ln(t_{10} - t_0)} \times \ln\left(\frac{90\%}{10\%}\right)}}$$

$$= \frac{S}{1 + \left(\frac{t_{50} - t_0}{t - t_0}\right)^{\frac{\ln\frac{90\%}{10\%}}{\ln\frac{t_{50} - t_0}{t_{10} - t_0}}}}$$

t_0 is the year immediately preceding the commercial launch: at t_0 the number of adopters is still zero.

The expression can also be linearised to derive the parameters α and β, assuming that t_0 is known:

$$\ln\left(\frac{1}{y}-1\right) = a - \beta \times \ln(t-t_0)$$

Differentiating this formula leads to:

$$\frac{dy}{dt} = \frac{\beta}{t-t_0} \times y \times (1-y)$$

This is similar to the differential equation of the logistic curve except that the coefficient of imitation $\beta/(t-t_0)$ is decreasing with time, so the modified logistic curve takes a long time to reach saturation. The model is also sensitive to the assumption made regarding t_0, so is more complex to use properly than the logistic model.

When t_{10} and t_{50} are assumed to be the same in a logistic and modified logistic model, the modified logistic will generate penetration levels which are much lower in the initial years, but with very high growth rate in this period, typically 100%-400% compared to 40%-80% for the logistic model. On the other hand, when demand in the first year is the same, the modified logistic curve typically grows a lot faster in the initial phase, reaching a high penetration level early on, but then takes more time to saturate. This is illustrated in Figure 9.8.

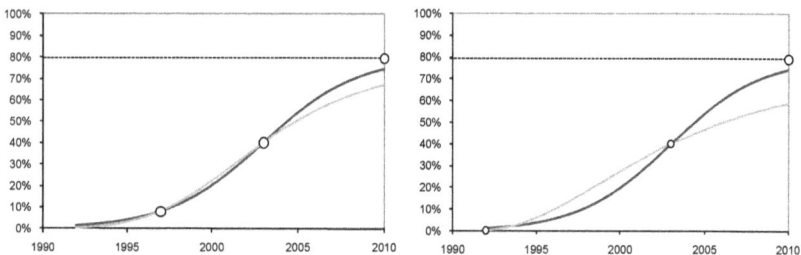

Figure 9.8: Comparison between a logistic curve (in blue) and a modified logistic curve (in green) [Source: INVESTAURA].

In practice, the price of electronics goods and high-tech products decreases quickly, making them rapidly affordable to the mass market, so that in most cases, the logistic model, or alternatively the Bass model will give the better results. The Gompertz and Weblus models are more relevant in cases where prices do not decrease rapidly.

3.6 Comparison between the five S-curve models

The main characteristics of the five S-curve models discussed above are summarised in Figure 9.9. The logistic model as well as the Bass model, which can be regarded as a generalisation of the logistic model, give the best results for the majority of innovation and have therefore been highlighted in the table above.

	Logistic (Fisher Pry)	Exponential	Bass	Gompertz	Extended logistic (Weblus)
S-curve shape	Symmetric around 50% penetration	Asymmetric	Symmetric around its inflexion point located between 0% and 50%	Asymmetric	Asymmetric
Behaviour modelled	Homogenous population of imitators, environment with no external influence	Homogenous population of innovators; adoption following mass media coverage; widespread knowledge available; limited interpersonal contact required to trigger the adoption decision	Innovators in early phase, imitators in later phases	Replacement of existing product; new technology is similar to previous technology	Heterogeneous population; adoption by few wealthy individuals first; income constraints for remaining adopters
Rate of change over time (dy/dt)	Increasing, then decreasing	Decreasing linearly	Usually increasing, then decreasing ($\beta > \alpha$)	Increasing, then decreasing	Usually decreasing
Parameters required	3	3	3	3	4 (3)
Parameter estimation	- Linear regression of historical data - Estimation based on $t_{10\%}$, $t_{50\%}$, (or $t_{10\%}$ and Δt) and saturation	- Linear regression of historical data - Estimation based on $t_{10\%}$, $t_{50\%}$, (or $t_{10\%}$ and Δt) and saturation	- Non-linear regression - Experience in realistic values for α and β (or $t_{10\%}$ and Δt)	- Linear regression of historical data - Estimation based on $t_{10\%}$, $t_{50\%}$ and saturation	- Linear regression of historical data - Estimation based on t_0, $t_{10\%}$, $t_{50\%}$, and saturation
Ease of use	Simple but symmetric pattern sometimes not realistic	Simple but applies in few cases only due to the very rapid increase to saturation	More complex due to iterative estimation of parameters or strong experience required to set α and β	Simple but applies in few cases only	Simple but saturation is reached slowly
Comment	**Best results when critical mass of early adopters has already been achieved and imitation leads to a rapid penetration increase**	Best results in innovative population where saturation is rapidly achieved within few years	**Most widely used model by marketers as it captures both innovators and imitators. Similar to logistic when α is small**	Best results to capture replacement demand or a heterogeneous population of adopters	**Useful when symmetry of logistic not acceptable. However, its tends to take too long to saturate or takes too low values in the early years**

Figure 9.9: Comparison between the five S-curve models [Source: INVESTAURA].

When 'keeping up with the Joneses' and imitation effects appear to be particularly important in the market dynamics, then the logistic model or its generalization the Bass model is probably the best one. When imitation effects are a lot less significant because price remains a barrier, or replacement without technological advantage dominates, then the modified logistic curve probably gives the best results.

In case you unsure whether to use the logistic model or the modified logistic model, proceed as follows:

- select a meaningful saturation level s
- calculate $z=\ln(1/y-1)$ and plot on a chart against time
- if a linear relationship appears (in the form of $a - \beta \times t$), then select the logistic model in this case. If the curve is slightly convex (curved upwards), then s is probably too high. The procedure can be repeated with lower values for s.
- if the curve is markedly convex, then it is worth checking whether the modified logistic model gives better results. In this case, plot z against $t'=\ln(t-t_0)$ on a chart. If the relationship is fairly linear, then use the modified logistic model in that case.

Although it is also possible to derive the saturation level s from regression analysis, we strongly recommend not doing so. Indeed, when few data points are available, the initial data are rather insensitive to the saturation level so that the estimate of the saturation level obtained from a regression is rather unreliable. On the other hand, when many data points are available, the saturation level is easier to forecast so that it might not have to be derived from the regression either.

3.7 When no historical data is available for regression

When you have to generate a forecast for a market where you have no historical data, then estimating the parameters from historical values and regression is not possible. In this case, you have no choice but to make meaningful assumptions, and maybe use benchmarks from other countries that are ahead.

You can proceed as follows:

- try and select what seems to be the best S-curve based on the product and market characteristics as summarised in Section 3.6
- develop your best guess for the saturation level that the market might achieve in the long term
- set the penetration level that you want or expect to achieve in the first year. This gives your first point
- set the time to reach 50% of saturation or alternatively the characteristic duration.

For instance, key mobile technologies like GPRS, MMS or camera functionality, required 3-4 years until all new handsets sold incorporated the technology. Assuming a 2-year replacement cycle, you need 5-6 years until all customers are enabled, so are potential users of the technology. Adding 2-3 years so they actually become users gives 7-9 years until saturation, so t_{50} set at 4-5 years is realistic, but probably a minimum.

Once have selected your S-curve, estimated the saturation level as well as defined two points on the curve, you can draw your forecast for all years. Also, as soon as new benchmarks or actual data become available, re-forecast.

4. Forecasts Must Have Predictive Power

When historical data are available, a very important step is to test the validity of the forecast generated by the model. Indeed, it can happen that a good fit (a high R^2) is the result of chance or is due to the high number of parameters used in the model, and is not reflection of a deterministic relationship, so that the forecast values give poor results. This problem is known as *overfitting*.

To test the forecasting validity of the model, the idea is to exclude the last historical data from the sample, perform a new regression, generate a forecast for the data point(s) that has been excluded before, and compare the forecast with the actual value. When few data are available in the sample, you should only exclude the last data point.

This procedure can be repeated for alternative S-curve models when the choice between various S-curves is difficult. Beware not to choose the S-curve that gives the best historical fit (the highest R^2) , but the one that has the highest predictive power.

To select the right model, we suggest that you proceed as follows:

- based on the dynamics of the market observed, determine which S-curve model might be expected to work best
- estimate how long it might take to achieve 10% penetration, 50% penetration, 90% penetration, based on experience or benchmarking
- fit the historical data to the model selected using regression analysis – in most cases this means using the Solver in Microsoft Excel® spreadsheet software
- calculate R^2, as well as the time to reach 10%, 50%, 90% predicted by the model
- repeat the last operation after excluding the last value in the time series, and perform a one-step forecast to check which S-curve gives the best forecast for the point that you have excluded
- rank the various S-curve using a mix of R^2 results (the quality of the fit) and the predictive power of the forecast
- compare the value obtained for t_{10}, t_{50} and t_{90} from the model with your personal guess, and if required fine tune the parameters of the S-curve manually, including the long-term saturation level.

Note that when you have too few data points, and penetration is still below 10% of the expected saturation level, then the regression results are not particularly stable, so use a critical eye to judge the validity of the results.

As application, let us look into the mobile telephony penetration in five European countries: France, Germany, the UK, Spain, and Italy. We compare three models: logistic ('imitators'), Gompertz ('replacement of existing product'), Weblus ('wealth constraint'). In a first step, we use 6 years of historical data for the period 1992-1997, generate a forecast for the following 6 years, and compare with actual penetration levels. We repeat the procedure, this time using 8 years of historical values (1992-1999) and generating a shorter forecast. We have assumed a saturation level of 70%, which was a very optimistic estimate back in 1997, but turned out to be too conservative.

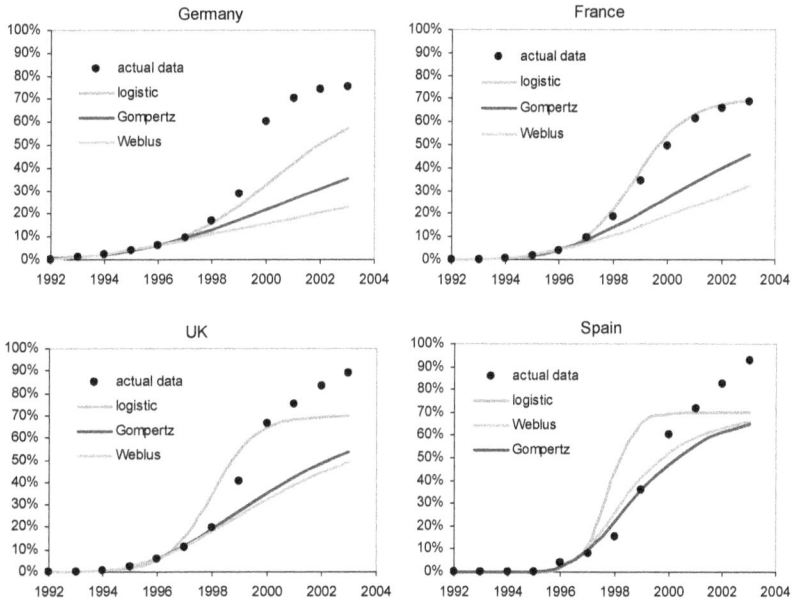

Figure 9.10: Model comparison based on 1992-1997 historical data [Source: INVESTAURA].

The logistic model usually generates the best forecast. The Gompertz and Weblus models generate time to saturation parameters that are too long and not realistic. In all countries, 4 to 5 years were required to reach 10% of saturation, which is rather long, except in Spain where it took only 3 years, probably the impact of external influence as Spain launched its GSM service later.

In the second forecast with more data point, the logistic model provides estimates for t_{90}: 9 years in France and the UK (correct), 12 years in Germany (too long: 10 years), 6.5 years in Spain (actually 7 years). In all countries t_{50} was estimated to lie between 6.5 and 7.5 years, except in Spain (5 years).

Finally, we have checked whether the Bass model provides any improvement on the logistic model, and the answer was negative as the innovation coefficient turned out to be very low and comprised between 0.001 and 0.005 and much smaller than β. β values were about 1, equivalent to a t_{90} of 9 years with an α of 0.001.

This forecasting exercise gives approximate results. The main difficulty however remains the estimation of the long-term saturation, which turned out to be underestimated by 10%-20 percentage points, except in France, where the forecast generated excellent results, predicting a 6-year forecast of 69% in 2003 against an actual value of 68%.

Looking at the results, you might feel disappointed by the lack of forecasting quality achieved by even the best model, especially in the short term. One way around this problem is to forecast demand on a quarterly basis when growth is extremely rapid, and review the forecast every quarter so as to include most recent data. In addition, a one-year forecast based one's best guess, the market current dynamics and competitor behaviour is usually more precise that the forecast generated blindly by an S-curve model, especially around the critical mass point t_{10} when the early majority starts being addressed. Therefore, you can include your one-year estimate in the sample of historical data and look for an S-curve that generates a medium term forecast that is consistent with your expectations. Alternatively, more complex models can be used, in which case read the following section.

5. More Complex Models

In this section, we discuss a number of alternative models available to forecast the diffusion of high-tech innovations. The objective is not to be comprehensive here, but rather to show a range of models that are sufficiently diverse and raise your curiosity to investigate the topic further in complementary books.

Taking a holistic view, the key steps in modelling are as follows:

- Specify a model with a set of deterministic equations, often non-linear, that are believed to replicate the dynamic of the diffusion process.

- Estimate the model parameters using regression techniques. When derivatives are used in the mathematical expressions, then they need to be transformed in expressions without derivatives before estimating the regression parameters.

- Generate a forecast for future time periods. When derivative are used in the model, numerical methods must be applied to produce the forecast: knowing the starting point conditions at t_k and a set of equations, forecast the state of the system at $t_k + \Delta t$.

- Check the predictive power of the model.

The first two steps bring considerable difficulties with them. As modelling of human preferences is more akin to psychology than hard-core science, the equations used to model demand will always be misspecified, so by their very nature produce results of average quality.

In the second step, regression can be difficult and produce biased estimators, or estimators that are unbiased, but with a variance that does not decrease as the sample size increases, so that the estimators remain imprecise.

In the second and third step, the challenge is also to transform partial derivatives in a manner that the numerical forecast is stable, i.e. truncation errors are not amplified but dissipated, and the numerical calculation converges to the solution of the set of equations before transformation when the time step gets small.

In practice, more complex models in demand forecasting tend to be very time consuming, so that before starting a simulation exercise, you should ask yourself whether adding more sophistication is worth the cost.

5.1 Using other explanatory variables than time

So far we have used only one explanatory variable in the S-curve models above: time. There are cases where you might want to use other explanatory variables. For instance, you might want to express demand as a function of price, and relate price decrease to time as competition increases. Very often, multiple equations will be necessary to capture the dynamic of the model.

Let us take a look at an example from the mobile telephony business:

- penetration can be expressed as a function of ARPU (Average revenue per user) as penetration increases when price decreases
- ARPU itself can be expressed as a function of price per minute (PPM) and minutes of usage per month (MOU)
- traffic is a function of PPM and of the mix between prepaid and postpaid subscribers, as prepaid customers generate a lot less traffic than postpaid users.

We therefore have a set of three relations with price and the percentage of prepaid subscribers used as explanatory variables – for which forecasts are assumed to be available – and MOU, ARPU and Penetration as explained variables. Based on previous experience, we specify the three equations as follows:

$$\text{Penetration} = s \times e^{-a \times \text{ARPU}}$$

$$\text{ARPU} = \text{PPM} \times \text{MOU}$$

$$\text{MOU} = k - b \times \text{Prepaid\%} - c \times \left(\frac{\text{PPM}}{\text{GDP}} \right)$$

s is the saturation level reached when ARPU is very low. The expression chosen for *Penetration* assumes that demand is price sensitive, with a being the price elasticity of demand. In the third equation, *MOU* decreases as *Prepaid%* increases, but *MOU* increases as *PPM* decreases.

The five coefficients s, a, b, c, k can be estimated through regression of historical data within one country, and when not enough data are available, through regression of data across multiple countries where the same dynamic applies (cross section analysis).

Using data for France, the UK, and Germany in the years 1997 to 1999, we have found that

$$\text{ARPU}(\text{€}) = 35.5 - 15.5 \times \ln(\text{Pen})$$

so deduct estimates for a and s: $a \sim 0.065$ and s ~ 9.9.

In addition, using data for the year 2002 from Merrill Lynch for 40 countries, MOU has been regressed on Prepaid% and PPM with the following result:

$$\text{MOU} = 210 - 90 \times \text{Prepaid\%} - 20 \times \frac{\text{PPM}}{\text{GDP} \cdot 10^{-5}}$$

We can therefore express penetration as a function of PPM and Prepaid% as follows:

$$\text{Penetration} = 9.9 \times e^{-0.065 \times \left[\text{PPM} \times \left(210 - 90 \cdot \text{Prepaid\%} - 20 \cdot \frac{\text{PPM}}{\text{GDP} \cdot 10^{-5}} \right) \right]}$$

We now focus on Germany to check the predictive power of the model and the quality of the forecast that it generates for the period 2000-2003. We first fine-tune the equation above for Germany to improve the quality of the fit to German historical data. This is achieved by using the Solver to minimise the sum of the residuals between the actual and the estimated penetrations, using historical data for the period 1992-1999. We find that the following formula provides a better fit for Germany:

$$\text{Penetration} = 4.1 \times e^{-0.050 \times \left[\text{PPM} \times \left(188 - 91 \cdot \text{Prepaid\%} - 20 \cdot \frac{\text{PPM}}{\text{GDP} \cdot 10^{-5}} \right) \right]}$$

Regarding the explanatory variables, we estimate that PPM will continue to decrease at the historical annual price decrease of 10% p.a. between 1999 and 2003, and assume that the portion of prepaid subscribers will continue to increase from 28% in 1999 to 50% in 2003. The results of the forecast for the three-equation model are shown in Figure 9.11.

The thee-equation model gives a somewhat better result than the logistic model, but only in the last two years of the forecast. On the other hand, this comes at a cost: the logistic model was considerably easier to apply. In addition, the three-equation model relies on forecasts for the share of prepaid subscribers and the price per minute for the period 2000-2003, and we were not able to predict that Prepaid% would increase from 28% to 53% in one single year rather than 4 years, so that the model substantially underestimates demand in the year 2000 to 2002. Had we been able to predict Prepaid% and to a lesser extent PPM correctly, then the forecast would have been very good indeed as shown under 'ex-post' in Figure 9.11, confirming the correct specification of the model. This tells us that results are very sensitive to a correct estimation of the prepaid percentage.

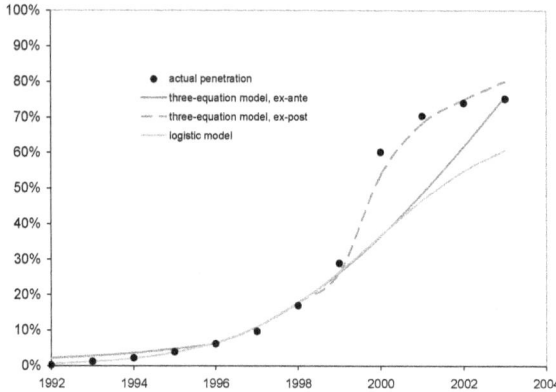

Figure 9.11: Comparison of the three-equation model with a simple logistic, German mobile penetration [Source: INVESTAURA].

In summary, in the example above we have set up a sophisticated model that provides insight into the explanatory variables and the drivers behind the take-up of mobile telephony. However we had to put significant effort to estimate its parameters, and largely failed at correctly estimating the explanatory variable Prepaid% in the first year of the forecast, thereby grossly underestimating demand in the initial years of the forecast.

5.2 Lotka-Volterra model of technological change

This model is derived from the mathematical ecology and the study of population systems, where it is known as the 'predator-prey' model. It states that the evolution of a population of two species is given by the following relationship as well as the initial value for y and z.

$$\frac{dy}{dt} = y \times (\alpha_1 - \beta_1 \cdot y - \gamma_1 \cdot z)$$

$$\frac{dz}{dt} = z \times (\alpha_2 - \beta_2 \cdot z - \gamma_2 \cdot y)$$

The model is similar to the logistic equation with an additional feedback term that captures the competing species and limits further growth. Intuitively, the model says that diffusion happens by contact within the same species (this is the proportionality of the diffusion coefficient to the current level y), but a ceiling applies to the population spread, in practice natural resources or the existence of a predator z to the species y.

In innovation diffusion, the Lotka-Volterra equations can be used to model the evolution of two competing technologies and their substitution. Other models have been specifically designed to capture multiple generations of a product and substitution of an older generation by a newer generation, for instance the Norton-Bass model. The Lotka-Volterra model can also be extended to more than two technologies, as has been done by Marchetti and Nakicenovic in their logistic substitution model, where each technology is modelled as a logistic and grows to saturation where it remains until it is replaced by a new technology. This could, for instance, be applied to successive generations of mobile telephony.

There are two long-term states to the system described above:

- If $\beta_1.\beta_2 < \gamma_1.\gamma_2$, the system is called competitive and one technology ('species') progressively drives the other one into disuse (out of existence). This is the most common case e.g. analogue mobile telephony versus GSM telephony, CD versus vinyl LP, DVD versus VCR, MP3 player versus the walkman. This is typical of technology substitution, and happens when a technology has a strong competitive advantage over another one.

- If $\beta_1.\beta_2 > \gamma_1.\gamma_2$, the system is inhibitive and the two technologies (populations) converge towards a saturation value. Two technologies coexist in parallel, e.g. CATV and satellite TV, LP and music cassette, cars and trains, TV and radio, Internet newspaper and paper newspaper. This happens when none of the technology has a strong competitive advantage over the other one, or the dominated technology still provide advantages for special applications.

A number of special and simplifying cases are worth mentioning:

- When y and z represent market share in the equation above, then their sum is equal to 1, and it can be shown in that case that y and z follow a logistic curve, one growing to 100%, the other one decreasing to 0%, so that the model is competitive in all cases.

- When three equations are used and the variables x, y, and z represent market shares, the model can be reduced to a Lotka-Volterra model with two equations only. The three-variable model is either fully competitive, with one technology reaching 100% and the other two converging to zero, or it is fully inhibitive with the three technologies converging to fixed values, or it is partially competitive and partially inhibitive, with two technologies converging to fixed values and the third one driven out of existence.

When $\gamma_1=\gamma_2=0$, the model reduces to a set of independent logistic curves. This means that the technologies are not competing against each other. When γ_1 and γ_2 are different from zero, the Lotka-Volterra cannot be solved analytically but one has to revert to numerical methods to estimate its parameters, assuming that historical data are available. For instance, the following iterative process can be used:

- assume values for the parameters, solve the differential equation and generate a forecast by using the Runge-Kutta method. The time step used in the Runge-Kutta method should be small so that the estimators are not biased by the approximation of the numerical integration.
- calculate the leased squares of the regression.
- vary the assumption for the parameters and minimise the leased square by iterating the calculation above.

We now apply the model to the case of CATV, satellite and terrestrial TV in Germany. This illustration shows how technology substitution can be modelled when similar technologies are competing for the same market. The base data are shown in Figure 9.12.

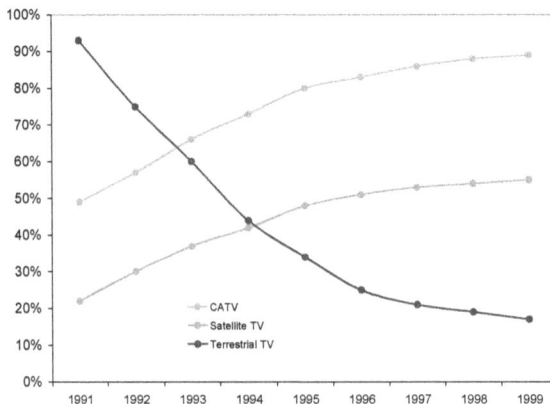

Figure 9.12: Household penetration of CATV, Satellite and Terrestrial TV [Source: see reference [9.13] in bibliography].

Note that the sum of the penetrations is higher than 100%, as some households use more than one access technology. The data are then converted into market share and the pattern that emerges on Figure 9.13 shows that CATV and Satellite are inhibitive and saturate at about 55% and 35% respectively, while terrestrial TV is still decreasing.

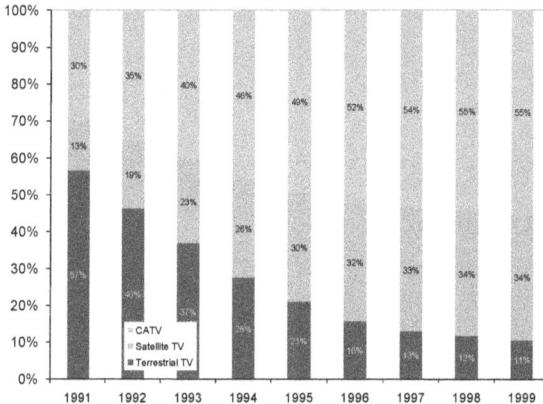

Figure 9.13: Respective market share of CATV, satellite and terrestrial TV [Source: INVESTAURA].

We reduce the three-equation model to two equations by taking the sum of the CATV and satellite penetration, which we call 'Non-terrestrial', and we fit a logistic curve to the 'Non-terrestrial' category, initially assuming that it saturates at 90%, and then using the Solver in Microsoft Excel® spreadsheet software to estimate the value of the saturation that minimises the residuals.

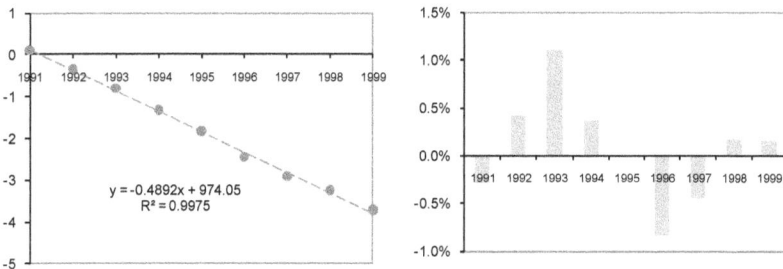

Figure 9.14: Fit of a logistic curve to the Fisher-Pry transformation ln(1/y-1), and corresponding residuals [Source: INVESTAURA].

The estimated saturation value is 91.6%, and the model is fully inhibitive. This implies a long-term level of 8.4% for terrestrial TV. The fit appears to be excellent, with a very high value for R^2. The residuals seem to be somewhat correlated (cyclical) but they are small so we do not have to be concerned here.

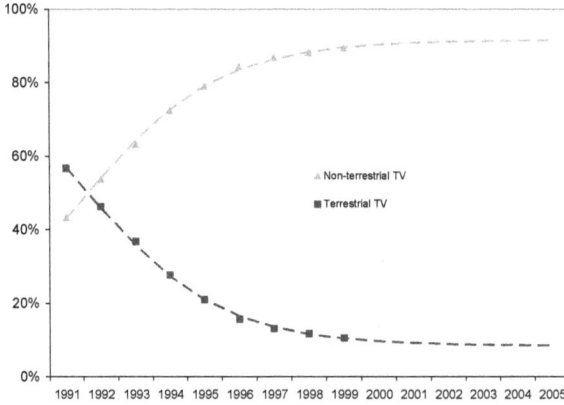

Figure 9.15: Forecast for terrestrial TV and 'Non-terrestrial' technologies [Source: INVESTAURA].

5.3 The KSIM model

The KSIM model developed by Professor Kane is a simulation model that focuses on the cross-impact of various variables or events on each other.

In traditional forecasting models, few endogenous variables are explained by a larger set of exogenous variables, and few endogenous variables interact on each other. Now, forecasting exogenous variables can be difficult as we have seen in Section 5.1 above, but in addition the estimation of parameters when jointly dependent variables exist in a set of equations is a challenging regression problem, as endogenous (explained) variables are exogenous (explanatory) variables at the same time.

The KSIM model takes the opposite perspective: it is essentially a set of jointly dependent endogenous variables and few exogenous variables capturing 'external' influences such as governmental decisions. Focus is not so much on the precise estimation of the model parameters or on the accuracy of the forecasting results, but rather on the lessons that can be learned from the simulation results. A side effect of building a simulation model is that it can provide significant insight into the issue at stake. Therefore, a simulation is not only valuable because of the forecasting results that it generates, but also as a process for developing a better understanding and improving communication within an organisation.

The KSIM model can be used to simulate the interaction of competing technologies, for instance, the impact of the launch of WiMax broadband wireless technology on UMTS, and vice-versa the impact of the launch of UMTS on WiMax. But a KSIM model can also include variables of different nature measured in various units, for instance the GSM penetration, the cost of a handset, the cost of a voice minute, the traffic per user per month, the status symbol of owning a mobile phone, health concerns and so on. A major benefit of the KSIM model is that it is equally comfortable with highly subjective qualitative parameters as well as with quantitative measurements.

The set of differential equations used in the KSIM model is also broad enough to capture many real world problems and provide meaningful analysis and policy recommendation, while benefiting from an elegant numerical solution. The KSIM model is probably the only dynamic simulation model that that can be constructed and used with limited resources and time, while capturing qualitative impacts that can only be roughly estimated.

To develop his simulation model, Professor Kane proceeded as follows:

- he developed a set of desirable properties (a 'theory') that the model should have
- he identified a set of differential equations satisfying the properties identified previously
- he provided a numerical solution to the differential equations that relies on simple mathematics
- he improved his model by taking into account that variables interact on each other in the long term not only through their absolute level, but also cross-impact in the short term through their change in absolute level.

The set of equations used by the KSIM model are as follows, with y_i being the variables impacting each other in the system, normalised to be comprised between 0 and 1, and N the total number of variables:

$$\frac{dy_i}{dt} = \sum_{j=1}^{N}\left(\alpha_{i,j} \cdot y_j + \beta_{i,j} \cdot \frac{dy_j}{dt}\right) \times y_i \times \ln(y_i)$$

$$= \sum_{j=1}^{N} I_{i,j} \times y_i \times \ln(y_i)$$

$\alpha_{i,j}$ and $\beta_{i,j}$ are the long-term and short-term impact of y_j on y_i respectively. To simplify the model, the $\beta_{i,j}$ can be assumed zero and we focus on long-term interactions only.

The numerical solution to the set of equations is given by:

$$y_i(t + \Delta t) = y_i(t)^{P_i(t)}$$

where the power function is given by:

$$P_i(t) = \frac{1 - \Delta t \times \sum \text{negative impacts on } y_i}{1 + \Delta t \times \sum \text{positive impacts on } y_i}$$

$$= \frac{1 - \Delta t \times \sum \text{negative } I_{i,j}(t)}{1 + \Delta t \times \sum \text{positive } I_{i,j}(t)}$$

A variable y_j has a negative impact on y_i when $I_{i,j}$ (or $\alpha_{i,j}$ if $\beta_{i,j}$=0) is negative, otherwise it has a positive impact.

In practice, you can proceed as follows to apply the model:

- identify the variables y_i to be used in the model, as well as their minimum and maximum values
- identify a variable representing the outside influences if relevant
- provide qualitative estimate of the impact of variables on each other; this can be done in a matrix format and using qualitative measures such as ++, +, 0, -, -- or their numerical equivalent 2, 1, 0, -1, -2
- translate qualitative variables to specific figures as appropriate
- agree on a set of initial values for the variables; normalise these values with the minimum and maximum values so that variables remain bound between 0 and 1
- calculate the power $P_i(t)$ for each variable $y_i(t)$
- run the model by calculating $y_i(t+\Delta t)$ and compare the results with historical data when some are available to calibrate the quantitative estimates of the cross-impact variables.

We now turn to two applications, starting with the mutual influence of UMTS, WLAN and WiMax. Our variables could represent the technology adoption level in a target population of business users, 0 indicating low adoption level, for instance because the technology is still at the prototyping stage, and 1 full adoption. The interaction matrix between the three technologies could look as follows.

impact of on	UMTS	WLAN	WiMax	Outside Intervention
UMTS	1	1	1	1
WLAN	1	2	1	-1
WiMax	-2	1	1	0

Figure 9.16: Matrix of cross impacts [Source: INVESTAURA].

The 'Outside intervention' variable is used to capture exogenous influences, here security concerns relating to WLAN (and therefore -1), as well as operator subsidies for UMTS terminals.

The starting values used in the year 2005 are 0.05 for UMTS, 0.3 for WLAN and 0.01 only for WiMax. All three technologies increase over time as the cross-impact parameters are mostly positive. The security concerns only have a minor impact on the WLAN take-up: try setting the parameter to zero and check that the results don't change much. WiMax is also negatively influenced by UMTS, but this is more than compensated for by the positive influence of WLAN that exercises a much larger impact due to its higher penetration. The results of the simulation are shown in Figure 9.17.

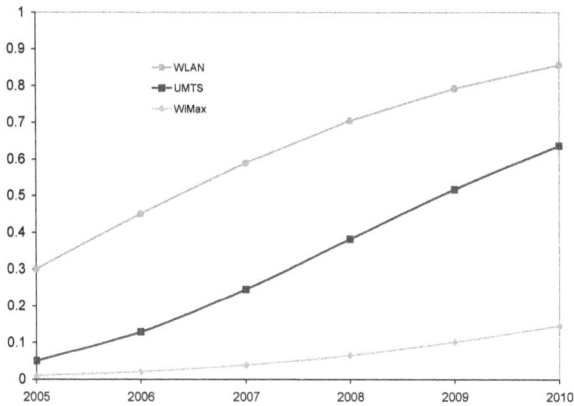

Figure 9.17: Forecast of UMTS, WLAN and WiMax penetration [Source: INVESTAURA].

Now let us turn to a more complex case and forecast the evolution of the GSM penetration. Note that the parameters in the cross-impact matrix do not have to be integer. Also parameters have been fine tuned so that the forecasting results are broadly consistent with historical data.

impact of on	GSM subs	Cost of phone	Traffic per user	Cost per min	Outside intervention
GSM subs	3	-1	1	-1	2
Cost of phone	-2	0	0	0	-1
Traffic per user	-1	1	0	-1.5	-1
Cost per min	-1	1	-1	0	1

Figure 9.18: Matrix of cross impacts [Source: INVESTAURA].

The 'Outside intervention' represents the massive subsidisation of handsets and the lowering of barriers to entry through the introduction of 'Prepaid' packages in the mid 1990s. Note the difference between the simulation results with and without the outside influence in Figure 9.19.

Now you might object that this is approach is very rough and, admittedly, the results need a fair amount of calibration of the cross-impact parameters. The main benefit though is that a complex system can easily be modelled in this way in Microsoft Excel® spreadsheet software, and the dynamics of the system be explored. Play with it! It will bring you new insights

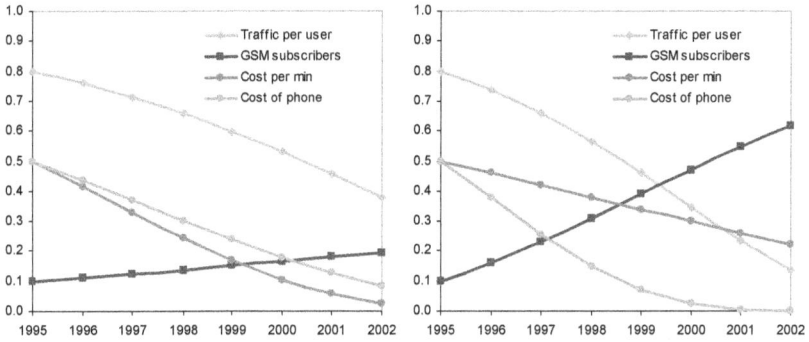

Figure 9.19: Results of the simulation: without outside influence on the left, with outside influence on the right [Source: INVESTAURA].

6. Monte Carlo Simulation

6.1 Introduction

We are closing this long chapter with the crown jewel of forecasting and simulation, named after an area in the city of Monaco well known for its casino and games of chance. Monte Carlo simulations are not limited to demand forecasting, but can be used on the supply side as well, and have a broad range of further applications.

A Monte Carlo simulation complements a forecast previously generated from average (expected) values for explanatory variables. The basic idea is that many parameters in a simulation are uncertain, so rather than assuming that they are known with precision, a Monte Carlo simulation takes the distribution functions of explanatory variables into account and calculates the distribution function of the explained variables. Even if you are only interested in average values, Monte Carlo provides better result estimates. Indeed, when models are not linear, which is the case most of the time, the expected value of a function is different from the function of the expected value: $E(f(x)) <> f(E(x))$. This happens whenever there is cross-correlation between variables, for instance between X and X^2, but also between Price and Volume of sales.

A Monte Carlo simulation runs a model a large number of times with inputs generated at random, but following distributions chosen in advance, and saves the results of the simulation in memory to calculate their distribution profile. This can be particularly useful in business planning for example to estimate the risk of making a loss or not achieving a certain target, and calculate confidence intervals around average values. Monte Carlo simulations are also invaluable in problems that can only be solved numerically. The beauty of Monte Carlo simulation is that they can be used in an extremely wide range of applications.

6.2 A simple illustration

Let us consider a first example: we have seen above that ARPU is the product of price per minute (PPM) and minutes of usage (MOU). Now let us assume that PPM is normally distributed with a mean of €0.30 and a standard deviation of €0.1, and MOU is uniformly distributed between 20 minutes and 300 minutes. To keep things simple we also assume that usage is independent of price. What is the expected value of ARPU?

To find the answer, first download a trial version of an excellent tool called RiskAMP (www.riskamp.com), and install it as Add-In in Microsoft Excel® spreadsheet software. Numerically the problem can be set as follows.

C1	PPM	=NormalValue(0.3;0.1)
C2	MOU	=UniformValue(20;300)
C5	ARPU	=C2*C3
C7	Average ARPU	=SimulationAverage(C5)
C8	Standard deviation ARPU	=SimulationStandardDeviation(C5)

Figure 9.20: Setting a simple Monte Carlo simulation problem in Microsoft Excel® [Source: INVESTAURA].

Then under the drop-down menu "Monte Carlo", select "Run Monte Carlo simulation…" with for instance 500 iterations. The results show that the average ARPU is about €48, the product of the average PPM (€0.3) and the average MOU (160 minutes), but the ARPU results are not normally distributed. The standard deviation of ARPU estimated by the simulation is €31.

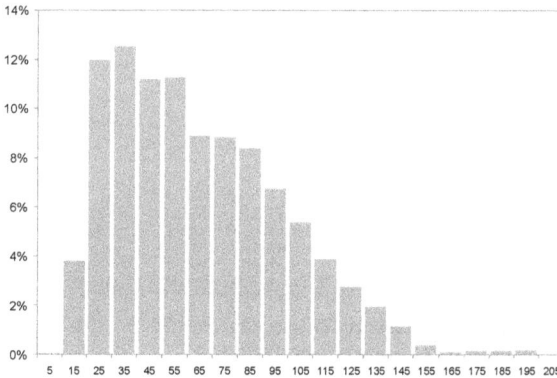

Figure 9.21: Distribution profile of the ARPU simulation [Source: INVESTAURA].

6.3 Demand forecast with uncertain parameters

Let us look at a second application using the Bass model to forecast the number of mobile TV subscribers in Germany between 2006 (year 0) and 2016 (year 10). We estimate that in the long term, the service will reach 10% of population penetration, so that the saturation level is about 8m subscribers. We also believe that it should take about 3 years to reach 10% of the long term saturation, however it could go faster, but it is unlikely to be less than 2 years, or slower, but unlikely more than 4 years. So we model t_{10}, the time to reach 10% of the saturation value, as a normal distribution with a mean of 3 years and standard deviation of 0.5 years. In 95% of the cases, t_{10} will be comprised between 3 years plus or minus two standard deviations. Equally for t_{90}, we believe that it should take about 8 years, but could be as low as 6 years or as high as 10 years, so we model t_{90} as a normal distribution with a mean 8 years and a standard deviation equal to 1 year.

Input parameters						
s	8,000,000					
t_{10}	3.088					
t_{90}	7.842					
t_{90}/t_{10}	2.539 β					
	α					
Calculation of alpha and beta						
Point A	10,000,000	5,000,000	2,500,000			
t_{90}/t_{10} estimate	1.32	1.3	1.4			
Point B	0	0	0			
t_{90}/t_{10} estimate	21.85	21.9	21.9			
Point C	5,000,000	2,500,000	1,250,000			
t_{90}/t_{10} estimate	1.33	1.4	1.4			
Estimated β/α	140.30					
Estimated α+β	0.91					
Estimated β	0.905					
Estimated α	0.006					

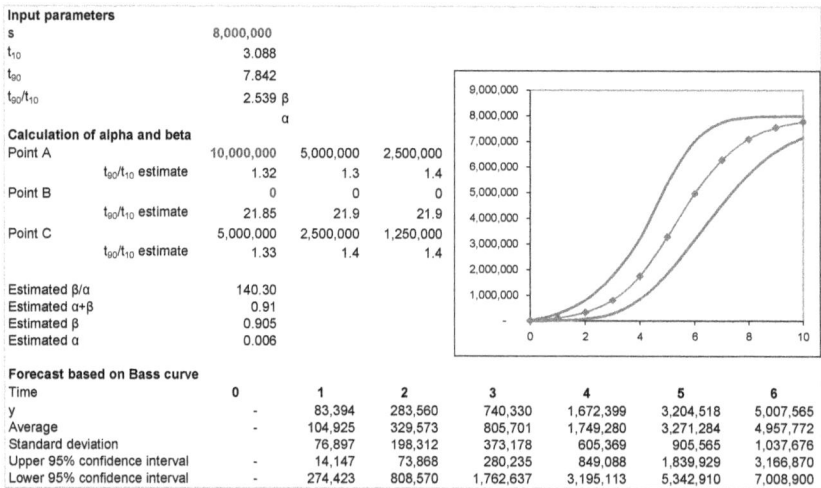

Forecast based on Bass curve							
Time	0	1	2	3	4	5	6
y	-	83,394	283,560	740,330	1,672,399	3,204,518	5,007,565
Average	-	104,925	329,573	805,701	1,749,280	3,271,284	4,957,772
Standard deviation		76,897	198,312	373,178	605,369	905,565	1,037,676
Upper 95% confidence interval	-	14,147	73,868	280,235	849,088	1,839,929	3,166,870
Lower 95% confidence interval	-	274,423	808,570	1,762,637	3,195,113	5,342,910	7,008,900

Figure 9.22: Mobile TV penetration forecast based on the Bass model and a Monte Carlo simulation [Source: INVESTAURA].

To run the model, we need to derive α and β from t_{10} and t_{90}. In Microsoft Excel® spreadsheet software, this can best be performed by 'bracketing' using the bisection method. The results of the forecasting exercise, including the 95% confidence interval, are shown in Figure 9.22. Note that the average number of subs in year 3 is not 800k (10% of 8m) but slightly more. Also, in the first year after launch, we can expect 107k subs with a 95% confidence interval of 11k-275k.

Note that the distribution of results is not normal either, otherwise the confidence interval, estimated by the "=SimulationPercentile" function of the RiskAMP Add-In, would be equal to the average plus or minus two standard deviations.

So if we are particularly risk averse, we would only order 11k handsets in the first year, but we need to have options to order up to 275k handset in case demand turns out to be much higher in that year.

6.4 Revisiting the penetration forecast from the 'three-equation model'

As a third example, we get back to the mobile penetration forecast from Section 5.1 above, expressed as a function of two explanatory variables: the price per minute PPM and the Prepaid share of subscribers. You will remember that we had to forecast PPM and the prepaid share, and that this was rather inaccurate. We now assume that the PPM price decrease between 1999 and 2003 is normally distributed with a mean value of -10% and standard deviation of 2% around the mean. We also assume that the average of the Prepaid share increases linearly between 28% in 1999 and 50% in 2003, but with a standard deviation of 2% around the average, so that in the extreme case (95% confidence interval), the Prepaid share would not increase by 5.5% points annually but between 1.5% points and 9.5% points.

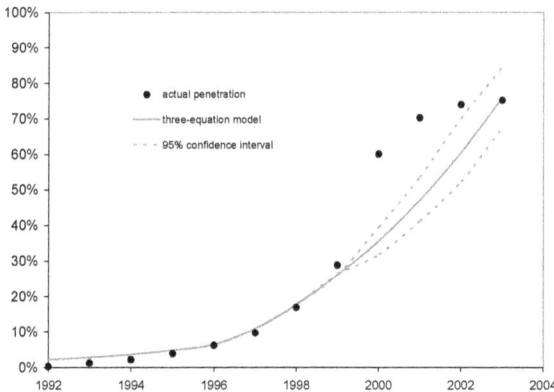

Figure 9.23: Forecast of mobile subscribers in Germany [Source: INVESTAURA].

The results of the simulation including the 95% confidence interval are shown in Figure 9.23. Here again, we failed to forecast the sharp increase in prepaid subs in year 2000, comparable to a temporary shock. On the other hand we now have a measure of uncertainty for our forecast results and know that the penetration in year 2003 should be comprised between 67% and 85% with an average value of 76%.

6.5 Monte Carlo simulation for a mobile TV business plan in Germany

In this last example, we include the cost side as well and look at the overall financial plan for mobile TV in Germany.

As before, we assume 8m subscribers in the long term. This time, we use a logistic curve to model the subscriber ramp-up, with the variables t_{10} and t_{90} assumed to be normally distributed. With a logistic curve, unlike the Bass model, we do not have to estimate α and β as the number of subscribers can be expressed directly as a function of t_{10}, t_{90} and time.

Our second unknown is the ARPU. We set the initial monthly fee to €10, decreasing at -10% per annum. The standard deviation of the initial monthly fee is €2, assumed to decrease over time by -15% per annum. The monthly fee is calculated as a normal distribution, and we also impose that it decreases over time, i.e. if the simulated value in year n is higher than in year $n-1$, then we take the value used in year $n-1$ for year n as well.

On the cost side, we assume a fixed cost for coverage that is constant over time. It is modelled as Normal(€100m, €15m) as its value at time zero is uncertain. We also include handset costs, modelled as Normal(€100, €10) at time zero, valid for an initial production volume of 100k handsets. We include a learning curve of -20% when production volume doubles, in order to model the decrease in handset costs over time. Note that the handset costs only capture the delta cost of the mobile TV functionality in a mobile handset, not the total handset cost. Finally, we assume that content costs are fully variable, as per a risk sharing with content providers, and equal to 40% of revenues.

The results of the simulation are shown in Figure 9.24. The chart shows the expected value for the cashflow as well as the confidence interval. The cashflow pattern for the project without uncertainty is also shown: this is used as a cross-check to see whether the traditional approach using average values would give the same result as the average obtained from the simulation model. Here this is only approximately the case: although there is no cross-correlation between variables in each year, we have added the additional constraint that the ARPU should be decreasing over time, and this constraint has introduced some auto-correlation in the ARPU series in the time domain.

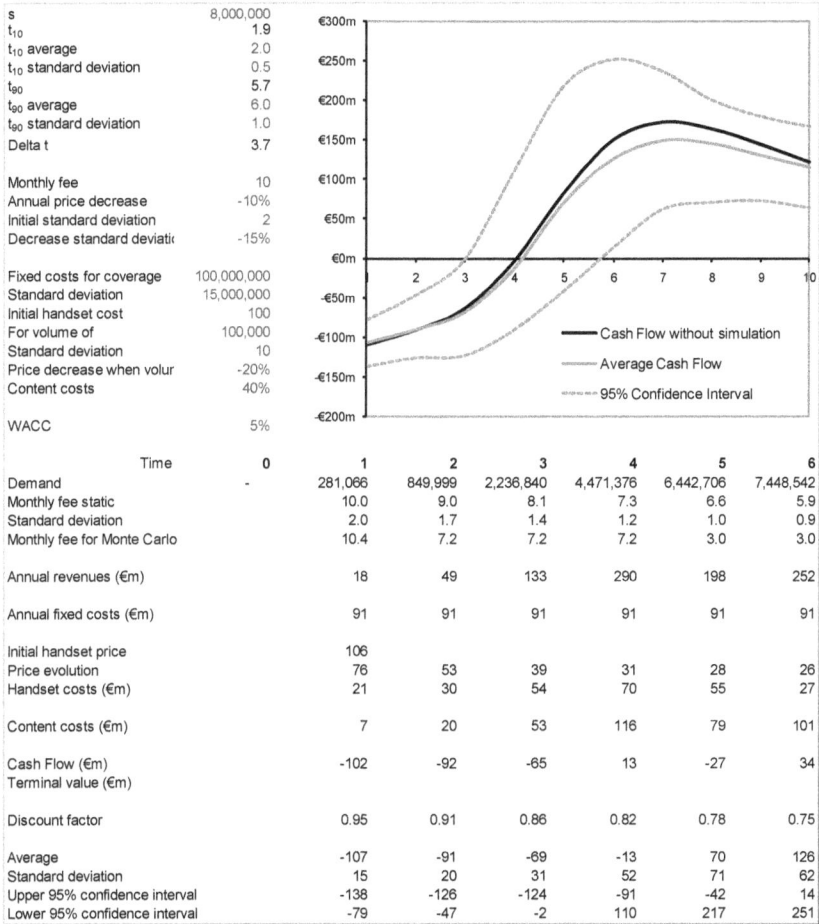

s	8,000,000
t10	1.9
t10 average	2.0
t10 standard deviation	0.5
t90	5.7
t90 average	6.0
t90 standard deviation	1.0
Delta t	3.7
Monthly fee	10
Annual price decrease	-10%
Initial standard deviation	2
Decrease standard deviatic	-15%
Fixed costs for coverage	100,000,000
Standard deviation	15,000,000
Initial handset cost	100
For volume of	100,000
Standard deviation	10
Price decrease when volur	-20%
Content costs	40%
WACC	5%

Cash Flow without simulation
Average Cash Flow
95% Confidence Interval

	Time 0	1	2	3	4	5	6
Demand	-	281,066	849,999	2,236,840	4,471,376	6,442,706	7,448,542
Monthly fee static		10.0	9.0	8.1	7.3	6.6	5.9
Standard deviation		2.0	1.7	1.4	1.2	1.0	0.9
Monthly fee for Monte Carlo		10.4	7.2	7.2	7.2	3.0	3.0
Annual revenues (€m)		18	49	133	290	198	252
Annual fixed costs (€m)		91	91	91	91	91	91
Initial handset price		106					
Price evolution		76	53	39	31	28	26
Handset costs (€m)		21	30	54	70	55	27
Content costs (€m)		7	20	53	116	79	101
Cash Flow (€m)		-102	-92	-65	13	-27	34
Terminal value (€m)							
Discount factor		0.95	0.91	0.86	0.82	0.78	0.75
Average		-107	-91	-69	-13	70	126
Standard deviation		15	20	31	52	71	62
Upper 95% confidence interval		-138	-126	-124	-91	-42	14
Lower 95% confidence interval		-79	-47	-2	110	217	251

Figure 9.24: Financial forecast for mobile TV in Germany [Source: INVESTAURA].

If you want to discount the cashflow projections to the present value, use the risk-free rate of interest and not the WACC. The reason is that the WACC captures both the time value of money and the risk of the project ex-ante. If we discount simulated cashflows, then the risk ex-post is actually nil. So we should only discount the future with the time value of money i.e. the risk-free rate of interest.

We obtain the following distribution. Be careful not to interpret this result as 'a distribution of NPV', a concept that is theoretically incorrect, as the NPV is the discounted value of expected free cashflows, so it can only take one value – showing a distribution of NPV would be double counting the risk.

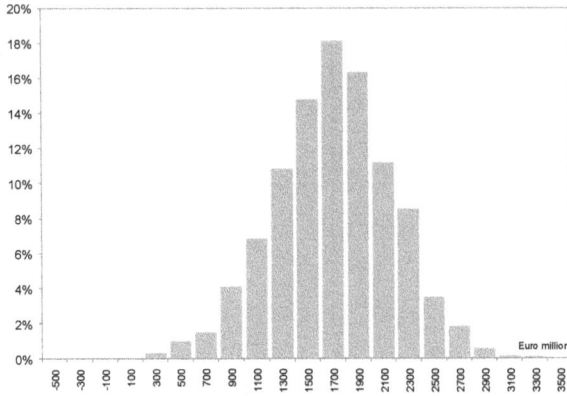

Figure 9.25: Distribution of discounted cashflows using the time value of money [Source: INVESTAURA].

Congratulations! You have covered a lot of ground on demand forecasting. As conclusion to this chapter, we have summarised some key lessons learned to keep in mind and get back to from time to time.

7. Lessons Learned from Demand Forecasting

- In all forecasting projections, you are using *models* to depict a complex reality, so do not trust model results blindly, but exercise judgment as much as possible.
- Complex models do not necessarily give better results than simple ones (for instance the logistic model). At the end of the day, it is better to be approximately right rather than precisely wrong.
- It is best to use a combination of forecasts, maybe building on different approaches, and take the average of the results.
- The forecast precision decreases quickly with the time horizon, so rely on short-term forecasts above all and update your forecasts regularly as new information comes in, rather than performing complex analysis too rarely. Also use Monte Carlo simulation to appreciate the uncertainty of results and derive confidence intervals.

To finish, remember the characteristics that make a good model.

- *parsimony*: as complex as necessary, as simple as possible
- *theoretically consistent*: check the signs of estimators in particular, and whether values are in the expected range
- *goodness of fit*: are R^2 values high?
- *predictive power*: as a high R^2 indicates high predictive power only in the sample considered, check that post sample the actual values are well approximated by the forecast as well and R^2 remains high, a sign of a good forecast.

## Part Four

Advanced Techniques

## Chapter Ten

Knowing Your Competitors

"When you are ignorant of the enemy but know yourself, your chances of winning or losing are equal. Know the enemy and know yourself, and in a hundred battles, you will never be defeated"
Sun Tzu, The Art of War, c. 400 BC

Traditionally, competition analysis involves collecting competitor data from a variety of sources, filtering the relevant from the irrelevant, structuring results into reports and newsletters, and drawing implication for a company's competitive strategy. If you do not know your competitors, you are running your business in blind mode. This could be fatal as you do not know what your relative strengths and weaknesses are, and cannot articulate why customers should do business with you rather than with someone else. So you need to look into what your competitors have to offer, how they position themselves in terms of image and price, and where they believe that their competitive advantage lies. In addition, you need to find out what your competitors are currently preparing and where their next move could be. This knowledge is invaluable as it helps you compete by differentiating your own offering.

In Part Three we have talked extensively about forecasting demand. To derive a revenue base line from the target market, you need to provide answers to the following questions: "How much of that demand can my business win?" and "What is a realistic market share?".

Estimating future market share is probably one of the most complex forecasting exercises, as market shares are constantly fought for and can rapidly decrease or increase, especially in industries that have not reached maturity yet. But why worry about market share at all? A high market share is particularly important in capital or R&D intensive businesses, where scale matters and can make the difference between a profit or a loss-making company. The initial costs of setting up a new mobile network or developing the next PC operating system are immense, but the marginal cost of transporting an additional Mbyte of data or distributing software licences over the Internet is close to zero.

Competition analysis is a wide area. Rather than trying to be comprehensive, the objective of this chapter is to provide an introduction to the topic and present a number of techniques for analysing industry structure and forecasting market share. We will follow an eight-step approach.

Overview of Chapter Ten

1. What's the Overall Battleground Like?... 229
2. Who are Your Current Competitors? 230
3. What do You Need Know about Your Current Competitors? 231
4. Where are Your Future Competitors Likely to Come From?.................... 233
5. What are Your Core Competencies, Comparative Advantage, USP?....... 234
6. Where and How do You Want to Compete in the Future? 236
7. What is Your Realistic Market Share?... 238
8. How to Beat the Competition? 241

1. What's the Overall Battleground Like?

Michael Porter's "Competitive Strategy" is a good starting point. It provides a framework for evaluating the attractiveness of a particular industry and identifies five forces determining the competition intensity that your business faces:

- *Suppliers:* how high is the bargaining power of your suppliers? Are alternative suppliers available or are you captive of any of them?

- *Customers:* how much bargaining power do your customers have? Can they choose between many or few alternative suppliers? Can they put pressure on price? How?

- *Substitute products:* what are the alternatives to your products, if any? What are the benefits of these alternative products? Is radical innovation likely to emerge shortly?

- *Rivalry among existing firms:* who are the main players in your industry? Are competitors few or plenty? How big or small are they? How aggressively are they fighting for market share? How high are barriers to exit?

- *Potential entrants:* who are tomorrow's competitors? Which background are they likely to have? How high or low are barriers to entry? How might they redefine the key success factors in the industry?

From Porter's five forces, the last three directly focus on competition. The issue of substitute products is important as your product will rarely be without alternative, and your customers can buy 'lateral' products to fulfil their needs. These alternative products either exist already or are emerging, and might cannibalise your core offering at some future stage.

Industry borders can be quite blurred, and you might not be fully clear of which industry you are competing in. If you are an airline, you are obviously competing in the passenger and goods air transport industry, but more generally you are in the long-distance transportation industry. You should include car, truck and train transportation in your target market, and in many countries fast trains have managed to capture most of the airline traditional business on distances of up to 500 km.

Knowing who is eating your lunch today can be tough, and knowing who will eat it tomorrow is even harder. This is the topic of our next two sections.

2. Who are Your Current Competitors?

To simplify the competitive landscape, it is usually valuable to break down your competitors into a number of groups that can be seen as homogeneous in the first approximation. In each group, competitors might have the same target market, comparable size and resources, and similar operational model. Competitor clustering is useful because companies in one cluster tend to have similar strengths and ways of competing. Clustering helps you understand in which group you are and identify who your direct competitors are. It also makes you ask whether this is where you want to remain, and how you can create a unique selling proposition for yourself.

The idea of clustering competitors in strategic groups is similar to that of grouping customers in customer segments.

• It helps create structure from apparently inextricable complexity. It simplifies the competitive landscape by structuring it. Each group will follow the same strategy to some extent.

• It improves your understanding of how your competitors are competing and where you are competing yourself. You should then focus your attention on the companies that belong to the same strategic group as you, analyse them one by one, and treat the other groups as secondary competition only.

• It can also help you prioritise between sales opportunities and focus your own resources, leaving aside opportunities where you have a lower chance of winning because a competitive group is better positioned to address them.

As always, nothing is static and competition changes over time, so you need to keep checking that the competitive groups are remaining valid over time, otherwise you will have to adapt your analysis to the new environment.

To build clusters, try any of the following dimensions:

• size, market share, growth, profit margin
• geography, target regions, global versus local presence
• target market segments, for example business versus consumer, or business customers further split in small, medium, and large, and consumers broken down in low / medium / high end, or according to

their lifestyle such as 'young and dynamic', 'family-oriented', 'mature and conservative'

- the breadth of competitors' product lines, their degree of diversification or focus on a single product
- their operational model and focus in the value creation, for example R&D, product line management, manufacturing, marketing, sales channel, and service.

Regarding the operational model, you can distinguish companies according to their degree of vertical integration in R&D, production, marketing and distribution channels. Some companies tend to do everything themselves while others outsource and focus on integrating what they buy from others. Some companies focus on the marketing of products manufactured by others, and see their own competence primarily in understanding customer requirements, designing products, their packaging and user interfaces; other companies are contract manufacturers. Some companies internalise their distribution channel, others externalise it and focus on R&D and product line management, and rely on partners who are essentially a distribution channel and add value in services and logistics.

Once you have collected data on competitors, try and identify the three most meaningful parameters of analysis for grouping them, and display the results in a Microsoft Excel® chart. Typically, sales or market share or some other measure of size will be displayed graphically by bubbles of various sizes with large competitors getting large bubbles, and small competitors smaller ones. The other two dimensions X and Y on your chart will vary from case to case, but should help you infer recommendations for your competitive strategy. Feel free to experiment: draw multiple charts, and find the ones that show the picture best. Don't forget to place your business on the chart as well. And don't over analyse either.

3. What do You Need to Know About Your Current Competitors?

Systematic competition analysis is often perceived as a tedious, time-consuming data collection task, and is unfortunately one of the most neglected activities in companies. Small companies focussing on a local or regional market and without the ambition to become a world leader will often be pleased enough to remain stable in size or grow at low to medium speed. Large companies will typically be very focused on their market share, but might analyse their direct competitors only in a very general way. In many cases they believe that their competitors are not directly observable so they cannot know what these are doing, or they believe that they already know everything that can be discovered in the public domain.

To be really useful, competition analysis should perform a deep dive in publicly available data, for example press releases and financial statements, and learn to read between the lines. But you can also collect information that cannot be found on the Internet or in company reports. These sources include:

• asking customers what other companies have offered them
• talking to the suppliers of your competitors
• talking to consultants and analysts about how they perceive your competitors
• talking to your competitors' staff on fairs.

A group needs to be assigned in your company, typically in a marketing, strategy or business development department, to structure the data collected and filter what is most credible and relevant from the rest. Your top management also needs to signal that competition analysis is an important topic and everyone should contribute. This can be facilitated by setting up an appropriate knowledge-management tool to support the data collection effort, and by providing incentives to collect feedback from your sales people.

Your knowledge-management tool should primarily focus on your direct competitors. In addition to the quantitative data listed in Section 2 above, you should also look for data of a qualitative nature, for example:

• their capabilities: management, employees, skills, finance
• their operational model: how they work, which value-chain component they focus on, where they add value
• how they win business: their claimed USP, their tactical sales approach
• how they maintain or develop flexibility to changing market environments.

4. Where are Your Future Competitors Likely to Come From?

If your current competitors are a concern, your future pain will usually come from disruptive new competitors, as new players come in all the time and many existing competitors disappear from the market. If you are in the telecom industry, had you heard of the Chinese company Huawei ten years ago? Do you often hear about Wang, DEC, Atari, or Commodore these days?

New competitors will come from various background and origins:

- *Different geographies.* Think about China in the hardware business, and India in the software and service businesses.

- *Extension of the product line from a related business.* For instance you are a mobile handset maker and an MP3 consumer electronics company such as Apple now taps into the mobile phone business; or vice versa, you are in the MP3 player market and a mobile phone supplier integrates MP3 functionality into its phone or launches MP3-only players. Do you remember the time when the camera market was dominated by players such as Kodak, Canon and Minolta? Did they see PC and consumer electronics players such as HP, Casio, Sony, Panasonic, and Samsung joining the game? Did Nokia see Apple coming into the mobile phone business? What will be the impact?

- *Forward or backward integration.* Some of your suppliers now want to be in your business. Maybe they have found out that there are some better profit margins to be made there. Or some of your customers don't want to buy from you anymore but in-source your activity.

- *Change in the regulatory or legal environment.* Barrier to entry might be lowered by the government, enabling new companies to enter the market, for instance when a government awards new spectrum licences to increase the competition among wireless operators.

If you can identify one or multiple future competitors, or at least the background and expertise that they might bring with them, try to describe them 1-2 years down the road as a story. Which strengths will they bring? Which angle of attack will they take? What might their first product be? How will they differentiate? How much market share might they capture?

5. What are Your Core Competencies, Comparative Advantage, USP?

In life, everything is relative. Once your competitive environment has become clearer, it is time to look inward and identify your core competences. This is more easily said than done. Most people – and companies as groups of people – are not good at reflecting on themselves and defining what their strengths really are. In a private circle you can draw on friends to give you feedback on what you do well and not so well. The equivalent in business is to draw on external advisors to benchmark you against others. Benchmarking can be done quantitatively for example look into your cost structure and compare R&D, manufacturing and sales costs with peer companies, or in a more qualitative manner. You can also undertake customer satisfaction surveys to learn more about yourself and how you are perceived by others.

Your *core competencies* might include any of the following:

- R&D capability
- project management skills
- management of partners
- low-cost production
- logistics
- know-how management
- purchasing skills
- M&A capability
- customer understanding
- branding
- visionary or and charismatic management
- and so forth.

From what you think your core competencies are, you can derive your *comparative advantages* by comparison with the core competencies of your competitors. You might find out that some of your core competencies are largely available to most of your competitors as well, so are not really differentiating. This analysis should also help you identify missing competencies that are strategic to acquire for your company's future and provide impulse to reinvent yourself.

Your comparative advantage might be anything from:

- valuable IPRs that generate high royalties
- short development cycle for new products
- an ecosystem of partner products enhancing your own product
- high production volume and just-in-time manufacturing capability
- strong negotiations skills and buying power
- unique process and distribution know-how supported by IT tools
- superior consultative selling skills supported by powerful CRM systems
- a widely recognised brand
- a culture that fosters innovation and can integrate new start-up acquisitions in a large corporation
- a top and middle management that knows how to motivate their staff to give their best.

And many more.

Finally, once your comparative advantages have been clarified, your *USPs* are nothing more than a rephrasing of your comparative advantage from the perspective of your customers or their end-users. Explain how your product offering creates value for them. Do you know companies that you can associate with one or more of the USPs below? Give it a try:

- the fastest and best quality MP4 compression algorithm
- an ability to design 'cult' products
- a wide product portfolio to serve the individual needs of micro-segments
- made-to-order capability with delivery within 3 days
- high quality products at the lowest cost
- a customer orientation that is pervasive in all areas of the company
- a cool brand that people emotionally connect with
- financial strengths that make the company resistant to external crises and guarantee financial continuity
- a top management that is widely recognised in the industry.

6. Where and How do You Want to Compete in the Future?

Strategy starts with the ability to say "No". In the context of competition, this means the ability to decide where you want to put all your weight and resources, and become a top tier player. Free yourself up! Where you want to compete is your decision. *Where* does not only mean geographically, but also in terms of customer segments, product portfolio, price and positioning in the value chain. Maybe it is time to wake up and put into question decisions that have been made so long ago in the past that nobody remembers why your company is competing the current way.

From the study of many industries, Porter has derived that there are three generic competing strategies that apply across the board.

Strategy One: Cost leadership

This requires low cost of production, high volume, low cost of distribution, and a mass-market approach. And more importantly a corporate culture and management that is completely dedicated to low cost in everything that they do, and breathe this philosophy every day. The danger of this strategy is that it tends to translate into cut-throat price wars creating one winner and many losers, and as everybody tries to be the winner, customers capture all the value while all suppliers, except perhaps one, struggle financially.

Strategy Two: Differentiation by bringing something unique to customers

Unlike cost leadership, there are numerous ways to compete in a differentiation strategy, creating room for many companies to be successful in the market. Typical differentiation strategies are:

- innovation. This requires strong R&D and trend-setting capability, as well as short development cycle.
- quality. Quality can mean all sorts of things, in particularly reliability, competence, short reaction speed, professionalism. Product quality requires strong process capability and system integration capabilities so that individual components best match each other. Competitive strategies focusing on quality might primarily address the premium market, but it does not have to be so (e.g. Toyota).
- service excellence. This requires efficient but affordable after-sales processes, and in case you are a service business, a passion for serving customers, looking at issues in an end-to-end way, and improving your processes continuously.

- perceptions including packaging and advertising. Many companies are successful not so much because of the quality of the products that they sell (these are largely commoditised) but because of their marketing approach. Think about big household product brands like washing powders, chocolate or jeans.

Strategy Three: Focus on a small market segment or a niche rather than the mass market

By narrowing your market focus, your target is to create for yourself a Unique Selling Proposition that larger competitors cannot match and provide your customers with something that perfectly satisfies their needs. This can again be a focus on cost leadership or a differentiated product offering.

A competing strategy based on differentiation does not mean that you can afford to forget costs, but that you are not primarily competing on a low cost and low price basis. So differentiation is really about finding the right trade-off between cost, innovation, quality and services. You need to push your analysis deeper and identify the right mix and how it makes most sense for you to compete, based on the value that you can bring to your customers. This is a value that they don't get from others today, and also not tomorrow due to your own efforts to continue developing and protecting your USPs.

A 'me-too' strategy is not good enough. Imitation can be a short-term by-pass, and god knows how imitation is easy on paper and how difficult it can be in practice. However this won't be sufficient in the long term. It is probably not worth competing in an area where you do not have USPs and cannot make a difference, because this will only lead to below average performance and profitability.

Make sure that there is an appropriate match between the size of the market that you want to address and your own resources. If the market is too large compared to your resources, then you are unlikely to be able to make a difference. You are like a drop in the ocean. You are running the risk of spreading your efforts too thinly across too many opportunities. Venture capitalists also prefer narrow, but well-defined markets where you can become the leader, rather than huge markets where you want to take 0.1% market share. On the other hand, you should not think too small either, otherwise you are acting too conservatively. If you believe that you are spreading your efforts too thinly on too many activities, scale down and focus on those segments where you are or have the potential to become a leader. If your addressable market is still too large compared to your means, then focus on segments of the value chain where concentration levels are higher, or where concentration is likely to happen. Concentrated industries have a reputation for being less competitive and more profitable.

As a start-up, you should choose your angle of attack so that you get maximum spinning from one market segment to the next. It is like a game of bowling. Start by putting all your resources on a market segment that is neither too small nor too large and where you can bring unique value, but make sure that this market segment gives you an evolution path towards a second segment leading to a third and so on. In the long term you could be addressing a much larger market.

7. What is Your Realistic Market Share?

Now let us go back to the practicality of how large a market share you can claim. Your target market share, as well as its evolution over time, is a function of three key factors:

- *Where the industry is in terms of maturity.* If the industry is still in its early stage with no industry leader, then you could in theory claim a high share in the long term. If on the other hand your industry is already pretty settled and you are coming in as a newcomer, then becoming even a Tier 2 player in this industry will be very difficult, unless you are a cost leader and can sustain this competitive advantage over time.

- *How you are currently positioned in the market.* This starts with your market share today, but also whether your current assets, sales channels, and reputation in the market position you well enough to claim more market share in the future. Or vice-versa if your current attempts to increase market share have not been quite as good as what your competitors have been doing recently, the best you can expect is to keep the status quo. In the worst case, and if you are honest with yourself, you are more likely to lose market share to others unless you do something radical.

- *Looking forward, which resources you are throwing at the game.* In one extreme case, with very large resources, you could buy market share with massive marketing campaigns and aggressive pricing, or M&A activities. In the other extreme case, with limited resources and low delivery volume, you will not be able to get the market share that your product deserves even if demand is overwhelming.

Obviously, your achievable market share depends on how narrowly or broadly you have defined your market. If the pond is small, then it should not be hard to become the largest frog.

Industry concentration: of gorilla, chimpanzees and monkeys

With regard to industry maturity, most industries are initially very fragmented as growth is overwhelming and even bad companies can survive. Then comes a period where growth slows down, customer expectations increase and the industry consolidates. A *gorilla* with a very high market share often emerges. In industries with extreme growth rates the gorilla might emerge early on, and maintain its position if it manages to grow fast enough. The gorilla can also emerge more slowly from one of the lead players, but in many cases, the industry makes sure that no single player acquires a dominating position, but settles on a couple of players of equal size. In some cases, the industry remains very fragmented.

- A typical gorilla has 40%-60% market share and more, and is followed by 2-3 *chimpanzees* with 10%-20% market each, and further behind and closing the tail 5-10 smaller *monkeys* with each 1%-5% market share. This is for instance the case in the IP router market with Cisco leading the pack as the gorilla.

- At the other extreme, the market remains fragmented with a large number of players, each owning no more than 5%-15% market share. This is still applicable to the PC industry to a large extent, as well as the IT service industry as a whole, which has somewhat consolidated and giants such as IBM, HP, Dell, Acer, Fujitsu Siemens Computers, Toshiba have emerged, but none is really able to claim a gorilla position, and as the barriers to entry are not high enough, new players appear all the time and put the status quo into question. Have you heard of Lenovo until recently? Well, the Chinese PC maker has taken over the IBM PC business in 2005, and was already large before.

- Alternatively, you can get the situation where three players have 20%-30% market share each, and a number of smaller players share the remainder with 5%-10% per company. This third model is applicable in many electro-mechanical industries like power generation and medical systems.

A fragmented industry might take a long time to consolidate, or might never consolidate if barriers to entry are low and/or barriers to exit are high. Also, some parts of the value chain might consolidate as they benefit from scale, while other areas in the value chain are more local by nature (for instance your hairdresser) and do not benefit from scale, so might never consolidate.

The industry concentration index HHI

The HHI index, named after its inventors Herfindahl and Hirschman, provides a useful measure of industry concentration. It is calculated as the sum of the squared market shares and is comprised between 1 (a monopoly) and 0 (a very fragmented industry comprising many players). An index lower than 0.1 describes an industry that is fragmented, and an index above 0.2 a concentrated industry. The three cases described previously have an HHI of respectively 0.25-0.3, 0.15-0.2, and 0.08-0.1. Competition typically decreases as the industry concentration index increases. In theory it is better to be in a concentrated industry, or in a medium-concentrated industry in a leading position. In a fragmented market, your strategy should be to carve out a niche for yourself in which you can increase you market share and claim premium prices for your products and services based on the outstanding value that you provide to customers.

To derive a market share forecast, you can benchmark your business against competitors and assess criteria by criteria how well you are positioned. You can then combine these results with an industry structure analysis and how fast the industry concentrates or has already concentrated. With good logic and common sense, you should be able to generate a reasonable market forecast. Then you need to check that your forecast market share makes sense, is achievable and consistent with your resource planning. Also, if you are winning market share very rapidly, who is losing market share to you, and why?

Always justify your market share assumption. 1% might be a lot if you are a small, unknown player with no resources in an existing market; or very small if you are the leader in a new emerging industry, in which case your market share should be high, but will probably go down over time. If you are already a large conglomerate, you might claim a long-term market share in a new business equal to the market share you currently hold in the industry, for instance 20%. But are you sure that innovation is not opening the door to new players, who are more agile than you and have no installed base? Is the *Innovator's Dilemma* not affecting you? The Innovator's Dilemma states that new products necessarily cannibalise existing ones and therefore can face strong opposition within an established company. If you are a large company, what are you doing to overcome the Innovator's Dilemma? If you are doing too little, then your market share in the new technology can only be smaller, maybe very much smaller, than you current market share. Vice-versa, if you have missed your market entry in the previous technology generation, but now put all your resources on the new opportunity, you could target a higher market share than your current position would seem to indicate. Nothing is static after all, competition is a game to be played and won every single day.

8. How to Beat the Competition?

Beating the competition requires the right mix of actions.

- It starts with careful *analysis* of customer needs, the competitive landscape, and development of how you want to compete in the market, including the identification of your USP.

- It requires *focusing your resources* on the target market and what it really important to your customer. Investing endogenously or exogenously via M&A might be required to acquire the skills that are missing to you to compete effectively.

- You must also make sure that *tactical measures* are undertaken to increase your market share, and grow faster than the overall market.

There is an excellent account of competitive strategy in Jack Welch's book "Winning". This is a great book that I strongly recommend reading – its addresses many more topics that competition alone. First of all, Jack Welch reminds us how dynamic and pragmatic competitive strategy is: it should not be lived as complex, nebulous and time-consuming analyses that remain the preserve of the boardroom, but a collaborative and from the ground up exercise involving fire fighters from multiple departments and leading to actionable decisions. Jack Welch recommends focusing on what he calls the 'Five Slides' that provides answers to five key questions. The five slides are as follows:

- Slide number one: "What does the playing field look like now?". This looks into your competitors, their market share, their strengths and weaknesses, and if possible benchmarks you against them.

- Slide number two: "What has the competition has been up to?". This addresses recent moves of the competition, their attempts to change the playing field, and the possible entry of new competitors.

- Slide number three: "What have you have been up to?". This explains what you have done in turn to gain a competitive edge, and reviews any competitive advantage that you might have lost.

- Slide number four: "What is around the corner?". This discusses the worst things that might happen in the coming year from a competition perspective, for instance a disruptive technology that could make your product obsolete. This part helps you not underestimate the competition, which is certainly not asleep but as active as you are and wants to win your business.

- Slide number five: "What is your winning move?". This sets out what can you do to change the competitive field and further win market share.

Get your strategy group, sales and product line management together every now and then to review the state of things, generate some lateral thinking and identify measures to improve your hit rate. The Five Slides above provide you with a guideline for structuring this event. The goal of strategy is to define how the objectives that you have assigned to your company will be reached. As you are not alone in the market, a strategy, to be successful, should include what your competitors are doing or are likely to do. Your strategy should define how you will compete, elaborate the Unique Selling Proposition that will form the core of your value proposition to your customers, and ensure that your competitive advantages are sustainable over time. This will require hard work and permanent attention to market evolution and competitive moves, as the market is constantly evolving.

Any market share forecast is only as useful as it is realistic, challenging but motivating, and aimed at reaching achievable targets. A market share estimate will help you plan your activities and resources, at least in the near term, and will have to be revisited regularly and defended over and over again. Many of your competitors' activities are not observable so there is always potential to be surprised. Try to anticipate, remain agile, and execute your strategy fast in order to keep the upper hand. Have fun competing in the market, remain fair, and watch out!

## Chapter Eleven

Value Chain and Business Model

"Our real problem is not our strength today, it is rather the vital necessity of action today to ensure our strength tomorrow"
Dwight D. Eisenhower, American President

The only constant in life is change. Analysing an industry and deconstructing its value chain is an effective way to identify the main players and the roles that they fulfil. This in turn will help define the business areas where you want to compete, as well as alternative business opportunities and business models. It sharpens your positioning and triggers tough but important questions: why do my business activities start here, and why do they stop there? It also helps you anticipate and prepare for major industry transformation.

Overview of Chapter Eleven

1. Introduction...244
2. Value Chains are Not Static 246
3. Examples of Value Chains...248
4. Selecting Your Position in the Value Chain and Business Model.............251
5. Impact on the Business Plan...253

1. Introduction

Value chains describe how a group of companies in an industry do business together, building up on each other and adding value to a product or service before it is sold to end-users. For simplification purposes a value chain is often depicted graphically as a linear series of activities. However, a trunk and branch structure, or even a web structure can be more appropriate when the business relationships are more complex and varied than the simple 'buy from the previous link in the chain, sell to the next link'.

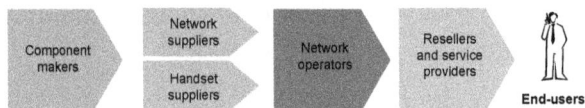

Figure 11.1: Top level view of the telecom value chain [Source: INVESTAURA].

Value chains can be depicted in various ways and a number of examples will be provided in this chapter.

Companies can be involved in more than one link of the chain, or focus on one segment only and diversify by enhancing their product portfolio rather than expanding their role across multiple value chain segments. At the top level, a value chain can be broken down in three to five main components. Figure 11.1 above provides a simplified view of the telecom business value chain. In most cases, each value chain component can be further broken down and there are many more players and interaction types than the top-level view initially indicates. This is illustrated in Figure 11.2, with the bold lines showing the main relationships between players while the thin lines show alternative relationships.

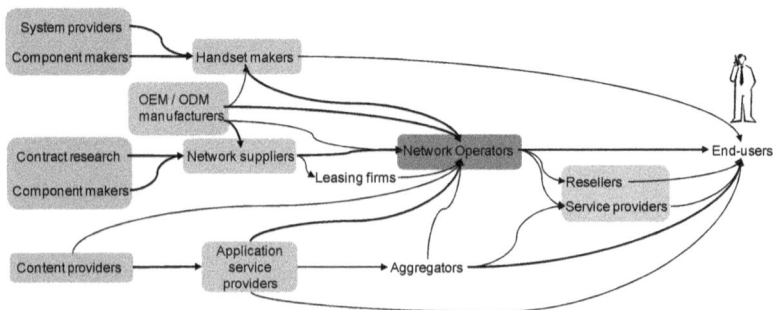

Figure 11.2: A more detailed view of the telecom value chain [Source: INVESTAURA].

The previous figure focuses on who sells to whom, and the arrows show the flow of products or services from one entity to the next. A monetary flow (cash) circulates in the opposite direction.

Although the terms *business model* and *value chain* are often used interchangeably, business model is a related but different concept. A business model focuses on one link or one company in the value chain and describes its operational model: how it does business, what it buys from other players, what its own contribution is, and who it sells to.

Business models also address additional aspects, such as:

- What are the main activities undertaken by a company?

- Who is the company selling to? Who is selling to the end-user? Who owns the end-user? Which channels are used? Which brand appears on the service or product? Who is billing and collecting money from the end-user? How are revenues shared between players?

- Who invests in what (assets)? How are other costs shared between players (e.g. marketing, customer care)?

- How is the money flowing between the players? Who is paying whom? Who is paying you?

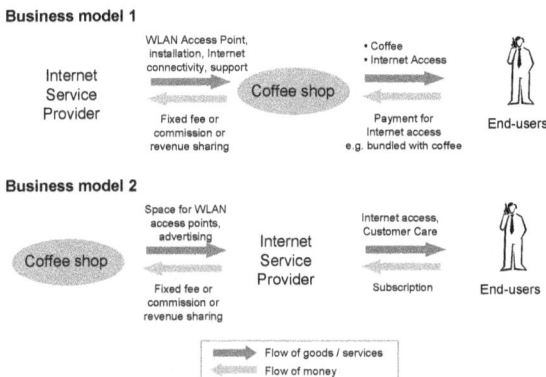

Figure 11.3: Alternative business models for a coffee shop Internet access over WLAN [Source: INVESTAURA].

How you generate revenues and who you sell to are questions that are not always easy to answer. For instance, although many Internet portals provide services to end-users, they do not generate revenues from them directly but are financed by third party advertisers, who themselves try to sell their products to end-users. There are also examples from brick and mortar businesses, for instance a coffee shop providing Internet access over WLAN as shown in Figure 11.3.

Is the coffee shop paying the Internet Service Provider (ISP) for the value provided by installing WLAN in the shop, which encourages customers to stay longer and consume more? Or vice-versa is the ISP, who has financed and installed the WLAN access points, paying the coffee shop a fee for the space and right to use the shop premises? Who is paying whom? Both are possible. The key questions are: who collects money from end-users, and how are costs and revenues split between the partners?

2. Value Chains are Not Static

The challenge in value chain analysis is that most industries, especially those with a high level of innovation and short product life cycles, the value chain is constantly changing as the industry is growing and maturing. Value chains often evolve along a common pattern:

- fragmentation followed by consolidation of companies within the same industry
- diversification across multiple segments of the value chain followed by specialisation and refocusing on core strengths
- vertical integration followed by horizontalisation, also called de-layering, within a value chain segment.

Waves of M&A activities, outsourcing and divestments are testimony to the permanent changes in the value chain. Typically, a new and fast-growing industry attracts a large number of players who are vertically integrated. Mergers then take place in order to create the scale required to lower costs and end-user prices and grow the market further. As the industry matures, innovation cycles shorten and it becomes difficult for a vertically integrated company to maintain speed and remain excellent in everything that it does in-house. At about the same time, business-to-business players emerge that can leverage scale synergies across multiple customers, resulting in lower costs, even after adding their profit margin. The value chain starts breaking up, with vertically integrated companies transforming former cost centres into profit centres. When an activity is not perceived as differentiating any more and third parties can provide it at a lower price, divestment and outsourcing become standard practices.

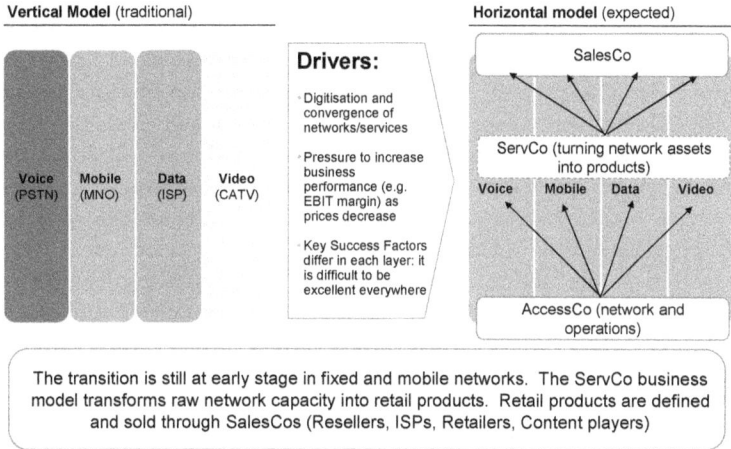

Figure 11.4: Evolution of the value chain from a vertically integrated model towards a horizontal structure [Source: Siemens AG].

Overtime however, dependency on one supplier can increase as backward consolidation takes place. When a large portion of the value creation is captured by key suppliers, the buyer's profitability can decrease, and this encourages re-verticalisation of the value chain. Professor C.H. Fine from the MIT University has developed a useful double helix model that captures the repeating pattern of consolidation, disintegration and reintegration. This model has been used to map the evolution of the mobile phone industry in Figure 11.5.

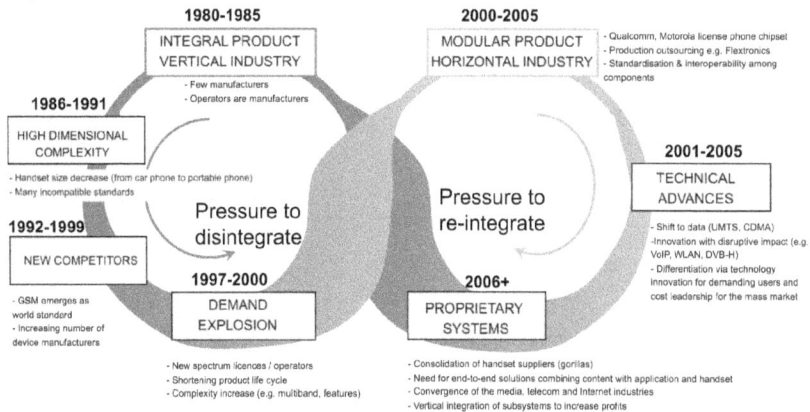

Figure 11.5: The dynamics of the mobile phone industry [Source: INVESTAURA, Pr. C. Fine].

Obviously, industries are not evolving at constant speed. Once players are deeply entrenched, the value chain often pauses for many years before evolving again. A critical mass of forces has to materialise and act in a self-reinforcing manner before a radical transformation can happen. In many cases key events that have the power to transform the value chain remain unnoticed for a long time. Take the PC industry for instance, a highly modular industry with many PC vendors and parts suppliers, but also an industry that witnesses gorillas such as Microsoft and Intel. Will the trends towards Open Source (for software development and licensing) and Software as a Service (rather than traditional software sale) fundamentally change the PC industry landscape? This is what many have expected but it has not happened so far and the value chain has not significantly evolved for more than 10 years. Maybe changes will come from a completely different area altogether.

3. Examples of Value Chains

In practice, how do you analyse an industry value chain? The first step is to identify the key players and group them according to the activities that they perform and their business relationships. The key activities form the links of the chain. Place the links at the top of a diagram, if possible in a linear series as the value chain is then simpler to depict and communicate.

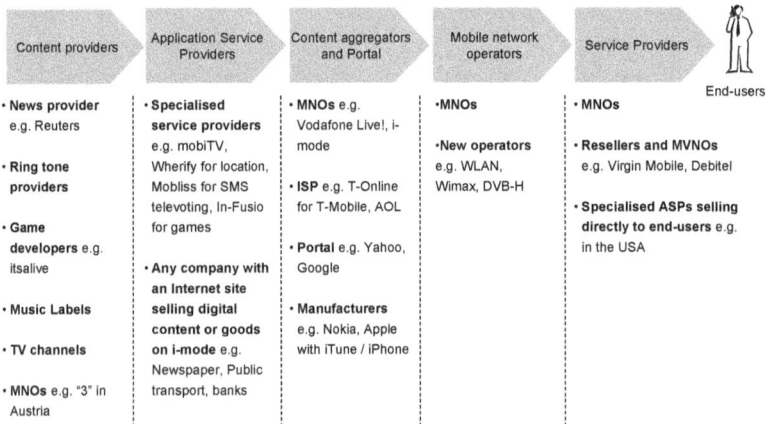

Content providers	Application Service Providers	Content aggregators and Portal	Mobile network operators	Service Providers
				End-users
• News provider e.g. Reuters	• Specialised service providers e.g. mobiTV, Wherify for location, Mobliss for SMS televoting, In-Fusio for games	• MNOs e.g. Vodafone Live!, i-mode	•MNOs	• MNOs
• Ring tone providers		• ISP e.g. T-Online for T-Mobile, AOL	•New operators e.g. WLAN, Wimax, DVB-H	• Resellers and MVNOs e.g. Virgin Mobile, Debitel
• Game developers e.g. itsalive	• Any company with an Internet site selling digital content or goods on i-mode e.g. Newspaper, Public transport, banks	• Portal e.g. Yahoo, Google		• Specialised ASPs selling directly to end-users e.g. in the USA
• Music Labels		• Manufacturers e.g. Nokia, Apple with iTune / iPhone		
• TV channels				
• MNOs e.g. "3" in Austria				

Figure 11.6: The mobile content value chain [Source: INVESTAURA].

Under each link, provide examples of companies or group of companies that perform similar activities. You can then focus on one link in the chain or one type of player, and analyse their business model further. Figure 11.6 and 11.7

show examples of value chains in the mobile content and TV broadcasting industries respectively.

The striking feature in the mobile content value chain is that it is largely dominated by mobile network operators (MNOs) acting as gatekeepers, who have historically undertaken massive investments to acquire spectrum licences and build mobile networks that provide next to full coverage. This predominance has led MNOs to capture the largest share of end-user revenues, typically 70%-90%, while the other players share the rest. On the other hand this has often been claimed as a barrier to the overall market development. Powerful players such as Nokia and Apple have recently started to put this status quo into question with the Ovi platform (for photos sharing, music, games, and location) and the iPhone/iTunes end-to-end solution respectively.

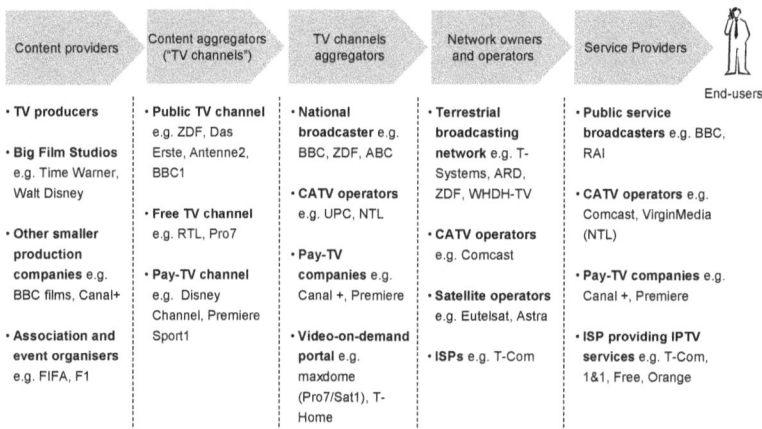

Content providers	Content aggregators ("TV channels")	TV channels aggregators	Network owners and operators	Service Providers
• TV producers • Big Film Studios e.g. Time Warner, Walt Disney • Other smaller production companies e.g. BBC films, Canal+ • Association and event organisers e.g. FIFA, F1	• Public TV channel e.g. ZDF, Das Erste, Antenne2, BBC1 • Free TV channel e.g. RTL, Pro7 • Pay-TV channel e.g. Disney Channel, Premiere Sport1	• National broadcaster e.g. BBC, ZDF, ABC • CATV operators e.g. UPC, NTL • Pay-TV companies e.g. Canal +, Premiere • Video-on-demand portal e.g. maxdome (Pro7/Sat1), T-Home	• Terrestrial broadcasting network e.g. T-Systems, ARD, ZDF, WHDH-TV • CATV operators e.g. Comcast • Satellite operators e.g. Eutelsat, Astra • ISPs e.g. T-Com	• Public service broadcasters e.g. BBC, RAI • CATV operators e.g. Comcast, VirginMedia (NTL) • Pay-TV companies e.g. Canal +, Premiere • ISP providing IPTV services e.g. T-Com, 1&1, Free, Orange

End-users

Figure 11.7: The TV broadcasting value chain [Source: INVESTAURA].

Contrast the mobile content value chain with the TV broadcasting value chain, where each segment of the value chain shows more diverse types of players. Owners and operators of the broadcasting networks have a less dominant role and capture about 10% of end-user revenues only, while content providers and aggregators get the lions share, typically 40%-50% of end-user spending.

From the mobile content and TV broadcasting value chains, future value chains and cooperation models between the mobile industry and the entertainment world can be derived, for instance for new business opportunities such as DVB-H (mobile TV).

As the previous examples show, a company is often involved in more than one link of the chain. This is partly explained by historical reasons as there was a time when the value chain was vertically integrated and a company had stakes in multiple related activities. This can also come from a company's diversification strategy to expand beyond its original role into neighbouring activities, to capture business opportunities and shifts in value from one link of the value chain to the next.

Sometimes, the value chain that emerges in a new sector is perceived as too long and too complex. This often explains why some emerging industries never develop to the potential that was originally forecast for them: there are simply too many 'hops' in the chain, too many incompatible systems, too many companies fighting for too little money, and maybe too much regulation. This has been the fate of positioning technologies and location-based services that emerged in mobile networks around 2001, but never managed to develop beyond a niche status, although they had attracted big names in the industry. The user interface and payment models were too complex and unattractive for end-users. Compare Figure 11.8 with the simple and straightforward value chain of portable navigation systems that have become very popular in cars: map providers, chipset vendors, device manufacturers, and sales channel. Four hops and nothing more!

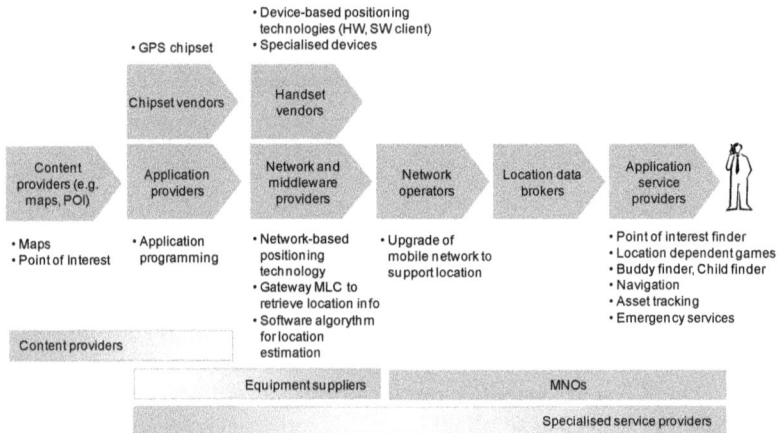

Figure 11.8: The location-based services value chain [Source: INVESTAURA].

Figure 11.8 also illustrates how players have taken multiple roles in the value chain. For instance, application service providers that are hosting and marketing services to end-users also often do their own application programming. Network and middleware vendors are also often providers of applications and handsets in an 'end-to-end' solution approach.

4. Selecting Your Position in the Value Chain and Business Model

Once the value chain has become clearer, the last step involves analysing the business drivers, competitive intensity and revenue share in each link of the chain and drawing some strategic recommendations, for instance a possible competitive move or diversification. Recommendations need to be crosschecked against resources available (cash, people, skills) in order to verify that they are practicable. Figure 11.9 illustrates this analysis from the perspective of a mobile phone supplier facing strong competition and looking for alternative business opportunities and a re-positioning.

Value chain link								Competitive intensity
Enabling technologies (battery, screen, camera, storage etc)	Sharp	NEC	Samsung	Sanyo	Hitachi	Toshiba	etc	High
Chipset	Freescale (Motorola)	STM (TI)	EMP (Ericsson)	Qualcomm	Agere (NEC)	Philips Semiconductors	Infineon etc	High
Operating system	Handset vendors proprietary **1**					Symbian Micosoft, Palm	Open source	Low
Integration	Nokia	Motorola	Samsung	LG	Sony-Ericsson	Palm, Dell, HP, RIM	etc	High
Application SW	Browser developer	Application developer	Application publishers	Handset vendors **2**				Medium
Services Providers	Operators				MVNOs	ASP e.g. RIM, Nokia, Apple		Medium

1 Understanding the needs of both end-users and operators for enabling technologies
  - Operators remain key buyers
  - Convergence of telco and entertainment industries
  - Durable partnering with selected peripheral suppliers / consumer electronics company could bring benefits

2 Strong level of competition among handset vendors
  - Limited success of mobile data so far, partially due to poor end-user interfaces and missing "plug-and-play" approach
  - New business models might boost product and mobile data business

Figure 11.9: The mobile handset value chain [Source: INVESTAURA].

One possible strategy would be to partner with a supplier of key technologies or a consumer electronics company to develop a stronger product capability and acquire better understanding of end-user needs. Another strategy would be to explore new business models and position oneself as provider of end-to-end solutions towards end-users, with very high quality integration between handset, user interface and application. The former strategy has been followed by Ericsson with Sony to form SonyEricsson, the latter strategy by RIM in the mobile email market, and more recently by Nokia and Apple.

The next example looks into the WLAN value chain and shows alternative options and business models that are available for service providers that want to be active in the field. The traditional model for a mobile or fixed network operator (MNO, FNO) is to control the value chain end-to-end and act as network provider as well as service provider towards end-users. However this strategy requires a significant investment in the WLAN network to get a critical mass of hot-spot coverage; furthermore, site owners might be reluctant to provide exclusive rights to one service provider if they want to address not only the customers of this service provider but other customers as well. Therefore, the alternative model for an MNO would be to buy WLAN wholesale capacity from aggregator of WLAN hot spots, and act as virtual network operator focusing on marketing and sales to end-users.

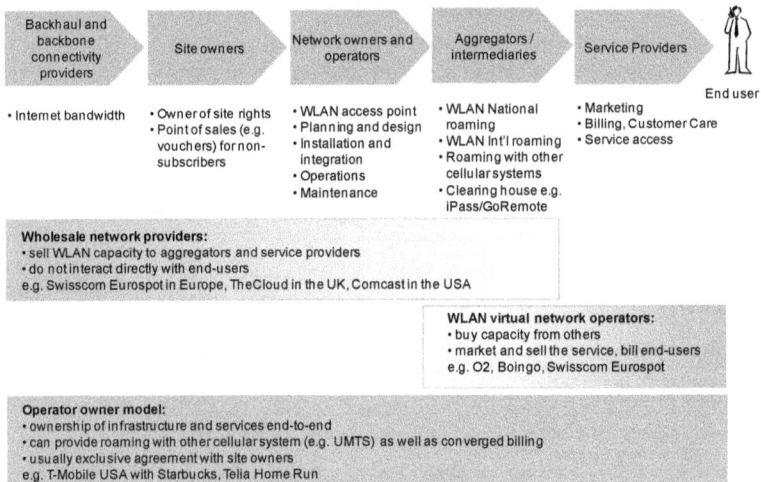

Backhaul and backbone connectivity providers	Site owners	Network owners and operators	Aggregators / intermediaries	Service Providers	End user
• Internet bandwidth	• Owner of site rights • Point of sales (e.g. vouchers) for non-subscribers	• WLAN access point • Planning and design • Installation and integration • Operations • Maintenance	• WLAN National roaming • WLAN Int'l roaming • Roaming with other cellular systems • Clearing house e.g. iPass/GoRemote	• Marketing • Billing, Customer Care • Service access	

Wholesale network providers:
• sell WLAN capacity to aggregators and service providers
• do not interact directly with end-users
e.g. Swisscom Eurospot in Europe, TheCloud in the UK, Comcast in the USA

WLAN virtual network operators:
• buy capacity from others
• market and sell the service, bill end-users
e.g. O2, Boingo, Swisscom Eurospot

Operator owner model:
• ownership of infrastructure and services end-to-end
• can provide roaming with other cellular system (e.g. UMTS) as well as converged billing
• usually exclusive agreement with site owners
e.g. T-Mobile USA with Starbucks, Telia Home Run

Figure 11.10: The WLAN value chain and alternative business models [Source: INVESTAURA].

In practice both business approaches have been implemented and there is no right or wrong model.

When faced with alternative business models, the choice should primarily be guided by:

- the company's strengths and resources that are currently available. For an existing company, these strengths will have been built in the past, however historical factors alone should not guide decision making as each company must and will have to reinvent its DNA from time to time, and develop or acquire new competencies that it does not have today.
- the competitive landscape and relative bargaining power between the various links of the value chain. This in turn will influence how the money is distributed across the chain and where higher profit can be generated.

Note that adopting a brand new business model is always a risky enterprise as the business model is unproven and the industry might not be mature or willing to let the new business model take root, especially if it is seen as disruptive and potentially threatening the status quo. Start-ups have to remain especially flexible: although it makes good business sense for a start-up to concentrate its strategy and resources on one primary model, it must react very rapidly to market feedback, and if necessary be ready to reinvent its core business model to survive.

5. Impact on the Business Plan

Why is the analysis of the value chain and the selection of a business model important from a business plan perspective? As we have seen above, this analysis helps identify alternatives and contributes to strategy definition. Beyond this, the economics of the business plan will differ markedly with the position that you plan to take in the value chain, as you will need different type of assets, resources and capabilities. This will translate into different risks, capital requirements, business set-up, success factors and financial results. Depending on your positioning in the value chain and business model, your business plan might be very R&D intensive, or very asset intensive, or require a lot of working capital, or a lot of manpower. Overall, analysing your value chain and business model should help you confirm the numerous qualitative and quantitative assumptions that you had to make to prepare the financial plan. It also increases your awareness of the business environment, helps anticipate shifts in the market and allows you to prepare business plans that are more robust.

## Chapter Twelve

Scenario Planning

"Uncertainty and mystery are energies of life. Don't let them scare you unduly, for they keep boredom at bay and spark creativity"
R.I. Fitzhenry, Vice President, Harper & Row

Sometimes, the environment in which a company operates is so uncertain that it seems that anything could happen. This is in particular the case when new technology and industries are emerging: the product is unclear, the applications and the end-user demand are unclear, the business model is unclear, and the competition is unclear. In this situation a scenario planning exercise is particularly useful to identify the main scenarios that might unfold and clarify how the future could look like. Scenario planning allows you to generate a first set of forecasts, identify the key signposts that distinguish one scenario versus another, and understand whether the company's current strategy and product roadmap are robust across multiple scenarios.

The good news about scenario planning is that there is no rocket science behind it: it is mostly straightforward and can be great fun. Ideally, it should be undertaken over a period of 4-6 weeks by a small group of people bringing various backgrounds and sufficiently diverse opinions to the table. In scenario planning you should be bold and think outside the beaten track to develop multiple pictures of the future world. These must be clearly different from one another to be valuable, but at the same time remain realistic. The forecasting horizon will typically be two or more product life cycles, and ranges between 4 and 30 years.

Following a review of the scenario planning methodology, we will go through a case study looking at Mobile TV with Digital Video Broadcast Handheld (DVB-H) as a major enabling technology. The DVB-H standard has been retained in Europe in 2004 to provide mobile TV type of services.

We would like to thank Gigaset Communications GmbH for its permission to reuse this material originally developed in the year 2004 as it was still part of Siemens AG. Note that the material is illustrative only and does not necessarily represent the current opinion of Gigaset Communications GmbH or Siemens AG.

Overview of Chapter Twelve

1. Methodology 257
2. Case Study: Scenario Planning for Mobile TV 258
3. Conclusion.. 265

1. Methodology

The methodology behind scenario planning can be broken down into six main steps.

Step 1

Scenario planning starts with a brainstorming session where issues that are likely to influence the business are collected in an open-minded manner. Be receptive to unusual ideas and do not apply any value judgment nor prioritise the issues at this stage.

Step 2

Draw the four quadrants of a matrix that has 'rather certain versus very uncertain' as its X-axis and 'low impact versus large impact' as its Y-axis. Position the issues identified in Step 1 in the matrix. From the 'Very uncertain', 'Large impact' quadrant, identify the key dimensions to be used to further define the scenarios.

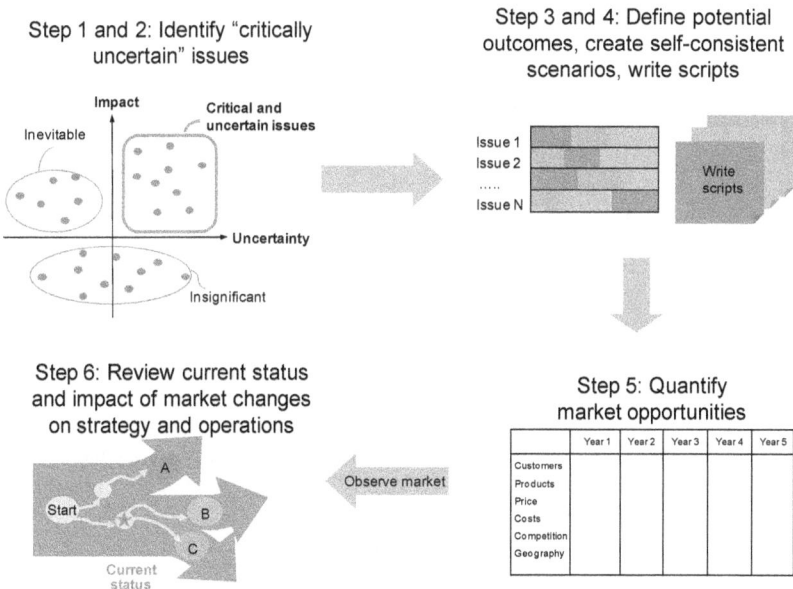

Figure 12.1: Overall scenario planning methodology [Source: INVESTAURA].

Step 3

Define the potential outcomes for the critically uncertain issues identified in Step 2. Group the possible outcomes of each dimension into a self-consistent scenario and define a minimum of three scenarios and a maximum of five. Each scenario should be clearly different from the others.

Step 4

Write the story behind each scenario and give it a title summarising its salient features. Also identify the signposts or observable events for each scenario, and prepare an indicative roadmap showing in which time frame the events are expected to materialise. From each market scenario, develop a business strategy. Identify 'no regret moves', which are actions that make sense whatever the future turns out to bring.

Step 5

For each scenario, translate the scenario script into a numerical forecast. To generate an average forecast, assign probability to each scenario and calculate the average of the scenarios.

Step 6

Observe the market and especially the signposts identified in Step 4. Update the scenario planning results accordingly, typically every 6 months, by repeating Step 4 and 5. Review the impact of the market evolution on your company strategy and operations.

2. Case Study: Scenario Planning for Mobile TV (DVB-H)

DVB-H stands for Digital Video Broadcast Handheld. It is a broadcasting technology derived from the digital TV standard Digital Video Broadcasting Terrestrial (DVB-T), to address the needs and limitation of mobile devices in terms of mobility, low battery capacity and smaller screens. In particular, DVB-H uses a time slicing scheme where power is switched off in time slots when no data are being transmitted to save battery power. Services are expected to include, but not remain limited to, TV programs, in particular if DVB-H is integrated with GPRS/UMTS networks that provide a return channel for authentication/billing as well as point-to-point connectivity for personalised downloads. Interactive TV, personalised TV, navigation support, electronic newspapers, and multiparty-gaming are some of the possible services that could come to the market by 2010.

End-users are expected to be consumers in the 12- to 25-year-old segment, and also business users between 26 and 45 as market research has shown that interest in mobile TV decreases beyond that age. Additional, non-TV services could also be developed to address the corporate needs, for example navigation.

Devices have been available since the first half of 2006 from leading manufacturers, in particular Nokia. Various device forms will coexist::

- mobile handsets, either in classical small-size form factor, or as entertainment devices with large touch-screens; mobile handsets will integrate DVB-H with GPRS/UMTS to provide additional service experience to end-users
- portable media players with integrated DVB-H receiver and recording capability
- PDAs with DVB-H extension modules.

The DVB-H business opportunity lies at the interface between the broadcasting and telecommunication worlds, and it has attracted the interest of a large number of players from both industries, in particular content providers, broadcast network operators and MNOs. The identification of DVB-H spectrum and the allocation process to interested parties are country-specific and vary widely within Europe. This is likely to delay the emergence of DVB-H services. Also the value chain and business models that are likely to emerge are still very unclear, which is a barrier to market development. At the end of 2007, only Italy had launched DVB-H services commercially.

In 2004, in light of the considerable uncertainty surrounding DVB-H and the timing of the technology introduction, a scenario planning exercise was undertaken within Siemens Communications to clarify the business opportunity, in particular generate a first handset volume forecast.

Step 1 and 2

The outcome of steps 1 and 2 is shown in Figure 12.2. Following a brainstorming workshop where a large number of issues were identified, the issues were positioned on the matrix and assigned a colour according to the topic that they relate to: orange for coverage issues, green for demand drivers, blue for MNO and value chain aspects, yellow for cost issues on the network side, dark purple for handset topics, grey for standardization, and white for other influences that could not be assigned to any of the category previously mentioned.

Each issue was positioned in the (Uncertainty, Impact) matrix and the key issues to be used as drivers for the scenario definition were then identified as shown in the top right-hand corner of Figure 12.2.

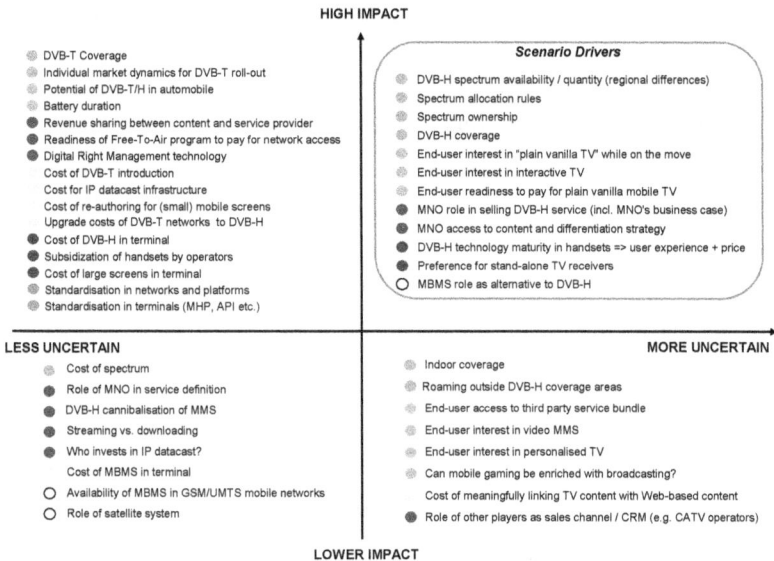

HIGH IMPACT

DVB-T Coverage
Individual market dynamics for DVB-T roll-out
Potential of DVB-T/H in automobile
Battery duration
Revenue sharing between content and service provider
Readiness of Free-To-Air program to pay for network access
Digital Right Management technology
Cost of DVB-T introduction
Cost for IP datacast infrastructure
Cost of re-authoring for (small) mobile screens
Upgrade costs of DVB-T networks to DVB-H
Cost of DVB-H in terminal
Subsidization of handsets by operators
Cost of large screens in terminal
Standardisation in networks and platforms
Standardisation in terminals (MHP, API etc.)

Scenario Drivers
DVB-H spectrum availability / quantity (regional differences)
Spectrum allocation rules
Spectrum ownership
DVB-H coverage
End-user interest in "plain vanilla TV" while on the move
End-user interest in interactive TV
End-user readiness to pay for plain vanilla mobile TV
MNO role in selling DVB-H service (incl. MNO's business case)
MNO access to content and differentiation strategy
DVB-H technology maturity in handsets => user experience + price
Preference for stand-alone TV receivers
MBMS role as alternative to DVB-H

LESS UNCERTAIN   **MORE UNCERTAIN**

Cost of spectrum
Role of MNO in service definition
DVB-H cannibalisation of MMS
Streaming vs. downloading
Who invests in IP datacast?
Cost of MBMS in terminal
Availability of MBMS in GSM/UMTS mobile networks
Role of satellite system

Indoor coverage
Roaming outside DVB-H coverage areas
End-user access to third party service bundle
End-user interest in video MMS
End-user interest in personalised TV
Can mobile gaming be enriched with broadcasting?
Cost of meaningfully linking TV content with Web-based content
Role of other players as sales channel / CRM (e.g. CATV operators)

LOWER IMPACT

Figure 12.2: Positioning of key issues on the (Uncertainty, Impact) matrix [Source: Siemens AG].

Step 3 and 4

In step 3, the potential outcomes for each scenario driver were discussed by the team and summarised as shown in Figure 12.3. Then four scenarios were defined by combining the outcomes of the scenario drivers, as shown in Figure 12.4. The four scenarios represent four different views of the future.

"no DVB-H spectrum" (blue scenario)

TV remains portable at best, but not mobile, as no spectrum is available for DVB-H services. The broadcasting industry priority concern lies in the transition from analogue to digital TV networks as well as the introduction of High Definition TV (HDTV) services. DVB-T set-top-boxes are pervasive in the home for plain vanilla or interactive TV. Portable DVB-T units are also available but remain niche products (e.g. auto, caravans, PCs). MNOs use Mobile Broadcast Multiple Services (MBMS) as multicast and broadcast technologies for video MMS services in mobile networks and to provide near video-on-demand TV channels in UMTS networks (e.g. news, sport).

#	Drivers	Outcomes		
1	DVB-H spectrum availability	No spectrum for DVB-H	Spectrum for about 10 TV channels	1 full Multiplex, about 30 TV channels
2	Spectrum allocation rule	Free or low cost, but some restrictions are imposed	Some free/low cost with restriction; rest is more expensive but no restriction	Spectrum is auctioned to highest bidder or allocated at medium level fee to players selected via beauty contest
3	Spectrum ownership	Spectrum in the hand of the Broadcast Network Operators	Spectrum in the hands of a few media / telcos	Spectrum in the hands of many players, each owning one channel
4	DVB-H roll-out	Only island coverage in country	Full coverage in country	
5	Demand for plan vanilla DVB-H TV	Limited acceptance, remains niche	30% of mobile users interested (at €10-€15 ARPU)	
6	Demand for interactive TV	10% of DVB-H enabled	50% of DVB-H enabled	
7	Willingness to pay	Low, people expect free-to-air (FTA) or low fee (€5)	High, incl. for premium pay TV (e.g. sport)	
8	MNO role in selling service	MNOs are not involved in value chain, used as return channel (e.g. SMS)	MNOs define and sells their own TV bundles under their brand	MNOs sell bundles of content players and act as sales channel, perform AAA
9	Availability of content	Public channel and private FTA are ready to provide content and expect low or no fee only	Private FTA see DVB-H as way to get into the pay TV field and expect high share of revenues	
10	Preference for stand alone receiver	Stand alone preferred	Integrated with cellular phone preferred	
11	DVB-H maturity in 2010	Low maturity (expensive, bulky, high battery drain)	High level of maturity (battery, light weight, wide spread availability in handsets, low additional cost)	
12	MBMS role in broadcasting	Limited bandwidth application (video MMS) for small to medium size communities	MBMS used as 1 x 64kbps TV channel as well. Unique differentiator for MNOs where DVB-H is not available	

Figure 12.3: Possible outcome of each scenario driver [Source: Siemens AG].

#	Drivers	Outcomes		
1	DVB-H spectrum availability	No spectrum for DVB-H	Spectrum for about 10 TV channels	1 full Multiplex, about 30 TV channels
2	Spectrum allocation rule	Free or low cost, but some restrictions are imposed	Some free/low cost with restriction; rest is more expensive but no restriction	Spectrum is auctioned to highest bidder or allocated at medium level fee to players selected via beauty contest
3	Spectrum ownership	Spectrum in the hand of the Broadcast Network Operators	Spectrum in the hands of a few media / telcos	Spectrum in the hands of many players, each owning one channel
4	DVB-H roll-out	Only island coverage in country	Full coverage in country	
5	Demand for plan vanilla DVB-H TV	Limited acceptance, remains niche	30% of mobile users interested (at €10-€15 ARPU)	
6	Demand for interactive TV	10% of DVB-H enabled	50% of DVB-H enabled	
7	Willingness to pay	Low, people expect free-to-air (FTA) or low fee (€5)	High, incl. for premium pay TV (e.g. sport)	
8	MNO role in selling service	MNOs are not involved in value chain, used as return channel (e.g. SMS)	MNOs define and sells their own TV bundles under their brand	MNOs sell bundles of content players and act as sales channel, perform AAA
9	Availability of content	Public channel and private FTA are ready to provide content and expect low or no fee only	Private FTA see DVB-H as way to get into the pay TV field and expect high share of revenues	
10	Preference for stand alone receiver	Stand alone preferred	Integrated with cellular phone preferred	
11	DVB-H maturity in 2010	Low maturity (expensive, bulky, high battery drain)	High level of maturity (battery, light weight, wide spread availability in handsets, low additional cost)	
12	MBMS role in broadcasting	Limited bandwidth application (video MMS) for small to medium size communities	MBMS used as 1 x 64kbps TV channel as well. Unique differentiator for MNOs where DVB-H is not available	

Figure 12.4: Four possible scenarios [Source: Siemens AG].

"DVB-H remains a niche" (green scenario)

MNOs are not involved in the DVB-H value chain so that DVB-H spreads slowly in the population. DVB-H spectrum is available as a subset of DVB-T spectrum, but not as full multiplex, providing capacity for about 10 channels. Coverage is limited to islands, in particular urban and suburban areas, covering 50%-70% of the population and the motorways. DVB-H is available as feature in a few high-end handsets, but end-users prefer stand-alone terminals due to high battery drain and large battery. The large media and TV groups dominate the mobile TV space and offer bundles that include public TV channels, private Free-to-Air (FTA) financed by advertising and a few pay-TV channels. Public TV and commercial content is not encrypted and mostly free. Pay-TV channels are encrypted, but take-up rate is low at about 10% of DVB-H users. Interactive services remain a niche and use SMS, voice or WAP as bearer for return channel. MNOs are used as bit pipes and AAA, Billing and Digital Right Management for Pay-TV are provided by pay-TV operators themselves. MNO provides video clips and the likes over MBMS, focusing on communities, but MBMS is not used as a TV bearer.

"DVB-H is a mass-market phenomenon, dominated by MNOs" (grey scenario)

MNOs play a key role in developing and selling the DVB-H service. One full multiplex or 30 channel equivalent of capacity is available for DVB-H services. Spectrum ownership is split between public TV, FTA private groups, pay-TV companies, some CATV operators and some MNOs, while other MNOs do not have spectrum. DVB-H is widely available in high- and mid-range handsets and the technology is mature. There is full coverage of the country with DVB-H. Some channels are FTA, others are encrypted (pay-TV, new interactive services, gaming etc.). DVB-H service acceptance is high among mobile users: end-users are ready to pay €10-€15 per month for pay-TV services and €5 service fee for FTA mostly to cover DVB-H handset subsidies. MNOs market their own TV service bundle, or market the TV bundle of a partner for example a CATV operator. MNOs provide AAA, billing and interactivity with their mobile content portal. Access to other bundles is not possible. MNOs take 30%-40% of end-user fees to cover their costs. MNOs without DVB-H spectrum enter into distribution agreements with pay-TV companies to distribute the bundles under the brand of the latter. These MNOs have low or no influence on the content distributed and play only a technical role in AAA, billing and interactivity. MBMS is not widely rolled out because video MMS are cannibalised by DVB-H and UMTS spectrum is reserved for unicast needs.

"DVB-H is a mass-market phenomenon, dominated by media companies" (orange scenario)

One full multiplex (30 channels) is available but no player owns more than 1-2 channels. DVB-H spectrum has been auctioned or allocated to a higher number of players who are attracted by a promising business opportunity. DVB-H is widely available in handsets, technology is mature. Some channels are FTA and financed by advertising, others are encrypted. End-users can subscribe the programs and services that they want and tailor their own bundles without restriction. This often results in more than one billing relationship, however there is no one centralised billing partner. Although MNOs and other players try to enter into commercial agreements with partners in a one-shop-shop approach and sell bundles, the landscape remains fragmented. MNO take 10%-20% of end-user fees. MNOs use DVB-H and MBMS programs to enhance their TV service offering and market about 5 channels under their own brand.

The following figure provides an overview of the four scenarios along four key dimensions: the availability of DVB-H spectrum, market demand, the role of MNOs in the business, and the usage of MBMS as a complementary broadcasting bearer.

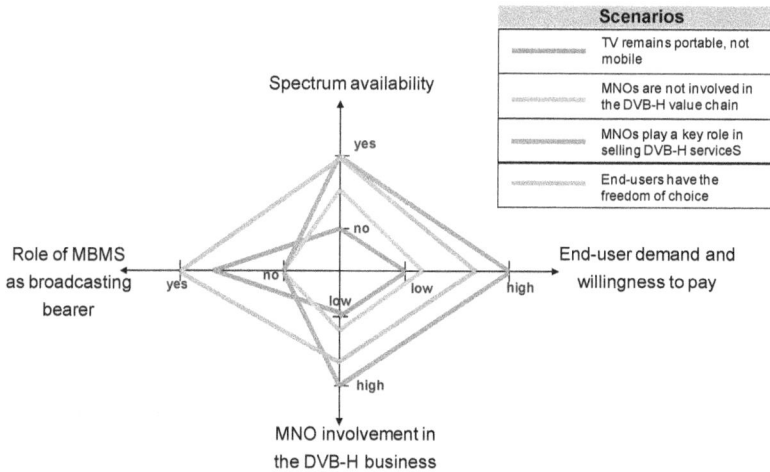

Figure 12.5: A simplified overview of the four scenarios [Source: Siemens AG].

Step 5

In step 5, a Microsoft Excel®-based model was set-up for the EU15 market. The model generated a forecast of the number of DVB-H handsets sold annually, the number of DVB-H users, the total revenues generated by end-users, the split of revenues between various participants in the value chain including MNOs, and an estimate of the infrastructure investment required. The forecasts were normalised to 100 inhabitants in each country.

Then, the particularities of each EU15 country were investigated and the probability that a scenario would happen in the individual country was estimated. The results were then scaled up to the total population in the 15 Western European countries. Figure 12.6 provides an overview of the results graphically and Figure 12.7 shows the model and assumptions made in the scenario "DVB-H is a mass-market phenomenon, dominated by MNOs".

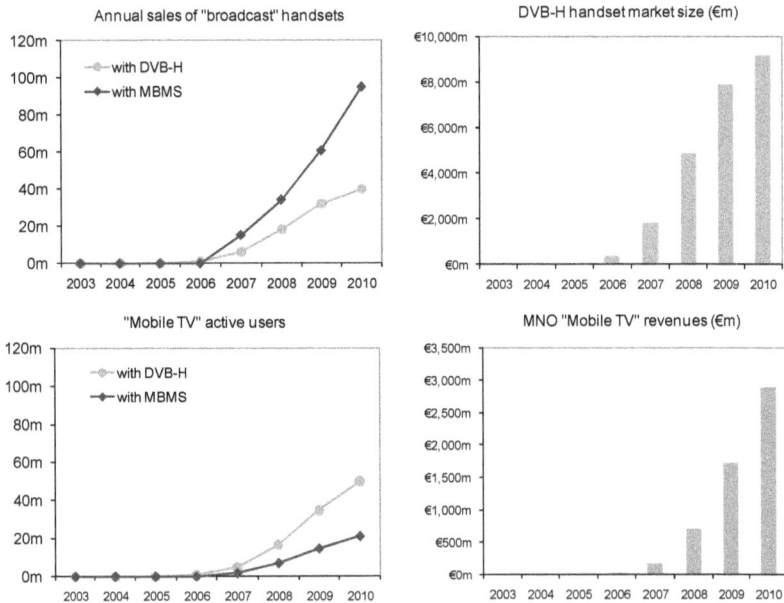

Figure 12.6: Handset Sales, Number of users and MNO revenues with DVB-H in EU15 [Source: Siemens AG].

Key market data	2003	2004	2005	2006	2007	2008	2009	2010
Country population (normalised to 100 people)	100	100	100	100	100	100	100	100
Mobile subscribers	69	72	74	76	77	78	79	80
# UMTS subscribers	0	1	3	7	14	24	36	49
# Handset sold in country p.a.	24	25	27	28	29	30	31	32
# Handsets sold with DVB-H p.a.	0	0	0	0.3	2	6	11	14
% handset sold	0%	0%	0%	1%	7%	20%	35%	44%
DVB-H handset market size	€0	€0	€0	€101	€591	€1,610	€2,724	€3,218
Average Selling Price (ASP)	€0	€0	€0	€338	€296	€268	€248	€230
# Handsets sold with MBMS	0	0	0	0	4	9	16	25
% handset sold	0%	0%	0%	0%	14%	30%	52%	78%
# DVB-H handset owners	0	0	0	0.3	2.3	8	17	25
# DVB-H users	0	0	0	0	2	6	12	18
DVB-H ARPU over average DVB-H user	€0	€0	€0	€10	€10	€10	€10	€10
DVB-H service revenues	€0	€0	€0	€13	€109	€433	€1,050	€1,764
MNO market share	80%	80%	80%	80%	80%	80%	80%	80%
Narrowband MBMS handset owners	0	0	0	0	1	3	5	8
Mobile TV MBMS handset owners	0	0	0	0	3	10	20	34
Mobile TV MBMS subs	0	0	0	0	0	0	0	0
Mobile TV MBMS ARPU	€0	€0	€0	€0	€0	€0	€0	€0
Mobile TV MBMS service revenues	€0	€0	€0	€0	€0	€0	€0	€0

Figure 12.7: Model logic and assumptions. The blue assumptions are valid for all scenarios, the green assumptions for this scenario only [Source: Siemens AG].

3. Conclusion

Scenario planning is a powerful technique. It can be used in demand and market forecasting as we have illustrated above, but also in strategy, R&D and portfolio management. Its full benefits are only revealed when the technique is applied on a regular basis rather than one-off, and linked to decision-making processes. When applied properly, it will greatly help businesses anticipate the future and position themselves adequately in an ever-changing world.

Valuing Business Opportunities as Real Options

"A wise man turns chance into good fortune"
Proverb

Methodologies used by practitioners in the financial industry evolve very slowly. Today the standard approach for valuing business opportunities is based on Multiples as well as the Net Present Value (NPV) and its operational equivalent the Economic Value Added (EVA®). However, this has not always been the case: it took 30 years for the NPV method to be widely accepted and used in business. Until the 1980s, other techniques were predominant and included P/E ratios, the use of the internal rate of return and pay-back period as selection criteria, on the basis that the shorter the pay-back period the better the project.

Today, practitioners start recognising the limitations of the NPV method for valuing businesses. In this chapter, we present a complementary technique that enhances the traditional NPV approach with the valuation of options that are embedded in the business opportunity, for instance the option to delay the decision to invest or the option to expand the project. Unlike financial options like *call* and *put* on shares, options in business ventures are said to be *real* because the underlying assets are real business assets as opposed to financial securities. The Real Options framework has been available since the early 1990s. Although not always easy to put into practice, valuations using Real Options bring new insights into the business opportunity and have been used successfully in a number of industries, for instance in mining and pharmaceutical. We expect that Real Options valuation will find more and more acceptance and become a standard tool in the next decade.

In this chapter, we start with a review of the NPV limitations. We will then discuss financial options and how they are valued using the Black-Scholes model. We then establish an analogy between an investment opportunity and a call option. A numerical example shows how to estimate the volatility of return sigma, one of the key parameters for option valuation. We then expand the framework to remove a number of limitations. Finally we discuss where and when it makes sense to apply Real Options and conclude on a number of industries where option valuation is currently widespread.

A note of caution before we start: the primary objective when valuing Real Options is to gain new insights as a business manager into a project opportunity, not to produce precise results. Therefore, making meaningful assumptions to simplify and solve Real Options problems is all right and always better than being precisely wrong. Results should always be understood as estimates: Real Options valuations, like NPVs, are based on models that approximate a complex reality.

Overview of Chapter Thirteen

1. Limitations of NPV Valuation 269
2. An Introduction to Financial Options 272
3. Valuing a Financial Option 273
4. Analogy between a Real Option and a Financial Option 275
5. Case Study: Valuing the Option to Invest in WiMax 276
6. How do You Estimate the Volatility Sigma? 279
7. Positioning the Project in the Option Space 282
8. Expanding the Framework: the Binomial Model 286
9. Recapitulation of the Real Options Methodology 293
10. When is it Worth Using Real Options Valuation? 293
11. Applications of Real Options 294

1. Limitations of NPV Valuation

The NPV assumes that the decision to start a project, as well as all other subsequent decisions, have to be taken at time zero (i.e. now) and these decisions, once taken, are irreversible. More generally, the NPV is based on a number of key premises:

- We cannot wait, but have to decide now or never. In reality, many decisions can be postponed, and managers do so, for instance request further analysis, additional R&D or a pilot project before proceeding to a full-blown launch.

- We go into this business, and stay in the business forever. In reality, managers can decide to scale back or abandon operations at a later stage.

- We go into this business, and stick to the original plan. In practice, managers remain flexible to changing market conditions. The NPV assumes that all future investments are pre-committed, whereas in practice this is never the case. Executing a strategy involves making a sequence of major business decisions, not deciding everything on day one. Managers do not follow a pre-determined plan blindly, but do consider and learn from how events unfold.

- We do not go into this business now, and we will never go. In practice, managers who initially decided not to be active in a sector can still decide to play at a later stage, for instance because the market conditions have improved.

The result is that NPVs are fundamentally flawed because they do not take into account the value of management flexibility to adapt to changing circumstances. If the market grows faster than anticipated, it is worth expanding operations. Technology innovation might also open the door to new and unforeseen applications. None of this is captured in the traditional NPV calculation. Real Options address this shortcoming: the value to wait before undertaking a major investment, the flexibility to enter a market with options to grow, scale down or abandon, or not enter a market now, but keep the option to participate at a later stage.

The traditional NPV can be interpreted as a 'floor'. In the ideal world where the cashflow forecast would be neither positively nor negatively biased, the NPV would still generate conservative results. This is problematic because it does not pay to be too conservative as it might lead to suboptimal decision-making and a firm might miss good opportunities.

There is ample empirical evidence that managers do not follow the NPV rule to the letter: investments are often made that cannot be justified by the NPV alone, and vice-versa companies often stay in a troubled business longer than an NPV analysis would recommend to do so: shutting down a business leads to an irreversible loss of tangible and intangible capital, and companies want to preserve the right to resume profitable operations later on. Managers' behaviour also demonstrates that decisions are often taken with an 'option' mindset, even if this happens unconsciously: projects which with low or negative NPV are undertaken on the basis that they are 'strategic', which in practice means that they open chances for future businesses. What companies are essentially doing is creating options for themselves and building up know-how for future opportunities.

If the NPV is negative, but close to zero compared to the size of the initial investment required, then this should not be a systematic 'no-go'. The decision to go ahead might be postponed and investments in R&D undertaken in the mean time to reduce technology risk. Or the project can go ahead now, but investment decision can be staged and performance be reviewed at regular milestones. In addition, uncertainty in market development and management flexibility to react to changes by expanding, contracting or abandoning the project also makes today's project value higher than in the static NPV approach.

In summary, when options and their values are taken into account, in many cases the value of the project with flexibility will be higher than zero, and in some cases substantially so.

In business life, three types of options can be encountered in practice:

- The option to defer an investment decision, in particular when uncertainty in the evolution of market demand is high and the project does not have priority due to limited resources.

- The option to expand an existing business at a later stage. In the initial phase, the business will focus on the most promising product or application and the business or portfolio will be enlarged later to address the remaining growth opportunities.

- The option to close down or sell a business or its assets, for instance when the current market share is too small and the business is more valuable to someone else. This is also called an abandonment option.

The first two types of options can be modelled as *call* options, the latter option is a *put* option. In the analysis below, we will focus on call options. Abandonment options usually have low value as assets are company or industry specific, and this makes their exercise price often negligible.

Some will say that the business options that have been identified can be added to the business plan and valued using the traditional NPV approach. But that is the whole point of Real Options: they do not make the identification of options redundant, but help value them correctly as an NPV calculation is not appropriate to value options. The risk profile of an option is different from the risk profile of the project as a whole, so discounting using the project WACC does not value the option correctly. The beauty of the Real Options framework is that it enhances the NPV approach: once the options have been valued, the total value of the business is the sum of the NPV and the value of the options.

Total NPV = NPV (without options) + Value of Options

Note that when the base cashflow forecast already includes an embedded option, the cashflows need to be restated by excluding the option cashflows and the option has to be valued using a separate technique. Only then can the value of the option be added back to the value (NPV) of the project without the option.

2. An Introduction to Financial Options

Before we can value Real Options, we need to understand how financial options are valued. In a second step, we can build an analogy between a real option and a financial option in order to value the real option.

On the stock market, an option is the right (but not the obligation) to buy or sell an asset (e.g. share, currency, oil or other commodities) at a predetermined price, at a certain date. *Calls* are options to buy, *puts* are options to sell. *European options* can only be exercised at expiry, whereas *American options* can be exercised at any time before expiry.

On the stock market, options, in particular on currencies, grain, metal and other natural resources, are useful to insure oneself from the risk of price changes. In addition options are also included in many financial instruments. In the US, many debt issues have embedded call provisions: the debt issuer can buy back the debt at a set price. This is equivalent to the debt-holder having sold a call option to the company issuing the debt. This protects the firm against interest-rate reduction in the case of fixed-interest debt. The value of the option translates into an interest-rate premium, or a lower issue price.

Many companies also issue convertible debt: the debt-holders have the option to convert their bonds into equity at a later stage. This form of financing can be seen as a bundle of straight debt and the option to acquire shares at a price known in advance. Companies also issue 'pure options' on their shares called *warrants*, for instance stock options to their staff. In addition, new share issues are associated with warrants that are detachable and can be sold separately, to ensure that existing shareholders are not worse off than new shareholders. But companies are not the only issuers of options: most options are 'written' i.e. sold by outsiders, especially banks.

Options are also pervasive in life and are included in many contracts. For example if you have bought a house and took a mortgage, it is very likely that your mortgage contract will have given you an option (a call) to reimburse the debt early on or an allowance for extraordinary instalments.

3. Valuing a Financial Option

We start with a review of how a European call is valued. A European call on a share is an option to buy the share at a set price, the exercise price X, at a certain date, t years into the future. It can be shown that the value of the call option today is fully determined by the following five parameters:

- The exercise price, X
- The current price of the share, S_0
- The time to expiry, t
- The standard deviation of the share return, σ (sigma)
- The risk-free cost of capital, r_f.

The return on the share is defined as total return including capital gains and dividend payments. Historically, looking at the period 1900-2000, the return on equities has averaged 6% in real terms (excluding inflation).

Black and Scholes have shown in a famous paper in 1973 that assuming that a number of assumptions hold true, the value of the call C can mathematically be derived by the following formula:

$$C = S_0 \times N(d_1) - X \times e^{-r_f \times t} \times N(d_2)$$

$N(d)$ is the cumulative normal (Gaussian) distribution.

$$N(d) = \frac{1}{\sqrt{2\pi}} \int_{-\infty}^{d} e^{-\frac{z^2}{2}}\, dz$$

d_1 and d_2 are given from the following expressions:

$$d_1 = \frac{\ln\left[\dfrac{S}{X \times e^{-r_f \times t}}\right]}{\sigma\sqrt{t}} + \frac{1}{2}\sigma\sqrt{t}$$

$$d_2 = d_1 - \sigma\sqrt{t}$$

At expiry, time has run out so t=0, and the value of the call is:

$$C = S_0 - X \quad \text{if} \quad S > X,$$

or 0 otherwise.

The Black-Scholes formula can be interpreted as follows: the value of the call today (C) is equal to the difference between the share price today (S_0) and the cost of exercising the option tomorrow $X \times exp(-r_f \times t)$, but adjusted for the probability $(N(d1), N(d_2))$ that the option ends 'in the money' i.e. that the share price at expiry is higher than X.

The assumptions of the Black-Scholes model are summarised below:

- Stock prices have a lognormal distribution i.e. stock returns are normally distributed and the variance of returns is constant over time. The normality assumption is only approximately correct, as we know today that distributions display a 'fat tail'. Also the variance of stock returns is not constant but fluctuating around an average value.
- Exercising of the option is only possible at expiry. This assumption is relaxed in the case of an American call.
- No distribution of dividend takes place before expiry. This assumption can also be relaxed latter.
- The market is efficient so no arbitrage is possible.
- There are no transaction costs.
- The company can borrow and lend money at the risk-free rate of interest.

The Black-Scholes model is exactly what it is: a model. It is only an approximation of reality but provides a useful mathematical expression for valuing simple financial call options.

4. Analogy between a Real Option and a Financial Option

Investing in a business or project involves spending money and acquiring assets, and this is equivalent to buying a share. We can therefore build an analogy between the real option to invest in a business and a European call, as shown in Figure 13.1:

Real option		European call
The investment required to acquire the assets of the project i.e. its stream of cash flows	X	The exercise price of the call option i.e. the price to pay to acquire the underlying
The value today of the stream of cash flows generated by the project. This is calculated by discounting cash flows by the WACC – also called the Present Value	S_0	The value of the underlying asset today, for instance a share of equity
The time available until the investment decision is taken	t	The time to expiry i.e. the time available to exercise the call option
The volatility (standard deviation) of asset rate of returns, as aggregate measure of the project risk	σ	The volatility i.e. the standard deviation of share returns – assuming share returns are normally distributed
The risk-free rate of interest: the discount rate to be used to calculate today's value of a payment known with certainty that will take place tomorrow	r_f	The time value of money i.e. the discount rate to calculate today's value of a risk free € to be paid tomorrow

Figure 13.1: Mapping between an option to invest and a European call [Source: INVESTAURA].

- The business opportunity will require an irreversible investment at a certain date, this is equivalent to X.

- Excluding the initial investment, the business opportunity will generate cashflows over a number of years that can be discounted using the project WACC to give the present value (PV) of expected future cashflows. This is equivalent to the value of the share today S_0 (cashflows from the business are similar to dividend payments).

- The investment X will take place in t years in the future, and as long as the investment has not take place, the decision to invest can be regarded as reversible. t can therefore be interpreted as the time to expiry.

- The cashflows generated by the business are uncertain, and this uncertainty can be captured by the variance σ (sigma), defined as the variance of Present Value returns.

- Finally, the business can invest money on a savings account at the risk-free interest rate r_f.

The standard valuation of the business opportunity today is given by the NPV:

$$NPV = S_0 - X / (1+WACC)^t$$

This can either be positive, in which case starting the project now is creating value; or be nil, in which case the project is neither creating nor destroying value but simply covering the cost of capital and shareholder expectations; or be negative, in which case the project today is destroying value and should not be undertaken.

Assuming that managers can delay the investment decision by t years without being ousted by the competition, then the business is in the fortunate position to wait, observe market conditions, undertake test marketing, update and refine the business plan. This flexibility is valuable, however it is not reflected in the NPV formula mentioned above. A more accurate estimation of the value of the business with flexibility is given by the Black-Scholes formula.

5. Case Study: Valuing the Option to Invest in WiMax

Let us look at a fictitious example. In early 2004, wireless spectrum for WiMax applications is sold by the telecom regulator in a European country for the fixed sum of €10m. A UMTS mobile operator is considering investing in WiMax technologies from 2006 onwards to provide broadband Internet access to consumers at home. Although the technology is not yet available in 2004 and still being standardised, the operator estimates that it would need to roll-out about 5,000 sites in Germany to cover the main urban and suburban areas at an investment per site of €30,000, with an initial roll-out of 3,000 sites taking place between the second part of 2005 and mid 2006 (X=€90m) and the remaining investment spread between 2007 and 2010.

Entering the market commercially in 2006, the operator believes that it can capture 10% of the broadband market share by 2010, estimated by analysts at 15m households in 2010. At the end of 2003, there were about 4m broadband customers in Germany, mainly using ADSL as access technology. A detailed bottom-up modelling has shown that the operator can expect to generate the following cashflows over the period 2006-2010. Beyond 2010, we have assumed that the cashflows remain constant (0% growth). The WACC of the business is 12%.

	2004	2005	2006	2007	2008	2009	2010
Subscribers	0	0	100,000	600,000	1,000,000	1,350,000	1,500,000
% of saturation			6.7%	40%	67%	90%	100%
Growth				500%	67%	35%	11%
Monthly ARPU			30	27	23	20	20
Revenues			€9m	€113m	€220m	€275m	€334m
EBITDA margin			-220%	16%	17%	16%	15%
Roll-out invesment			€90m				
Invest % of revenues				18%	9%	7%	7%
CAPEX			€90m	€20m	€20m	€20m	€23m
Cash flow excluding roll-out			-€20m	-€2m	€18m	€24m	€27m
Total roll-out invesment, H2 2005		€90m					
WACC							12.0%
Terminal value at End 2010							€127m
Discount factor	0.89	0.80	0.71	0.64	0.57	0.51	0.45
DCF (2006-2010)	€19m						
DCF (2010-2020)	€57m						
DCF 2006-2020 (S)	€76m						
NPV early 2004	€0m using WACC to discount X						
NPV early 2004	-€8m using r_f to discount X						

Figure 13.2: Discounted Cashflow calculation for a WiMax operator [Source: INVESTAURA].

The discounted cashflow generated by the project over the period 2006-2020 is worth €76m at the beginning of 2004. Including the initial investment X, the NPV of the project in 2004 is €0m if the WACC is used to discount X, and -€8m using 5% to discount the initial rollout investment. The latter is more correct as the value of the investment X is relatively certain. The negative NPV reflects the challenge of entering the high-speed Internet-access market rather late and having to compete with fixed-line operators. On this basis, the spectrum licence should not be acquired and the project be abandoned.

However, the decision to build up the network does not have to be undertaken today: the major rollout investment in 2006 is not pre-committed. Instead, the company could invest a small amount of money to set-up a pilot network and undertake test marketing in 2004 and 2005, and use results to resolve some of the uncertainty surrounding this project. Acquiring the spectrum licence today creates the option of building the network and launching services tomorrow.

In any project, time available before investing is valuable for two reasons:

- All other things being equal, you would rather invest later than sooner as you can earn the time value of money of the planned investment by placing the money in the bank and earning a risk-free interest rate. This first source of value is reflecting in the Black-Scholes formula via the term $exp(-r_f . t)$ which is used to discount X, the initial investment cost.

- The second and more important source of value comes from the opportunity to resolve uncertainties while waiting. Some of this uncertainty will resolve itself on its own, whereas other uncertainties should be resolved by proactive management of the opportunity, for instance undertaking additional research. If the business opportunity turns out to be less attractive that you initially thought, you do not have to make the investment. Time preserves your ability to participate in good opportunities while insulating you from bad ones.

Assuming that the pilot project and the test marketing cost the company €5m in 2004, the option can be valued using the Black-Scholes formula with the parameters (X = €90m, S_0 = €76m - €5m, t = 1.5 years, σ = 60%, r_f = 5%). This gives a value of €16.4m. This is higher than the initial investment required to create the option, equal to the licence costs. So acquiring a licence for €10m makes sense because it opens the possibility for a business opportunity later. Also, investing in WiMax is keeping a potential new competitor away as WiMax applications might cannibalise the core UMTS business of the mobile operator.

Sensitivity analysis was also undertaken on the value of the call to better appreciate the impact of σ (sigma) and of t on the value of the call.

σ	X	t=1	t=1.5	t=2
40%	€ 80	€ 9	€ 12	€ 15
	€ 90	€ 6	€ 9	€ 12
	€ 100	€ 4	€ 7	€ 10
60%	€ 80	€ 15	€ 19	€ 23
	€ 90	€ 12	€ 16.4	€ 20
	€ 100	€ 10	€ 14	€ 18
80%	€ 80	€ 20	€ 26	€ 30
	€ 90	€ 18	€ 23	€ 28
	€ 100	€ 15	€ 21	€ 26

Figure 13.3: Sensitivity analysis of the option value [Source: INVESTAURA].

6. How do You Estimate the Volatility Sigma?

In a Real Options valuation, the parameter that managers find the most difficult to estimate is the volatility sigma of project returns. In addition, the value of the call is particularly sensitive to sigma. A number of approaches are available.

Educated guess

The simplest method is to use an educated guess. Most stock funds and stock indices have a one-year volatility in the range of 10% to 40%. Volatility of individual companies is higher and commonly between 15% and 60%. Volatility of individual projects is even higher. Sensitivity analysis can be used to quantify the impact of various estimates of sigma on the call value. Note that the volatility of a share of equity is not the same as the volatility of a firm because firms not only use equity, but also debt financing, and debt influences the volatility of equity and vice-versa. Also note that a firm, as a collection of projects, has a lower volatility than individual projects.

Alternatively, you could use a comparable project: if a similar project is available as a benchmark, you can observe the historic volatility of the project return and use it as a base for sigma. On the stock market, this would be equivalent to checking up the volatility of the share returns and its evolution over time. When a share option is traded on the market, you can reverse engineer the value of sigma with the help of the Black-Scholes formula. The derived volatility is called the implicit volatility. It is the volatility of the equity, not the volatility of the firm, which will typically be lower.

Project returns are normal

The second approach is to exploit the assumption that project returns are normally distributed i.e. the distribution of the project present values is log normal. You can then proceed as follows: ask yourself by how much the value of the assets to acquire (S_0) is likely to increase within the period of time t. Let us call the percentage increase u. By how much is it likely to decrease? Let us call the percentage decrease d (d should be positive). Estimates of the standard deviation sigma are then given by the following formula:

$$\sigma_u = \frac{\ln(1+u)}{\sqrt{t}} \qquad \sigma_d = \frac{\ln\left(\frac{1}{1-d}\right)}{\sqrt{t}}$$

Simply take the average between both values to get an estimate of sigma. In our WiMax example from Section 5, managers believe that the present value of the project might increase by 100% or decrease by 60% within a year. This gives us two estimates for sigma: 69% and 92%, leading to an average of 80%. The difficulty with this approach is that it is very approximate as people are rarely capable to take the time factor correctly into account and estimate the increase or decrease relating to the time period considered.

An alternative approach is to estimate the variance of the Present Value S_0 and derive the variance of project returns. To estimate the variance of S_0, ask managers what would be the maximum value that they would imagine for S_0 if the future turned out to be different than forecast. If S_{max} is the maximum value for S_0, then let us define:

$$k = \frac{S_{max} - S_0}{2 \times S_0}$$

This would be equivalent to a 95% confidence interval and provides an estimate for the variance of S_0. Then an estimate for sigma is:

$$\sigma = \sqrt{\ln(1 + x)}$$

$$x = \frac{-(k+1) + \sqrt{(4k^2 + 2k + 1)}}{3/2}$$

In the example above, let assume S_{max} to be €200m. Then $k = 0.91$ and $\sigma = 57\%$.

Monte Carlo simulation

The last method, and certainly the more complex, but also the more accurate, is to generate a Monte Carlo simulation of possible project values and rates of return, and estimate the volatility as the standard deviation of rate of return.

The key in this approach is to generate a meaningful distribution of project present values. The present value is the discounted value of expected future cashflows (ex-ante). The expected cashflows must be discounted at the appropriate discount rate reflecting the risk of the project. Note that generating a simulation of future cashflows and discounting ex-post with the WACC is wrong, because there are not *expected* cashflows but *realised* cashflows.

The present value at time zero is already known: this is $S_0 = PV_0 = PV_{WACC}$, the traditional present value of the project obtained by discounting expected future cashflows using the WACC of the project. Rather than generating a distribution of present value at time zero, we generate a distribution of present value at time 1 as follows:

1. Run the Monte Carlo simulation for year 0 only, i.e. draw values from the various parameters and simulate the cashflow at time 0.

2. Derive the cashflows in the following years as expected future cashflow, based on the additional information of what has happened at time zero, i.e. the realised subscriber base, revenues, costs and cashflow at time zero. In most models, the forecast in year n+1 will follow a set of causal and deterministic relationships from what has happened in year n, so generating cashflows for the year 1 to year N (the last year) can be undertaken in Microsoft Excel® spreadsheet software, based on the value observed in year 0.

3. Calculate the present value of the project at time 1, based on the expected Free Cashflows of year 1 to year N. Assuming that the project volatility and risk is constant, the project WACC can be used to discount these cashflows to year 1.

4. The rate of return between year 0 and year 1 is then given by:

$$RoR = \ln\left(\frac{PV_1}{PV_0}\right)$$

5. As the Monte Carlo simulation for year 0 parameters runs, the rate of return RoR becomes a random variable as PV_1 whereas PV_0 remains constant. Its standard deviation can be calculated with the following function from the RiskAMP Microsoft Excel Add-In:

= SimulationStandardDeviation(RoR)

The standard deviation obtained is an estimate of the standard deviation of the project returns, and is consistent with the project WACC that was assumed.

We have applied this approach to the WiMax example using the RiskAMP Add-In for the Monte Carlo simulation. The primary uncertainty is the number of subscribers at launch and in the following years. We assume that the number of subscribers at end 2006 is normally distributed with an average of 100,000 subs and a standard deviation of 30,000 subs. This means that in

95% of the cases, the number of subscribers in 2006 will be comprised between 40,000 and 160,000. To calculate the number of subscribers in the following years, we use a fixed S-curve profile normalised at 100% in year 2010. After 5,000 iterations, we obtain an estimate of 22% for the standard deviation of return. This is much lower than the standard estimated from the other methods. Even if not all risks have been factored into the Monte Carlo simulation, the values estimated previously for sigma look high.

7. Positioning the Project in the Option Space

In this section, we discuss the issue of optimal timing for project start: is it better to undertake the project now or wait and start later? This is analogous to the issue of exercising the option: when is it optimal to acquire the share, knowing that while doing so, the option is 'killed'?

Essentially, we would like to compare the value of undertaking the project now i.e. committing resources and money immediately, versus keeping the option alive and retaining the flexibility to undertake the project later.

The Black-Scholes formula above show that the five parameters used to calculate the value of the call can be reduced into 2 parameters only: $S_0/(X \times e^{-r_f \times t})$ and $\sigma\sqrt{t}$.

The first of these parameters can be re-defined as the NPV quotient NPV_q: this is the quotient of the Present Value of expected future cashflows and the Present Value of the initial investment. The second parameter is the volatility over the period t, also called cumulative volatility.

The standard NPV formula for undertaking the project in t years from now is:

$$NPV = S_0 - \frac{X}{(1 + WACC)^t}$$

if X is as uncertain as the project expected cashflow stream. This NPV does not include the value of flexibility and can be called the 'NPV without flexibility'. If X is assumed to be known with certainty or at least with a lot more certainty that the revenue and other costs streams, then a risk-free rate of interest should be used instead of WACC.

The NPV$_{\text{without flexibility}}$ then becomes:

$$NPV_{\text{without flexibility}} = S_0 - \frac{X}{(1 + R_f)^t}$$

where R_f is the annual risk-free interest rate. This NPV is lower than the NPV calculated using the WACC.

If a compound interest rate r_f is used instead, then:

$$r_f = \ln(1 + R_f)$$

giving for the NPV without flexibility:

$$NPV_{\text{without flexibility}} = S_0 - X \times e^{-r_f \times t} = S_0 \times \left(1 - \frac{1}{NPV_q} \right)$$

This formula shows that there is a one-to-one relationship between NPV$_q$ and NPV$_{\text{without flexibility}}$, and provides an interpretation of the NPV quotient: it is a way to normalise NPV to make it independent of the size of the business. A positive NPV$_{\text{without flexibility}}$ is equivalent to an NPV$_q$ larger than 1 and a negative NPV$_{\text{without flexibility}}$ implies that NPV$_q$ is comprised between 0 and 1.

The term $\sigma\sqrt{t}$ describes the variance of returns over the period t. When t=1, then the term reduces to the annual variance. The more time is available to exercise the option i.e. the longer the time available until the decision cannot be postponed anymore, the higher the uncertainty is, and the more valuable the option and the business are if it is possible to act on this uncertainty.

Varying the value for NPV$_q$ and $\sigma\sqrt{t}$, a table called the *option space* can be generated giving the value of the call expressed as a percentage of S_0. We have also positioned the WiMax project as a black dot in Figure 13.4.

In the top line, time has run out and the NPV reduces to NPV$_{\text{start now}}$ = S_0-X. The decision to invest depends whether NPV$_q$ is larger than one ("invest now", in dark blue) or smaller than one ("invest never", in grey).

NPVq

σ x sqrt(t)	0.5	0.55	0.6	0.65	0.7	0.75	0.8	0.85	0.9	0.95	1	1.05	1.1	1.15	1.2	1.25	1.3	1.35	1.4	1.45	1.5
0.1	0.00	0.00	0.00	0.00	"invest never"		0.00	0.00	0.01	0.02	0.04	0.07	0.10	0.13	0.17	0.20	0.23	"invest now"		0.31	0.33
0.2	0.00	0.00	0.00	0.00	0.00	0.01	0.01	0.03	0.04	0.06	0.08	0.10	0.13	0.16	0.18	0.21	0.24	0.26	0.29	0.31	0.33
0.3	0.00	0.00	0.01	0.01	0.02	0.03	0.04	0.06	0.08	0.10	0.12	0.14	0.16	0.19	0.21	0.24	0.26	0.28	0.30	0.32	0.34
0.4	0.01	0.02	0.02	0.04	0.05	0.06	0.08	0.10	0.12	0.14	0.16	0.18	0.20	0.22	0.24	0.26	0.28	0.30	0.32	0.34	0.36
0.5	0.03	0.04	0.05	0.07	0.08	0.10	0.12	0.14	0.16	0.18	0.20	0.22	0.24	0.26	0.26	0.29	0.31	0.33	0.35	0.36	0.38
0.6	0.05	0.07	Area 4: "probably never"					0.16	0.18	0.20	0.22	0.24	0.25	0.27	0.29	0.31	0.33	0.34	0.36	0.37	0.39	0.40
0.7	0.08	0.10	0.12	0.14	0.16	0.18	0.20	0.22	0.24	0.26	0.27	0.29	0.31	0.33	Area 1: "may be now"				0.40	0.42	0.43
0.8	0.12	0.14	0.16	0.18	0.20	0.22	0.24	0.26	0.28	0.29	0.31	0.33	0.34	0.36	0.38	0.39	0.40	0.42	0.43	0.44	0.46
0.9	0.15	0.17	0.20	0.22	0.24	0.26	0.28	0.30	0.31	0.33	0.35	0.36	0.38	0.39	0.41	0.42	0.43	0.45	0.46	0.47	0.48
1	0.19	0.21	0.24	0.26	0.28	0.30	0.32	0.33	0.35	0.37	0.38	0.40	0.41	0.43	0.44	0.45	0.46	0.48	0.49	0.50	0.51
1.1	0.23	0.25	0.28	0.30	0.32	0.34	0.35	0.37	0.39	0.40	0.42	0.43	0.45	0.46	0.47	0.48	0.49	0.51	0.52	0.53	0.54
1.2	0.27	0.29	0.31	0.34	0.35	0.37	0.39	0.41	0.42	0.44	0.45	0.46	0.48	0.49	0.50	0.51	0.52	0.53	0.54	0.55	0.56
1.3	0.31	0.33	0.35	0.37	0.39	0.41	0.43	0.44	0.46	0.47	0.48	0.50	0.51	0.52	0.53	0.54	0.55	0.56	0.57	0.58	0.59
1.4	0.35	0.37	0.39	0.41	0.43	0.45	0.46	0.48	0.49	0.50	0.52	0.53	0.54	0.55	0.56	0.57	0.58	0.59	0.60	0.60	0.61
1.5	0.39	0.41	0.43	0.45	0.46	0.48	0.50	0.51	0.52	0.54	0.55	0.56	0.57	0.58	0.59	0.60	0.61	0.61	0.62	0.63	0.64
1.6	0.43	0.45	0.47	0.48	0.50	0.51	Area 3: "may be later"		0.58	0.59	0.60	0.61	0.61	0.62	0.63	0.64	0.65	0.65	0.66		
1.7	0.46	0.48	0.50	0.52	0.53	0.55	0.56	0.57	0.58	0.59	0.60	0.61	0.62	Area 2: "probably later"				0.66	0.67	0.68	0.68
1.8	0.50	0.52	0.53	0.55	0.56	0.58	0.59	0.60	0.61	0.62	0.63	0.64	0.65	0.66	0.66	0.67	0.68	0.69	0.69	0.70	0.70
1.9	0.53	0.55	0.57	0.58	0.59	0.61	0.62	0.63	0.64	0.65	0.66	0.67	0.67	0.68	0.69	0.70	0.70	0.71	0.71	0.72	0.72
2	0.57	0.58	0.60	0.61	0.62	0.64	0.65	0.66	0.67	0.67	0.68	0.69	0.70	0.70	0.71	0.72	0.72	0.73	0.73	0.74	0.74

Time has run out and projects with positive NPV should be undertaken

Area 1: NPVstart now is positive but we might want to wait if "leakage value" is not too high

Area 2: NPVq is higher than 1 so the project is promising. However, NPVstart now is negative so we should wait

Area 3: NPVq is lower than 1, however the call value is significant - higher than NPVwithout flexibility

Area 4: NPVq is lower than 1 and the call value is low compared to NPVwithout flexibility

Here we can not wait anymore and the project has negative NPV so should not be undertaken

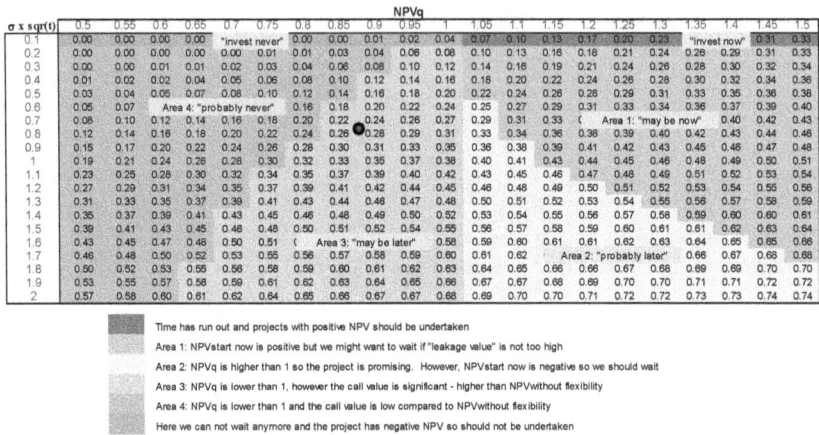

Figure 13.4: Value of a European call expressed as a percentage of S_0 [Source: INVESTAURA].

The option space also shows four additional areas, two of them are 'in the money' and the two others 'out of the money':

- Area 1 in light blue: projects in this area have NPV_q larger than 1 and $NPV_{start\ now}$ is positive, so the project could be undertaken immediately. However, if there is no 'leakage value' of waiting, then it is preferable to wait and invest X later rather than now, because nothing is lost in doing so, and something can be gained: experience from obtaining additional insight from the market and reducing the remaining uncertainty while the investment is delayed. Therefore, the timing to invest can be optimised by delaying investment, while there is an opportunity to reap additional reward. If this sounds counter-intuitive, think about an option on a share that you do not plan to sell immediately after exercising the option but keep it in the long term: in this case there is no value in exercising the option early, even if the current share price is above the exercise price. The capital required to cover the exercise price can be invested elsewhere in the meantime, for instance in the bank at the risk-free interest rate.

- Area 2 in green: in this area, NPV_q is larger than 1 so the project is creating value, however the $NPV_{start\ now}$ is negative so it does not make sense to invest now. The delta value between now and expiry only comes from the fact that the investment (budget) X can be placed in the bank and earn interest while waiting t years. However, assuming all other things remain equal, the option will end 'out of the money' at expiry once time has run out and the option has moved up the table and to the left as

- $\sigma\sqrt{t}$ and NPV_q decrease with time. Measures should be undertaken (active management) so that the odds of the project improve, either by increasing S, or decreasing X, or both. This allows the option to move to the right of the table towards the blue area so that the value of the option increases, and ends 'in the money' at expiry.

- Area 3 in orange: the NPV_q is lower than 1 but the project has a call value that is larger in magnitude than $NPV_{without\ flexibility}$ (which is negative). Unlike Area 2, the value generated by placing X in the bank is not sufficient to compensate the negative value of the project. However, as the value of the call is large enough, the project has potential to end in the money i.e. in the right hand side of the table. Like Area 2, Area 3 is particularly interesting as we are sitting on the borderline. We might be able to undertake actions to improve the chances of the project. If the uncertainty can be acted on, for instance if there is enough time for this or the impact of our action is high enough to turn a negative NPV into a positive one, then we can reap the benefits of a successful project. Area 3 is the area where it is most valuable to use Real Options valuation to 'save' valuable projects that would otherwise be scrapped on the basis that they are NPV-negative.

- Area 4 in pink: in this area the project NPV is negative and the value of the call is low compared to the magnitude of negative NPV. In principle, the project could be left to mature and further develop, but it is rather unlikely to develop positively in the future, so it is probably best to abandon it because it is too far away from being 'in the money'.

The option space above is a useful tool to compare alternative projects and options and actively manage a portfolio of opportunities.

We now look into how to expand the Black-Scholes model to capture more realistic (but also more complex) cases and remove some limitations that are imposed so far.

8. Expanding the Framework: the Binomial Model

The application of the Black-Scholes model is based on a number of assumptions that do not always hold in practice. The main caveats are summarised below:

- While the decision to invest has been delayed, positive cashflows or market share might be lost to the competition. This is equivalent to a share paying a dividend (and the share price going down by the same amount as a result), whereas the exercise price of the call option on the share is not adjusted as a result. For a new business, the impact might remain limited, because the cashflows generated in the first one or two years by new ventures are usually limited, and no significant disadvantage of late entry is created. To capture the (negative) impact of late entry and the 'first-mover advantage' of competitors, a competition model would be required as well.

- So far we have assumed that the option can only be exercised at one point in time: at expiry. This problem can be solved by using an American call rather than a European call. As long as the underlying share does not pay a dividend, equivalent to the absence of a permanent loss to the competition, it can be shown that it is optimal to wait until expiry to exercise the American call, and the value of the American call is the same as the value of the European call. Intuitively, the reason is that if there is nothing to lose from waiting before investing, it is better to spend the money later and wait in the mean time to learn how the business opportunity is developing. On the other hand, when there is 'leakage value', it can be shown that if the dividends paid out are high enough (equivalent to positive cashflows generated by the business lost forever to the competition), early exercise of the American option creates more value. Unlike European calls, there is no closed formula to value American calls, i.e. we have to revert to numerical methods to estimate the value of the call.

- The Black-Scholes formula assumes that the exercise price is known with certainty. This might be true for the option on a share, but is only partially true for an investment decision. When new and unproven technologies come into play, the exercise price can only be approximated. One way to get over this problem is to perform sensitivity analysis of the value of the call on the exercise price. The assumption that X is known with certainty is much more problematic in the case of 'put' options. In this case a project is usually abandoned because of poor demand conditions for a product and business performance. The disposable value of the business is likely to be strongly affected by market conditions applying at that time, unless the price has been agreed in advance in a contract with a potential buyer, or unless the business and its assets (tangible, intangible) can be 'redeployed' to another industry, which is often not the case.

- The Black-Scholes model only addresses one of the simplest options: the option to delay investment. It can also be used to value the option to expand. In practice, business opportunities often contain more complex options. There can be multiple options available simultaneously e.g. the option to invest in A or in B, or compound option i.e. the option to invest in A tomorrow opens the option to invest in B the day after tomorrow. This is especially the case when investment or R&D expenditure are staged. This means that the business has an option on an option. For example you could have a compound option to invest, with the second option also having the flexibility to be delayed by up to 2 years.

The good news is that the framework presented above can be expanded to include all these aspects with the use of a binomial model. In a binomial model we build a tree structure modelling how the value of the opportunity is expected to change over time, then map the options that are available for the business at each point in time, then identify the optimum decisions based on what creates the highest value and finally calculate the value of the business and its embedded option by moving back to the present.

The binomial model is particularly powerful for a number of reasons:

- it allows you to calculate the value of fairly complex options capturing a full range of management flexibility
- it helps you identify the optimum decisions at each step
- the binomial model is consistent with the Black-Scholes model as it includes the European call as a special case. It can also be shown that the binomial valuation converges to the Black-Scholes formula when the number of steps used for the binomial calculation become high
- finally the binomial model makes the valuation more transparent and avoids the black-box problem of the Black-Scholes formula.

The binomial model states that in each time step, the value of the project can only move up or down and takes two alternative values. The values of the up and down movements are related to the volatility of the project returns and calculated from the following relationships:

$$u = e^{\sigma \times \sqrt{\frac{t}{n}}} \qquad (u > 1)$$

$$d = e^{-\sigma \times \sqrt{\frac{t}{n}}} \qquad (d < 1)$$

A tree structure for the WiMax project is shown in Figure 13.5. We have used three steps here, and with time to expiry equal to 1.5 years, each step is equivalent to 6 months.

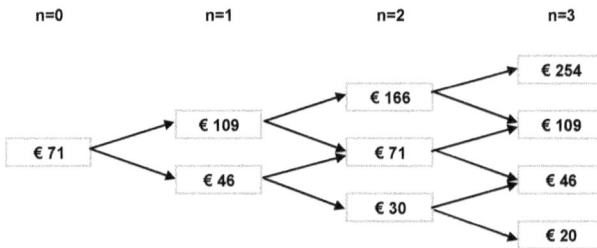

Figure 13.5: Binomial tree for the WiMax deferral option (n=3, σ=60%) [Source: INVESTAURA].

The following step is to map the flexibility of management on the tree diagram. In this case, the only flexibility available is at termination with the option to invest €90m or not. Investing before is not worthwhile because there is nothing to lose from waiting.

Then, the optimal decision-making is determined for each node of the tree and the pay-offs are calculating, starting from the end. At n=3, the company should go ahead with the project only if the value of the project is larger than the cost of investment. This is the case when the value of the project is worth €254 or €109, but not if the value of project has gone down, for instance because the ARPU and market size have been revised downwards. The pay-offs at n=3 are calculated as Max(S-X, 0). If the project is not undertaken, the value of the project is zero. The values of the pay-off are shown in green to colour mark that management flexibility is available at this step in the form of undertaking the project or not.

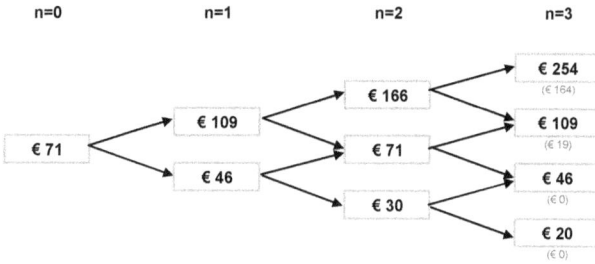

Figure 13.6: Pay-off at expiry for project WiMax [Source: INVESTAURA].

The following step is to discount the pay-offs available at n=3 to step n=2. The common mistake here is to use the WACC for discounting: this leads to the wrong answer because the riskiness of cashflows changes based on where we are in the tree and the decisions that are made at each step. A discounting based on the WACC assumes that all decisions had been taken in advance at time zero, which is one of the NPV flaws.

Rather than calculating the risk of the project at each stage, we discount the future pay-offs with the risk-free rate of interest for the period, and use so-called 'risk-neutral probabilities'. These are the fictitious probabilities that the value of the project has gone up or down between n=2 and n=3, in order to generate a risk-free project return.

The risk-free interest rate over one step and the risk-neutral probability that the present value of the project has gone up are:

$$r = (1 + R_f)^{\frac{t}{n}} - 1$$
$$p = \frac{(1+r) - d}{u - d}$$

The discounting formula then simply becomes:

$$PayOff_n = \frac{p \times PayOff_{n+1}^{up} + (1 - p) \times PayOff_{n+1}^{down}}{1 + r}$$

We can now apply the previous formula to calculate the pay-offs at n=2.

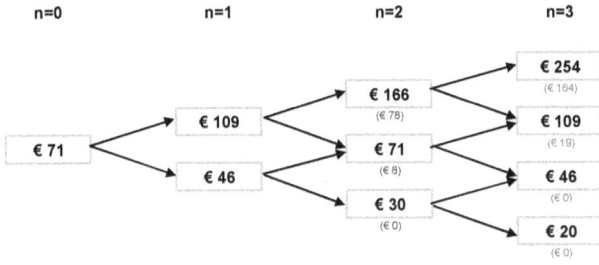

Figure 13.7: Pay-offs at n=2, shown in blue [Source: INVESTAURA].

The same procedure is repeated until n=0. The pay-off obtained at time zero is equal to the option value. In the WiMax case, we obtain a value of €16.9m, which is very close to the value obtained from the Black-Scholes formula (€16.4m).

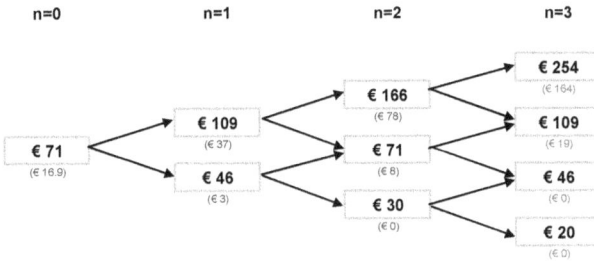

Figure 13.8: Pay-offs at n=0 [Source: INVESTAURA].

If we were to increase the number of steps, the call value calculated from the binomial model would converge towards the Black-Scholes value. Practice shows however that very few steps are necessary to estimate the call value, typically 2 to 3 only.

Now let us assume that the competition is expected to enter the market at some time between n=1 (6 months from now) and n=3 (18 months from now), and this would result in a loss in the value of the project of €30m at n=1. We capture the loss by reducing the project value by €30m at this stage. This also has the effect of reducing the future project value beyond n=1 in the binomial tree. At n=3, the project is out of the money most of the time except in the upper case; in the three other cases it does not make sense to enter the market. The value of the call today is now reduced to €6.6m.

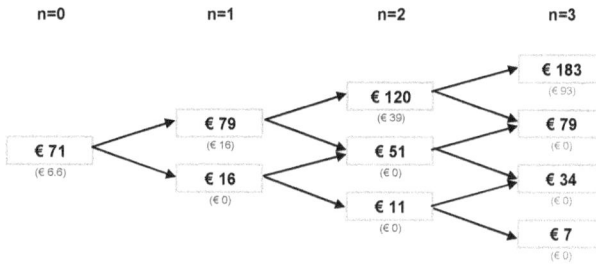

Figure 13.9: Impact of late entry and increased competition [Source: INVESTAURA].

However, let us assume that at n=1, the management has additional flexibility to enter the market early and invest at that time rather than waiting until n=3. This could prevent competitive entry, or at least prevent the permanent loss of €30m in the value of the project. At n=1, we now have the choice between keeping the option to invest alive, i.e. invest at expiry only, or to invest 'ex-ante' i.e. before the loss of value to the competition. If we do so at n=1, the value of the project is €79-€90+€30= €19 in the upper case, and €16-€90+€30= -€44 in the lower case. While investing early is not attractive in the lower case, it makes sense to invest at n=1 in the upper case as the value is higher than the option to wait: the value ex-post is €16 only, as shown in Figure 13.9. Therefore if we are in the upper case at n=1 we should invest. We now have the equivalent of an American call, with the option to invest before expiry if it is valuable to do so. If the impact of the competition had been lower, for instance €5m only, then it would have been more valuable to keep the option open and early investment at n=1 should not take place. The flexibility of entering the business early has now increased the value of the call by €1m to €7.7m as shown in Figure 13.10. If the cost of the licence is €10m, it does not make sense to acquire the license though.

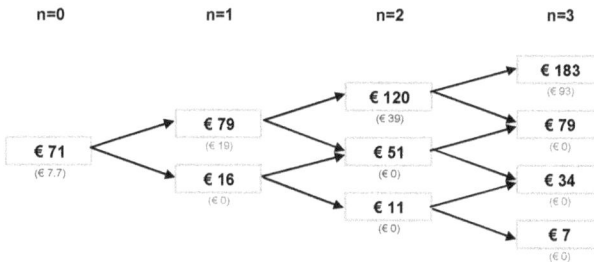

Figure 13.10: Flexibility to invest early at n=1 [Source: INVESTAURA].

Now let us assume that the business has an additional option: the option to resell the WiMax license at anytime in the future for the value of €10m. We can change the decision-making rules at n=1, 2, and 3 to reflect this additional option. The binomial tree shows us that if the project value goes down, the WiMax licence will be resold. Also the project (call) value now increases to €15.5m.

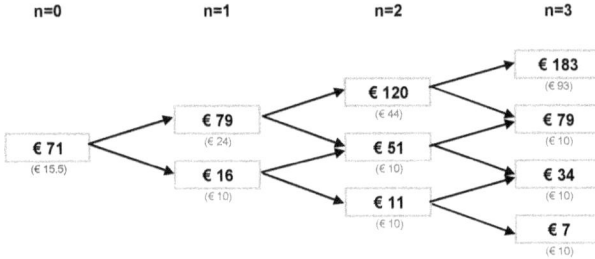

n=0	n=1	n=2	n=3
			€ 183 (€ 93)
		€ 120 (€ 44)	€ 79 (€ 10)
	€ 79 (€ 24)	€ 51 (€ 10)	€ 34 (€ 10)
€ 71 (€ 15.5)	€ 16 (€ 10)	€ 11 (€ 10)	€ 7 (€ 10)

Figure 13.11: Flexibility to resell the WiMax licence at n=1, 2 or 3 [Source: INVESTAURA].

To summarise, we have started with a project that had an NPV of -€8m excluding the licence costs, assuming that the investment is committed today. However, as the market entry can take place later, the network build-up can be committed later and we have the option to launch in 1.5 years or stop the project at that stage. This flexibility increases the project value before licence costs to €16.9m, so the overall value of waiting is €16.9-(-€8)=€24.9m. However competition will eat our lunch if we do not launch in the first 6 months, so we need to take this effect into account with the option to invest in 6 months from now: the value of the project is now reduced from €16.9m to €7.7m (and not €16.9m-€30m). In addition we can resell the licence at any time, so the value of the project now grows again from €7.7m to €15.5m. This value is the combination of the flexibility to delay investment up to 18 months, to invest as early as 6 months if the market is promising, to stop the project and resell the licence at any time if the market looks less promising. The value of the call is also giving us an indication of the maximum price to pay for the licence: €15.5m. Acquiring the licence is what is creating the call in the first place.

9. Recapitulation of the Real Options Methodology

The binomial model is a very powerful way to factor all sorts of options that are available in a business opportunity. In this section, we would like to summarise the key steps necessary for a Real Options valuation. We propose a five-step methodology as set out in Figure 13.12.

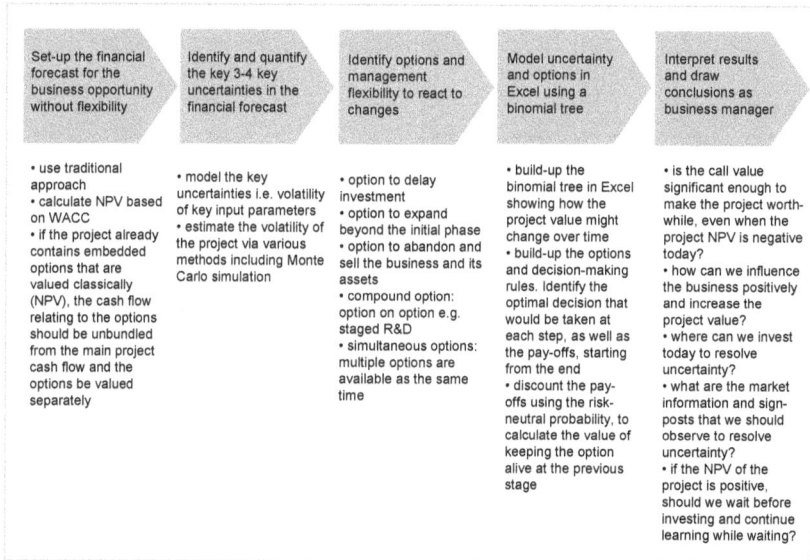

Set-up the financial forecast for the business opportunity without flexibility	Identify and quantify the key 3-4 key uncertainties in the financial forecast	Identify options and management flexibility to react to changes	Model uncertainty and options in Excel using a binomial tree	Interpret results and draw conclusions as business manager
• use traditional approach • calculate NPV based on WACC • if the project already contains embedded options that are valued classically (NPV), the cash flow relating to the options should be unbundled from the main project cash flow and the options be valued separately	• model the key uncertainties i.e. volatility of key input parameters • estimate the volatility of the project via various methods including Monte Carlo simulation	• option to delay investment • option to expand beyond the initial phase • option to abandon and sell the business and its assets • compound option: option on option e.g. staged R&D • simultaneous options: multiple options are available as the same time	• build-up the binomial tree in Excel showing how the project value might change over time • build-up the options and decision-making rules. Identify the optimal decision that would be taken at each step, as well as the pay-offs, starting from the end • discount the pay-offs using the risk-neutral probability, to calculate the value of keeping the option alive at the previous stage	• is the call value significant enough to make the project worthwhile, even when the project NPV is negative today? • how can we influence the business positively and increase the project value? • where can we invest today to resolve uncertainty? • what are the market information and signposts that we should observe to resolve uncertainty? • if the NPV of the project is positive, should we wait before investing and continue learning while waiting?

Figure 13.12: Five steps for valuing real options [Source: INVESTAURA].

10. When is it Worth Using Real Options Valuation?

Valuing options is a relatively complex undertaking. It requires identifying the option(s), splitting the overall cashflow forecast in multiple components in case the option was embedded in the overall cashflow forecast, structuring an analogy between the real option and a financial option, setting the parameters correctly, including sigma, valuing the option, and interpreting results. This is clearly not worth the pain when the project is strongly NPV positive or strongly NPV negative. Another way to look at it is that when projects have large positive or negative NPVs, the options that might be embedded in this project remain too small to fundamentally change the overall picture and are not worth estimating.

When the project is borderline the NPV is close to zero, and low in any case compared to the size of the investment commitment. These are the green and orange areas that we have identified above in the option space. Applying option valuation is particularly insightful in this case. Using option valuation is only valuable when we have tough decisions to make, i.e. the project is neither particularly good nor particularly bad. A second necessary condition is that time to expiry or uncertainty is high enough so that there is strong likelihood that we will receive new information and learn while the option is kept open. A final prerequisite is that management has the flexibility to react to new market conditions and can improve the odds of the project. Like a good and conscientious gardener that regularly waters his unripe tomatoes, removes the weeds and protects his future harvest from worms and birds, managers must proactively manage business opportunities to transform them into pearls.

11. Applications of Real Options

Generally, most contracts between buyer and seller contain options and the framework presented here can be used to value those options.

Although not still widely used in the industry due to the complexity of the approach, Real Options find applications in a number of areas, in particular pharmaceutical, resource extraction (oil, mining) and utilities.

- Pharmaceutical companies have a large portfolio of products and undertake R&D not in one step but in stages. The time to develop a new drug usually spans 10 to 20 years, and only few products will ever reach market introduction. At any one stage, the R&D undertaken opens the option to go to the next phase, and eventually to commercialise the product. All this takes place in a highly uncertain environment for the end product. The Real Options approach is particularly valuable when there are a large number of products to value and benchmark against each other.

- In the oil industry, oil-producing companies buy the rights to develop areas that have uncertain prospects for production. Drilling is the equivalent of R&D. It is performed to estimate the value of the opportunity as the costs of exploitation are uncertain e.g. depth and ground constitution. Also, optimal timing for exploiting the opportunity depends on the oil price evolution in the market.

- In utilities and especially electricity, companies face a trade-off between strong economies of scale for large and expensive plants (typically fired by coal), versus the possibility to invest in smaller plants that have a higher unit cost of production, but cost less to build (typically fired with gas). As the market demand and respective prices of coal and gas are uncertain, Real Options are useful to correctly value the flexibility of choice between multiple production methods.

Real Options can also help value start-ups that currently hardly generate revenues. A start-up is essentially nothing more than the option to develop a successful business at a later stage. Investment in start-ups, like R&D, takes place in phases with various types of venture capitalists at each stage. If the option is still valuable at the end of each phase, then the start-up can go to the next phase and initiate a further round of funding, and use the money to invest in further product development or expand its market reach. The high valuations achieved in the 'New Economy' can at least be partially explained by options embedded in start-ups, and options on options. The huge valuations achieved by loss-making start-ups quoted on the stock exchange come from the huge amount of uncertainty that these companies face: their volatility is very high, and volatility increases option value. Also the volatility on an option is higher than the volatility of the stocks, and many start-ups are more like an option than a stock, so as a shareholder invested in a start-up, you own something very similar to a call option, not a share of equity, and this can result in huge changes in option value, including losing your entire investment.

Finally when trying to introduce Real Options valuation as a methodology within a company, it is important to take the company's specific situation into account and current practice used by business and financial managers. Some companies are already very mature in their current business planning and valuation techniques, and can be particularly receptive to the Real Options approach. It is useful to have a 'godfather' at high management level to support the successful introduction of a complementary valuation methodology that builds up on traditional NPV valuation. In companies that are not so advanced, the standard NPV approach is likely to be more successful, enhanced with sensitivity analysis and maybe scenario analysis.

Conclusion

Did MNOs Overpay for Their UMTS Licence?

"May you look back on the past with as much pleasure as you look forward to the future"
Paul Dickson, writer

Ten years after the auctioning of UMTS licences in Europe (from April 2000 to September 2001), a tantalising issue remains: did MNOs overpay for their licence? This is not a vain question when you consider that the average UMTS licence reached the horrendous price of £4.5bn in the UK and €8.4bn in Germany, with 5 and 6 licences awarded respectively. In Germany, the total licence costs were equivalent to €620 per head of population and 2.5% of the country GDP in that year! Also, the delays in network build-up, the initial lack of handsets, the late launches of commercial services in 2004 rather than 2002, and finally the rather lukewarm enthusiasm from end-users so far show that the short- and medium-term business opportunities from UMTS services were largely overestimated at the time.

But let us remain fair and not forget that the telecom industry looked quite different in the year 2000, and operators, facing strong subscriber growth in most countries (+60% on average in Europe, and in some countries up to +100% in 2000), had good reasons to be optimistic. Hindsight is always an exact science and it is all too easy to see things clearly in retrospect.

Methodologically, we therefore have to be careful to differentiate between an ex-ante view based on the market beliefs at the time of the auction, and an ex-post analysis taking today's perspective. So we first have to restate the original question: did MNOs overpay for their UMTS licence *based on what they knew at the time*?

1. Economic Theory

Economic theorists, in particular those who have designed the auction procedures in the UK and Germany, believe in the principle of rationality of bidders and clearly answer "No" to the question that we are raising here. Indeed, it can be shown that bidder *rationality* is a sufficient condition for auctions designed as 'multiple-round simultaneous ascending second-best price' to be *efficient* in the sense that the winners are the bidders who can make the best use of the asset.

Most of microeconomic theory is normative and studies how things should be, not how they are. In particular it makes the hypothesis that individual agents are rational, acting so as to achieve their most preferred outcome, subject to their knowledge and capabilities. The issue of rationality is very debatable in itself: even considering the limited knowledge and high uncertainty surrounding UMTS at the time, in particular regarding customer willingness to pay for mobile data services, were decision makers not blurred by the hype of the 'New Economy' that dominated the second part of the 1990s, and took decision emotionally rather than rationally?

And was it really optimal and economically efficient to treat incumbent and new entrants mostly in the same manner and have them pay the same price in the auction? Let us look 'ex-post' at some empirical evidence.

2. Empirical Evidence: New Entrants versus Incumbents

Looking at MobilCom and Quam, formally Group 3G, who both acquired a UMTS licence in Germany in July 2000 but scrapped their UMTS plan a few years later, the answer is clear: the hefty capital investments in UMTS licences have put enormous strain on the business of new entrants and their providers of finance, France Telecom for MobilCom, and Telefonica/Sonera for Quam, eventually decided to pull the plug. In 2005, Mobilcom emerged from bankruptcy and merged with its former fixed-line and ISP subsidiary freenet.

For the history: in February 2003, MobilCom filed for bankruptcy following its incapacity to refinance its debt and a 99% decrease in share price from its height of 2000; in December 2003, it returned its licence to the German regulator. As for Quam, after launching a GSM network as MVNO in December 2001, it shut down operations 12 months later, missed its UMTS roll-out targets in December 2003 and finally returned its dearly acquired licence as well.

From the 16 UMTS licences that were originally awarded to new entrants in Western Europe, 11 have been returned by their owners to the regulators who issued them. The remaining five licences are held by two companies.

- H3G in the UK, Italy, Sweden and Austria. H3G has had to face heavy competition in the countries where it is operating. In mid 2007, H3G had 7.5m in Italy (10% market share), 4m in the UK (6%), 0.5m in Austria (4%) and about 0.6m in Sweden (6%).

- Xfera in Spain. Xfera was awarded a UMTS licence in March 2000. Its original shareholders were Spanish building companies, the Scandinavian operator TeliaSonera and the French group Vivendi. After much trouble, and a shareholder reshuffle in June 2006, service was finally launched in December 2006 under the brand Yoigo. The company has a very limited UMTS coverage and relies on a GSM national roaming agreement with Vodafone. Yoigo has positioned itself as a simple, low cost mobile telephony provider, and has signed partnership with large supermarket chains and shopping malls to distribute its products. Yoigo has entered the Spanish market at a time when the market is already heavily saturated. Its objective is to reach 0.9% market share at the end of 2007 and 10% in 2015.

From today's perspective, acquiring a UMTS licence was a bad deal for most new entrants. Those who participated in auctions and have been wiped-out since then know that they have lost a lot of money in the process. The licence winners of the time have been suffering from the "winner's curse" ever since. As the auctioning process in most countries was designed with equal treatment between operators, with no discrimination according to operator market share and limited differentiation between incumbent and new entrants, the latter were forced to pay the same price as larger players, who ran the risk to be excluded from the market in the long term if they did not have a UMTS licence, and therefore had a very strong motivation to fight for a licence.

However, the picture for incumbent is less clear. In Germany, the four incumbent mobile operators are fully committed to UMTS and launched commercial services in 2004. We will therefore focus on incumbent operators in the remainder of this chapter.

3. Impact of UMTS Auctions on Operators' Share Price

A possible approach followed in research has been to use 'event analysis'. This consists in investigating the evolution of the MNO share prices a few days before and after the closing of the auction and looking for 'abnormal return' (see reference [14.1]).

Event analysis of share prices in the phase March 2000 to July 2001 has shown that a learning effect has taken place in the market. There is some evidence that in the spring 2000, the market rewarded licence winners and penalised losers, while in the summer 2001, at the end of the licensing process in Europe, the stock market rewarded losers and penalised the winners that had paid dearly for their UMTS licence in the past. A second learning effect has been that the prices of the UMTS licence per head of population have gone down over time as shown in Figure 14.1.

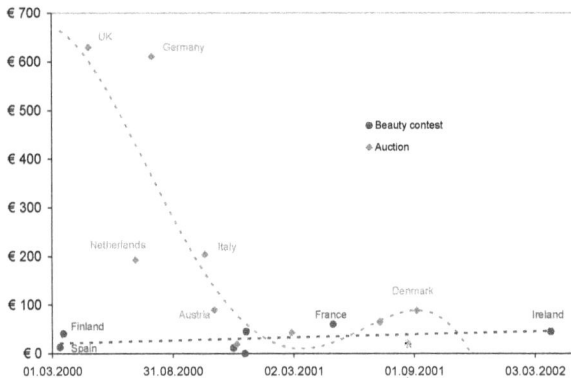

Figure 14.1: UMTS licence price per capita in EU15, Norway, and Switzerland [Source: public information].

The turning point for understanding what UMTS licences were really worth seems to have been the Austrian auction in November 2000. France Telecom and Deutsche Telekom, which won licences, were penalised by negative abnormal returns. Interestingly, BT, KPN and Vodafone, which did not bid, but had previously acquired expensive UMTS licences, displayed even larger negative abnormal returns. The latter players might have been punished for previous expensive 'wins', as well as for not taking advantage of the 'cheap' Austrian auction. As an example, the abnormal negative return of the Vodafone share compared to the NASDAQ translated into £19bn of the £160bn market capitalisation wiped out by the market as a result. Note that

Vodafone had previously spent about £30bn in the UK, Germany, the Netherlands and Italy on UMTS licences.

Event analysis indicates that the market in late 2000 believed that the incumbent winners in the first four UMTS auctions in the UK, Germany, the Netherlands and Italy had overpaid for their UMTS licence. Unfortunately, as market capitalisation of companies is correlated with fair company values only in the long term, event analysis is only a reflection of market sentiment at the time and does not tell us what the fair price for a UMTS licence should have been. We therefore return to the modelling of value drivers in the next section to derive a more precise answer.

4. Total Value of UMTS for Incumbent MNOs

In this section, we analyse the question from the point of view of a first-tier player, typically an incumbent operator with a market share like T-Mobile or Vodafone in Germany. The price paid for a UMTS licence could ex-ante be justified by three arguments:

Argument 1

The prospects of the UMTS technology as enabler for new data applications that could not be provided on GSM/GPRS networks. In the UMTS case study of Chapter 2, we have seen that the UMTS data business could be valued at about €6bn at the end of 1999.

Argument 2

The requirement to expand the life of the GSM licence and the mainstream voice business beyond the 2010 timeframe. Indeed, GSM spectrum has been allocated to MNOs in the early 1990s with a 10-20 year licence duration, so that most spectrum licences were expected to terminate around 2010, and in some cases before that time. Back in 2000, a year of fantastic customer growth, there was clearly a need to 'insure' the long-term prospect of a profitable voice business, and reduce the uncertainty of what would happen after the GSM license expiry. In Chapter 2, we have valued this business opportunity at about €10bn.

Argument 3

The attempt to force bidders out of the race and thereby avoid the emergence of new MNOs and increased competition in the country. This is called a 'predation strategy'. This argument was certainly valid in Germany, where 7 bidders entered the race for 6 licences. As one of the bidders dropped out in Round 125 when the licence price reached €2.5bn, the auction could have stopped there, but Vodafone and T-Mobile bid further to take hold of an addition frequency carrier (2x5Mhz), or exclude one or two of the potential new entrants (or a smaller GSM incumbent, which was rather unlikely). As none of the new entrants would drop, the auction continued for another 48 rounds until T-Mobile stopped bidding. The licence price had inflated from €2.5bn to €8.4bn in the meantime. Although the predation strategy of the two large operators seemed to have failed at the time, Vodafone and T-Mobile have indirectly reached their goals with the dropout of Mobilcom and Quam three years later.

To put a price on predation, we need to estimate the impact of increased competition on the incumbent with six players on the market rather than four at the time. The main differences between the two scenarios would have been:

- a loss of market share in the voice and data business leading to lower revenues, all other things remaining equal
- a reduced EBITDA margin due to a smaller number of subscribers to cover the same fixed OPEX
- increased competition intensity resulting in lower end-user tariffs, increased marketing expenses to acquire new subscribers and retain existing ones, and overall additional pressure on profitability margins.

In the following pages we will quantify the loss of market share for a large MNO following the market entry of new players. We will then estimate the reduction in EBITDA and EBIT margin following increased competition. Rather than setting up a detailed business plan and cashflow calculation, we will use a number of rules of thumb and historical data to derive an estimate of the predation strategy.

Figure 14.2 shows what the typical market shares were in early 2001 for MNOs according to their rank of entry in a market. The long term market share of new entrant is lower because they have had a coverage disadvantage for a long time, their brand was not as strongly established, and they had less time to build up their customer base.

Considering that a fifth or sixth operator would enter a saturated market in terms of subscriber level we believe that 10% is the maximum market share that a single new entrant could claim at the time, and 15% if two new operators were to enter the market together. Assuming that this market share gain would imply a market share loss for existing operators that is proportional to their market share before the entry of new players, then T-Mobile would have faced a potential loss of 4-6 percentage points of market share.

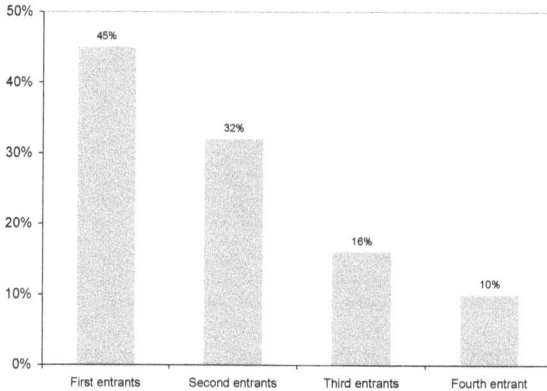

Figure 14.2: Average Market share of Western European MNOs in March 2001 [Source: EMC].

To derive the impact of the market share loss on the MNO value, we need an estimate of the MNO enterprise value at the time of the auction. The enterprise value is measured as the sum of the equity value (market capitalisation) and debt value (estimated from the MNO balance sheet). The shares of telecom companies were largely overpriced in the hype of the 'New Economy', so not a reliable reflection of the business fair value. Instead, we are using data from the end of 2003, when the share prices had returned to more realistic levels.

Operator	Equity value	Debt value	Entreprise value	No. of subs	EV per sub	2003 EBITDA	EBITDA multiple
Vodafone	€ 129bn	€ 15bn	€ 144bn	130m	€ 1105	€ 20bn	7.2
Orange	€ 46bn	€ 3bn	€ 49bn	49m	€ 984	€ 7bn	7.4
TIM	€ 37bn	€ 1bn	€ 38bn	36m	€ 1066	€ 6bn	6.9
Telefonica Moviles	€ 36bn	€ 5bn	€ 41bn	33m	€ 1244	€ 4bn	9.2
O2	€ 13bn	€ 1bn	€ 13bn	20m	€ 661	€ 2bn	6.4

Figure 14.3: Enterprise value per subscriber at 31 December 2003 [Source: INVESTAURA, Cortal Consors, company annual reports]

Large mobile operators in Europe were valued at about €1000 per subscriber at the end of 2003. With 26.3m subs in Germany for T-Mobile in December 2003, this translates into a €26bn Enterprise Value at the same date. Taking 5 percentage points off a 42% market share from T-Mobile at that date leads to a loss of value of 5/42 x €26bn ~ €3bn. The remaining value would be about €26bn-€3bn = €23bn.

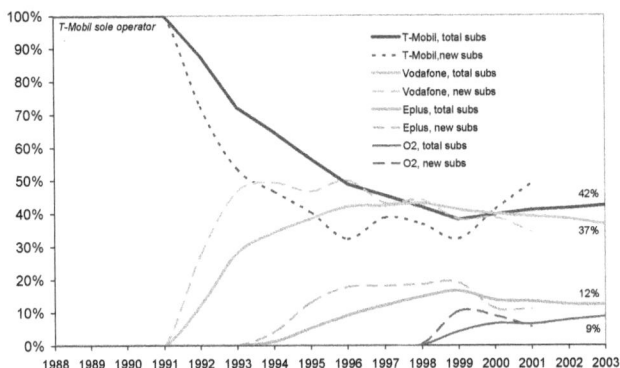

Figure 14.4: Evolution of market share of total and new subscribers in Germany [Source: Operator data, INVESTAURA].

The second factor to take into account is the reduction in profit margin due to lower prices, higher marketing costs and stable fixed costs. The following figure shows the how the EBITDA margin relates to the market share of the operator.

With a market share decreasing by 5 percentage points, the EBITDA and EBIT margins would have decreased by 1-2 percentage points as there were fewer subscribers to cover the same fixed costs. We also assume that increased competition intensity would lower prices and lead to a decrease of another 2-3 percentage points of EBIT. Assuming that the EBIT margin would have worsened by 5 percentage points in total, a large incumbent would have seen its EBIT margin decrease from about 25% to 20%. Assuming that Free Cashflow and entity value is reduced in the same proportion, the company value would have gone down by 20%, leading to a loss of 20% x €23 or about €4.5bn measured at the end of 2003.

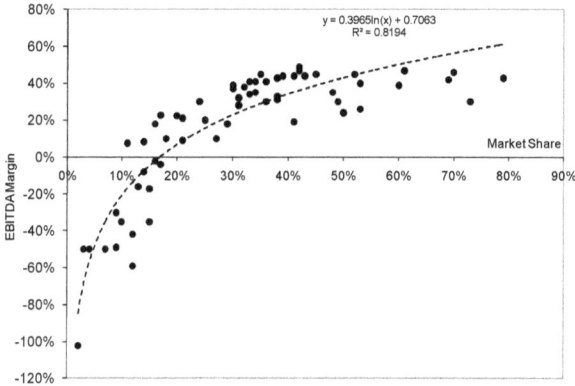

Figure 14.5: EBITDA margin as a function of market share in Germany, UK, France, Spain and Italy [Source: operator data from 1997-2000, INVESTAURA].

Adding the impact of reduced market share and lower margin, the loss in company value would have been of the order of €3+€4.5 = €7.5n. This rough calculation overestimates the impact of competitive entry because market share loss will take place over a period of 5 -10 years, not in one step. However, it provides us with an upper bound, and we see that the market entry by one or two additional competitors would have implied a loss in enterprise value of a couple of billion Euros for a Tier1 operator in Germany. To get a more precise estimate, we would need to perform a bottom-up analysis and calculate the Enterprise Value as the net present value of future cashflows, discounted to the beginning of the year 2000, and estimate the delta between a scenario with increased competition and a status quo scenario with four operators in the market.

To summarise our findings:

• the standalone UMTS data business was worth about €6bn
• the protection of the GSM voice business was worth about €10bn
• the avoidance of increased competition was worth somewhere in the range of €3bn-€7bn.

In total, the benefits of owning a UMTS licence could be valued ex-ante by a German MNO at about €20bn in 2000. From this perspective, a price of €8.4bn looks appropriate for a large incumbent after all.

Annex: A note on Regression

Regression is the art of fitting a mathematical model to a sample of data and estimating the model parameters that generate the best fit. The mathematical model contains one or more dependent variables (also called explained, or endogenous variables) and one or more explanatory (also called independent, or exogenous) variables. To perform a regression you can proceed as follows:

- specify a model, if possible using theory as a starting point
- estimate the model parameters, usually using least squares estimation
- check the statistical significance of the estimators from the t-test
- check that the model is correctly specified, from an analysis of R^2 and the residuals

Subsequently, a forecast for the dependent variables can be generated from the explanatory variables. It is also good practice to check the predictive power of the model as shown in Chapter Nine Section 4. This is done by excluding the last observation from the sample, calculating the estimators, generating a forecast for the excluded observation and comparing the forecast with the actual value.

When there is more than one independent variable, people talk about multiple regression analysis, which is a generalisation of the single variable case. When there are multiple dependent variables, a matrix formulation is necessary and the mathematics gets more involved, but the principles remain the same.

Overview of the Annex

1. Least Squares Estimation (LSE) 310
2. Test of Significance 310
3. Quality of the Fit: R^2 and Adjusted R^2 311
4. The Problem of Multicollinearity 312
5. Plotting the Residuals 312
6. The Problem of Autocorrelation 313
7. The Problem of Simultaneous Equations Models 314

1. Least-Squares Estimation (LSE)

In practice the most common regression method consists of minimising the sum of the residual squares, which can be shown to be a particular case of the more general Maximum Likelihood Estimation. Instead of taking the squares of the residuals we could have taken their absolute value; intuitively, rather than giving equal weight to the residuals in the sum, the squared residuals give more weight to those points that are further away from the regression line.

Estimators derived from LSE have desirable statistical properties and are said to be Best Linear Unbiased Estimator (BLUE):

- when the model is linear, the estimators can be expressed as a linear function of the observation
- the estimators are unbiased: this means that the expected value of the estimator is equal to the true value of the parameter that it estimates
- they have minimum variance: this means that unbiased estimators calculated by other methods than LSE have larger variance.

Linear models are those where the explained variable is a linear function of the estimated parameters, but not necessarily a linear function of the explanatory variables. When the model is not linear, the least squares estimators cannot be expressed explicitly as a function of the observed data, but have to be calculated by iteration using numerical optimisation algorithms. In practice, the Levenberg-Marquardt routine is often used for non-linear least squares estimation as it works very well.

2. Test of Significance

The significance of the explanatory variables is checked by calculating the t-statistic for each estimator, defined as the ratio of the estimator to its standard error.

$$t = \frac{\hat{\beta}}{\hat{\sigma}_\beta}$$

A t value higher than +1.96 or lower than -1.96 indicates that the regression coefficient is statistically significantly different from zero with 95% probability. When t is higher or lower than +2.57 / -2.57, the statistical significance increase to 99%. This assumes a very large number of data points. When fewer data points are available, which is often the case, the threshold value for the 95% and 99% significance are higher. For instance, in a 7-datapoint and 2-parameter regression model, the values are 2.57 for 95% significance. When the number of degrees of freedom is higher than 20, the "2 t" rule of thumb applies: the explanatory variable is 95% statistically significant when the t value is larger or smaller than +2 and -2 respectively.

When an estimator is not statistically significant, the corresponding explanatory variable should best be excluded from the regression, as the probability is high that the 'true' value of the estimated parameter is zero.

3. Quality of the Fit: R^2 and Adjusted R^2

The quality of the fit or overall model significance is given by the R^2 value, also called the coefficient of determination. It states how much of the variation in the dependent variable is explained by the explanatory variables. The higher R^2, the better the quality of the fit.

R^2 is equal to 1 minus the sum of the squared residuals normalised by the variation of the dependent variable around its mean.

$$R^2 = 1 - \frac{\sum u_i^2}{\sum (y_i - \bar{y})^2}$$

A low R^2 indicates that a large portion of the dependent variable is not explained by the independent variables currently included in the model, so additional explanatory variables should be looked for. Alternatively, this can be a sign that the model is misspecified.

On the other hand, one should not exaggerate the importance of R^2 compared to the individual significance of the explanatory variables, as the value of R^2 increases as the number of explanatory variables increases, but increasing the number of explanatory variables might create problems of multicollinearity (see next section).

Also, to compare the quality of the fit provided by two alternative models for the same explained variable, it is necessary to compare the values of R^2 normalised by the number of explanatory variables. This is called the adjusted R^2 and is lower than R^2. It is better to use the adjusted R^2 as R^2 gives an overly optimistic picture of the quality of the fit.

The adjusted R^2 is derived from R^2 according to the following relation:

$$\text{Adjusted } R^2 = 1 - \frac{N-1}{N-k} \times \left(1 - R^2\right)$$

N is the number of observations, k the number of parameters in the model. *N-k* is also called the degree of freedom.

4. The Problem of Multicollinearity

When regressing an explained variable on a number of explanatory variables, it is important not to let the number of explanatory variables grow too large as multicollinearity problems will arise. Multicollinearity happens when there is correlation between two or more explanatory variables, for instance when X, X^2, X^3 are used simultaneously as explanatory variables. The estimators become unstable in this case and can vary a lot with the inclusion of new data points. The variance of estimators also increases, so that although estimators remain unbiased, they are not precise. In the extreme case of perfect collinearity, there is no unique value for the estimators.

Multicollinearity also leads to lower t values, and explanatory variables are more often rejected whereas R^2 might remain high. This is the classic symptom of multicollinearity. In order to avoid excluding explanatory variables too early when a model is likely to exhibit multicollinearity, the explained variable can be regressed on each explanatory variable individually and the significance of the estimators checked with the t statistic in order to find those variables that should not be rejected.

A solution to the multicollinearity problem is to combine the correlated explanatory variables into a 'meta' variable and regress the explained variable on the meta variable as well as the remaining variables. This is the approach used in 'principle component analysis'.

5. Plotting the Residuals

Plotting the residuals also provides a very useful way to crosscheck the validity of the model. If the model has been correctly specified, the residuals should be randomly distributed.

If this is not the case, typically a pattern will emerge, which indicates one or more of the following problems:

- an important explanatory variable has been omitted resulting in a specification bias, and additional explanatory variables might solve the problem
- the model does not have the correct functional form, so additional models could be investigated, including varying the value of parameters assumed by default in the model
- the residuals are autocorrelated, in which case the least square estimators do not have minimum variance.

6. The Problem of Autocorrelation

Autocorrelation happens when the residuals are not statistically independent of each other. This can happen because of multiple reasons, for example when there is a time delay between changes in explanatory variables and their impact on explained variables, as well as when an explained variable is influenced by one of its lag values (this is called autoregression).

When autocorrelation happens, the least square estimators, although unbiased, are not efficient anymore: they do not have minimum variance. The difficulty in this case is that estimators have large variance and the t test of significance cannot be applied anymore to accept or reject explanatory variables. When the nature of the correlation is known, the model can be transformed into another model where autocorrelation does not happen anymore.

When autoregression happens, the situation is even worse as the residuals are not only autocorrelated but the lag value of the explained variable is correlated with the residuals. In this case, the leased square estimators are biased, but also inconsistent, so that they do not converge to the true value as the sample size increases, and the bias does not disappear asymptotically. LSE is misleading in this case and other methods have to be applied to produce unbiased estimators. One such method is to replace the lagged explanatory variable by a proxy variable with which it is correlated, but that is not correlated with the residuals. This is called the method of instrumental variables. Alternatively, one has to revert to Maximum Likelihood Estimation.

7. The Problem of Simultaneous Equations Models

Simultaneous models are multiple equation models in which one of the explanatory variables appears as an explained variable in a second equation as well, so that it is both explanatory and explained variable. The distinction between explanatory and explained variable becomes blurred and the jointly-dependent variables are said to be endogenous. The least square estimators are biased, but also inconsistent as the explanatory variables are not independent of the residuals.

In this case, consistent estimators can be generated by applying a two-stage least squares regression:

- regress the endogenous variables on all the exogenous variables in the model
- replace the endogenous variables in the original model where they appear as explanatory variables by their estimated value from the previous regression used as proxy.

Bibliography

This short bibliography provides a diverse collection of business books, university textbooks, research papers and Internet links. The references are grouped according to the chapter that they (mostly) relate to. If you have limited time for further reading, start with the reference at the top of each list.

Chapter One: Structuring a Business Plan

[1.1]   *Business Plans for Dummi*es, Paul Tiffany and Steven D. Peterson, Wiley Publishing, 2nd Edition, 2005

[1.2]   *http://www.score.org/template_gallery.html,* Business Plan for a Start-Up Business, The Score organization,

[1.3]   *The definitive business plan*, Richard Stutely, Financial Times Prentice Hall, 2nd Edition, 2002

[1.4]   *Planen, Gründen, Wachsen*, McKinsey&Company and Redline Wirtschaftsverlag, 4th Edition, 2007 (in German)

[1.5]   *Praxisratgeber Existenzgründung*, Sandra Bonnemeier, dtv, 2005 (in German)

[1.6]   *Entrepreneurship*, Miroslaw Malek and Peter K. Ibach, dpunkt.verlag, 1st Edition, 2004 (in German)

[1.1] is an excellent book that is full of practical examples and is very enjoyable to read. [1.2] is a great template that asks all the right questions and can be used as guideline when writing a business plan in Microsoft Word. [1.3] is a more numerical book that looks how business plans can be prepared in practice in the Microsoft Excel spreadsheet software. [1.4] is addressed at start-ups and would-be entrepreneurs, while [1.5] looks into the practicalities of setting up a new business. [1.6] is a very good book covering all the important issues relating to entrepreneurship.

Chapter Three: What can we Learn from the dot.com Crash?

[3.1]   *The Top Ten Lies of Entrepreneurs*, Guy Kawasaki, Harvard Business Review, January 2001

[3.2]   *The (mis)Behavior of Markets – A Fractal View of Risk, Ruin and Reward*, Benoit B. Mandelbrot and Richard L. Hudson, Basic Books, New York 2004

[3.3]   *Origins of the Crash: The Great Bubble and Its Undoing*, Roger Lowenstein, Penguin Books, 2004

[3.4]   *wie wir waren, die wilden jahre der web generation*, Constantin Gillies, Wiley, 2003 (in German)

[3.5]   *www.businessplanarchive.org*

[3.1] is a short and witty article written by a venture capitalist based in Silicon Valley who advises would-be entrepreneurs how they can improve their pitch when seeking funding. [3.2] is an excellent book from Benoit Mandelbrot, the inventor of the fractals, showing how risky markets really are. [3.3] and [3.4] provide a perspective on the New Economy bubble and an explanation of the dot.com crash. For those of you who are nostalgic of the dot.com years, [3.5] provides a repository of business ideas that have died in young age.

Chapter Four: Understanding Financial Statements

[4.1]   *Understanding Company Financial Statements*, R.H. Parker, Penguin Books, 6th Edition, 2007

[4.2]   *The elements of Accounting, An Introduction*, G. Whittington, Cambridge University Press, 1992

[4.3]   *Analysis for Financial Management*, Robert C. Higgins, McGraw-Hill, 7th Edition, 2004

[4.4]   *Principles of Corporate Finance*, Richard A. Brealey and Stewart C. Myers, MacGraw-Hill, 6th Edition, 2000

[4.1] is an excellent introductory book to financial accounting, providing a good overview of the topic. [4.2] focuses on accounting from the angle of double-entry book keeping. [4.3] provides a concise but superb exposition of financial analysis, including ratio analysis, forecasting and valuation, and although not specifically discussing financial statements, is strongly worth reading. [4.4] is the bible in corporate finance, covering capital budgeting, financing, ratio analysis, valuation and many more topics.

Chapter Five: Valuing Businesses

[5.1]   *Valuation: Measuring and Managing the Value of Com*panies, Tom Copeland, Tim Koller and Jack Murrin, McKinsey&Company, Wiley, 2nd Edition, 1996

[5.2]   *Strategic Valuation of Companies*, Alan Gregory, Financial Times Executive Briefings, 2nd Edition, 2001

[5.3]   *Portfolio Theory and Investment Management*, Richard Dobbins, Stephen Witt and John Fielding, Blackwell, 2nd Edition, 1994

[5.4]   *From dividend yield to discounted cashflow: a history of UK and US equity valuation techniques*, Janette Rutterford, Accounting, Business and Financial History, Vol. 14, No. 2, pp. 115-149, 2004

[5.5]   *Best Practices in Estimating the Cost of Capital: Survey and Synthesis*, Bruner, Eades, Harris and Higgins, Financial Practice and Education, Spring/Summer 1998

[5.6]   *Estimating the cost of capital for fixed and mobile Significant Market Power operators in Sweden*, Draft Report for Post & Telestyrelsen, Andersen Management International A/S, 2003

[5.1] is the 'bible' from McKinsey on the topic of valuation. [5.2] is a UK perspective on valuation, including an interesting exposure on the cost of capital and historical data on the risk premium. [5.3] provides some theoretical background about betas and the management of portfolio of equities. [5.4] provides an historical perspective on how valuation techniques have evolved during the 20th century, from dividend yield to P/E ratios to discounted cashflow. [5.5] is an excellent overview of practices used by practitioners to estimate the cost of capital. [5.6] looks into the calculation of the WACC for fixed and mobile operators, and emphasises that considerable judgement is required to turn the theory into practice.

A huge amount of current and historical financial data can be found on finance.yahoo.com.

Chapter Seven: Forecasting is an Art

[7.1]   *Guide to business modelling*, John Tennent and Graham Friend, The
        Economist Books, 2001

[7.2]   *Basic Econometrics*, Damodar N. Gujarati, McGraw-Hill, 4nd Edition,
        2003

[7.1] is a good guidebook on business modelling, focusing on the
practicalities of setting up models in Microsoft Excel® spreadsheet software.
[7.2] is a reference text book on econometrics, including a good coverage of
parameters estimation via regression analysis.

Chapter Eight: Forecasting on the Supply Side

[8.1]   *Digital Nomad*, Tsugio Makimoto and David Manners, Wiley, 1997

[8.2]   *Is there a Moore's law for bandwidth?*, IEEE Communications Magazine,
        October 1999

[8.3]   *Key components for 3G devices*, Report No. 15, UMTS Forum

[8.1] is a visionary book on the evolution of technology and the impact on
our life style. [8.2] is a research article on Moore's law. [8.3] is one of the
many reports from the UMTS Forum.

Chapter Nine: Forecasting Demand

[9.1]   *Diffusion of Innovations*, Everett M. Rogers, free press, 5th Edition, 2003

[9.2]   *Crossing the Chasm*, Geoffrey A. Moore, HarperBusiness, 3rd Edition,
        2002

[9.3]   *Inside the Tornado*, Geoffrey A. Moore, HarperBusiness, 2nd Edition,
        2004

[9.4]   *Prognoserechnung*, Peter Mertens and Susanne Rässler, Physica-Verlag
        (Spinger), 6th Edition, 2004 (in German)

[9.5]   *The International Takeoff of New Products: The Role of Economics, Culture,
        and Country Innovativeness*, G. Tellis, S. Stremersch, E. Yin, Marketing
        Science, Vol. 22, No.2, pp.188-208, Spring 2003

[9.6]   *Information Technology Innovations: General Diffusion Patterns and Its Relationships to Innovation Characteristics*, J. Teng, V. Grover, W. Güttler, IEEE transactions on engineering management, Vol. 49, No. 1, February 2002

[9.7]   *The Dynamics of Energy Systems and The Logistic Substitution Model*, C.Marchetti and N.Nakicenovic, IIASA Research Report, RR 79-13, 1979

[9.8]   *A Primer on Logistic Growth and Substitution: The Mathematics of the Loglet Lab Software*, P. Meyer, J. Yung, J. Ausubel, Technological forecasting and social change, Vol.61, No. 3, pp. 247-271, 1999

[9.9]   *Diffusion of Technology Generations: a Model of Adoption and Repeat Sales*, P.I. Bass and F.M. Bass, Working Paper, 2001

[9.10] *A New Modelling Approach Investigating the Diffusion Speed of Mobile Telecommunication Services in EU-15*, A.N. Giovanis and C.H. Skiadas, Technical University of Crete, 2002

[9.11] *New Product Diffusion Acceleration: Measurement and Analysis*, C. Van den Bulte, Marketing Science 19-4, pp. 366-380, 2000

[9.12] *A Primer for a New Cross-Impact Language – KSIM*, Prof. Julius Kane, Technological forecasting and social change, Vol. 3, 1972

[9.13] *Übergang vom analogen zum digitalen terrestrischen Fernsehen*, Arbeitsgruppe DVB-T Einführung der Deutschen TV-Plattform, Juni 1999

[9.1] is a reference book written by the 'father' of the diffusion of innovations. [9.2] and [9.3] are excellent books on marketing products in the various phases of the S-curve, the Chasm describing the transition between the early adopters and the early majority, and the Tornado the exponential growth phase in the early majority. [9.4] is a good book on forecasting for those who like mathematics and can read German. [9.5] to [9.12] are research papers. [9.13] is a report on the introduction of DVB-T in Germany.

Chapter Ten: Knowing Your Competitors

[10.1] *Competitive Strategy: Techniques for Analyzing Industries and Competitors*, Michael E. Porter, Simon & Schuster, 2004

[10.2] *Winning*, Jack Welch, HarperCollins, 2005

[10.3] *Mastering the Dynamics of Innovation*, James M. Utterback, Harvard Business School Press, 1994

[10.1] is the famous book from Michael Porter on competitive strategy. [10.2] is an excellent and pragmatic book from Jack Welch, the former CEO of General Electric: [10.3] shows how innovation and competition reshape the industry landscape.

Chapter Eleven: Value Chain and Business Model

[11.1]   *Clockspeed: Winning Industry Control in the Age of Temporary Advantage*, Charles H. Fine, Sloan School of Management, MIT, 1998, Perseus books

[11.2]   *The Innovator's Dilemma*, Clayton M. Christensen, Harper Business Essentials, 3rd Edition, 2003

[11.1] is an excellent good book on industry dynamics and value chain evolution. [11.2] shows how disruptive technological change can be.

Chapter Twelve: Scenario Planning

[12.1]   *Learning from the Future: Competitive Foresight Scenarios*, Liam Fahey and Robert M. Randall, Wiley, 1998

[12.2]   *http://www.well.com/~mb/scenario_planning/*

[12.1] is a reference book on scenario planning, while [12.2] is a website specialising on scenarios.

Chapter Thirteen: Valuing Business Opportunities as Real Options

[13.1]   *The pricing of Options and Corporate Liabilities*, Fischer Black and Myron. Scholes, Journal of Political Economy, Vol. 81, No.3 pp- 637-654, May-June 1973

[13.2]   *Real Options: a Practioner's guide*, Tom Copeland and Vladimir Antikarov, Texere Publishing, 2003

[13.3]   *The Options Approach to Capital Investment*, A.K. Dixit and R.S. Pindyck, Harvard Business Review, May-June 1995

[13.4]   *What's it Worth? A General Manager's Guide to Valuation*, T. Luehrman, Harvard Business Review, May-June 1997

[13.5]   *Investment opportunities as Real Options: Getting Started on the Numbers*, T. Luehrman, Harvard Business Review, July-August 1998

[13.6]   *Strategy as a Portfolio of Real Options*, T. Luehrman, Harvard Business Review, September-October 1998

[13.7]   *A Real-World Way to Manage Real Options*, T. Copeland and P. Tufano, Harvard Business Review, March 2004

[13.8]   *Valuation and the New Economy*, Merill Lynch, a report from the 9 May 2000

[13.9]   *Monte Carlo Estimation of Project Volatility for Real Options Analysis*, Pedro Manuel Cortesao Godinho, Journal of Applied Finance, 2006

[13.1] is the seminal paper by Black and Scholes on the valuation of financial options.   [13.2] is an excellent book on the application of Real Options. [13.3] to [13.7] are business articles on Real Options.   [13.8] looks into the valuation techniques used in the New Economy.   [13.9] addresses the application of Monte Carlo simulation in order to estimate the volatility of project returns.

Conclusion

[14.1]   *Spectrum auctions and regulation of mobile carriers: impact on share prices*, Leonard Waverman, London Business School, December 2003

[14.1] is a research article on the auctioning of UMTS licences.

Index

A

Accruals 68, 71
Acid test 86
Adjusted R^2 311
ADSL 38, 167, 277
Amortisation 74, 79, 80, 82, 83
Applications 45, 48, 158, 162, 173
ARPU 42, 50, 52, 55, 144, 157, 159, 205, 216, 220
Autocorrelation 137, 313
Autoregression 313

B

Balance Sheet 69, 76, 80, 87
Bass 191, 197, 218
Battery 167, 258
Benchmarking 49, 81, 143, 154, 155, 180, 234
Beta 132, 135, 136
Biased 96, 105, 135, 160, 203, 208, 269, 313, 314
Binomial tree 287
Black-Scholes 273, 278, 279, 282, 286
Brands 79

C

Call option 129, 130, 271, 272, 273, 275
CAPEX 49, 52, 67, 90, 111, 170
Capital Employed 80, 82, 84
Capital turnover 84, 85, 112, 122
CAPM 132
Cash in excess 87, 108
Cash ratio 86
Cashflow 31, 67, 70, 71, 72, 96, 108, 139, 220, 221, 275, 277, 280
CATV 48, 207, 208, 262
Characteristic duration 184, 189, 192, 193, 194
Coefficient of imitation 189, 192, 193, 196
Coefficient of innovation 191, 192, 193
Competition 28, 60, 144, 227
Competitive strategy 229

Consolidation 239, 246
Content 45, 48, 50, 52, 55, 220, 248, 262
Costs 49, 145, 170, 174, 236
Critical mass 179, 183, 184, 192, 193, 248, 252
Cross-checks 50, 112, 143, 157
Cross-impact 211, 212, 213, 214
Current assets 74, 76, 77, 85, 86
Current cost 77, 127
Current ratios 85, 86

D

Debt 76, 77, 85, 87, 88, 89, 124, 127, 136
Debt cover ratio 88
Debt-to-equity ratio 87
Depreciation 66, 68, 74, 75, 82, 107
Differentiation 29, 236, 237
Diffusion speed 184
Dividends 69, 71, 73, 122, 124, 134, 286
Driver tree 85
DVB-H 167, 255, 258

E

Early adopters 179, 183, 190, 191
Early majority 179, 183, 186, 202
EBIT margin 53, 82, 85, 102, 103, 106, 111, 120, 123, 175, 306
EBIT multiple 103, 105, 107, 121
EBITDA margin 82, 102, 306, 307
EBITDA multiple 103, 105, 107
Elasticity 157, 204
Equity 76, 124, 131, 136, 279
EVA 104, 116
Experience curve 171
Exponential 190, 197
Extended logistic 195, 197
Externalities 183, 193

F

Fibre 166, 171
FIFO 78
Fisher-Pry 188, 197, 209
Forecast 42, 46, 65, 90, 96, 110, 149, 165, 177, 240, 242, 264, 309

Fragmentation 239, 246
Free Cashflow 52, 72, 108, 109, 114, 119, 124, 146, 222

G

GAAP 66, 74, 78, 80, 83
Gearing 87, 88, 106, 125, 136, 137
Gompertz 194, 197, 201
Goodwill 66, 74, 79, 80, 83, 117
GSM 38, 39, 40, 41, 44, 53, 152, 201, 214, 215, 303, 307

H

Handset 171, 172, 199, 214, 219, 220, 233, 251, 259, 264
HHI 240
Historical Cost 77, 127

I

IFRS 74, 78, 79, 80, 83
i-mode 155
Industry analysis 229
Inflation 77, 78, 92, 113, 121, 126, 127, 134, 145
Innovators 179, 190, 197
Intangibles 74, 79
Interest cover ratio 88
Inventories 76, 77, 78, 84, 86, 111
Invested Capital 82, 83, 84, 117, 118
IRR 138

K

Key drivers 34, 42, 260
Key ratios 81, 90
KSIM 211

L

Laggards 180
Late majority 179, 182, 186, 195
Learnings 58, 143, 223
Least-Squares Estimation 310
Lessons learned 143, 223
Leverage 84, 87, 105, 107, 125, 126, 136
Licence 56, 233, 249, 276, 278, 291, 292, 299, 300, 301, 302, 303, 307
LIFO 78
Linear model 310

Liquid ratio 86
Liquidity metrics 85
Liquidity ratio 85
Logistic 187, 188, 192, 196, 197, 198, 201, 205, 207, 209, 223
Loss 72
Lotka-Volterra 206

M

M&A 80, 99, 241, 246
Market share 144, 183, 207, 209, 227, 238, 305, 306, 307
Marketing 24, 27, 49, 174, 182, 185, 186, 191, 194, 237
Memory 170
Mobile content 248, 262
Mobile data 45, 158
Mobile TV 172, 182, 218, 220, 258
Monte Carlo simulation 216, 280
Moore's law 166, 173
Multicollinearity 312
Multiples 102, 121, 267

N

Network externalities 183
New Economy 57, 60, 295
Non-linear model 310
NOPAT 83, 102, 111, 112, 122
NPV 58, 108, 222, 267, 269, 276, 277, 282, 289, 292

O

Operations 30, 71
OPEX 49, 52, 67, 74, 84, 145, 174

P

P/E 60, 106, 267
Performance ratios 89
Perpetuity 111, 113, 117, 120, 121, 122
Price elasticity 157, 204
Profit and Loss 68, 73
Profitability metrics 82
Put option 271, 272

Q

Questionnaire 160
Quick ratio 86

R

R² 156, 200, 210, 311
Radio capacity 49, 167, 171
Real Options 267
Regression 132, 135, 154, 155, 156, 190,
    191, 195, 197, 198, 200, 203, 204, 208,
    209, 309
Residuals 156, 192, 205, 209, 312, 313
Risk premium 60, 132, 133
Risk-free rate 127, 132, 133, 134, 221,
    273, 283
Risks 32, 96, 124, 253, 282
ROA 84
ROE 83, 84
ROI 84
ROIC 83, 84, 85, 102, 103, 106, 111, 113,
    117, 118, 119, 120, 121, 122

S

Sales channel 29, 145, 172, 174, 180, 231,
    238
Sales multiple 103, 105, 120, 121
Satellite 207, 208
Scenarios 24, 34, 42, 54, 56, 255, 261, 304
S-curve 178, 186, 188, 197, 199, 200, 202,
    204, 282
Segmentation 27, 43
SG&A 32
Simultaneous equation 314
SMS 54, 150
Stability metrics 87
Subscribers 43, 44, 152, 155, 205, 218,
    219, 220, 306
Sunk costs 59, 145

T

Tariff 51, 54, 55, 157
Tax 66, 72, 75, 76, 83, 107, 114, 124, 136,
    146
Terminal Value 110, 111, 117, 120, 123,
    138, 146
Times burden covered 88
Times interest earned 88
Traffic 46, 51, 204, 205
t-test 310, 312

U

UMTS 37, 47, 171, 213, 214, 258, 262,
    276, 299
Unbiased 131, 203, 310, 312, 313
USP 23, 29, 234, 235, 237, 241

V

Valuation 53, 56, 60, 77, 78, 79, 80, 86,
    93, 146, 267, 303
VAT 73
Volatility 273, 279, 288, 295

W

WACC 54, 83, 109, 114, 122, 124, 137,
    146, 221
Weblus 195, 197, 201
WiMax 213, 214, 276, 283, 288
WLAN 213, 245, 252
Working capital 77, 86, 111, 112, 119,
    146, 253

www.ingramcontent.com/pod-product-compliance
Lightning Source LLC
Chambersburg PA
CBHW021550210326
41599CB00010B/380